A NEW CALL TO HOLINESS

Other works by DR. J. SIDLOW BAXTER

AWAKE MY HEART
A full page of devotional Bible study for every day in the year. A Special Lent and Easter section is included.

DOES GOD STILL GUIDE?
Answers this important question of our modern times. Designed in simple style to meet the need of the general reader.

EXPLORE THE BOOK
A basic, progressive, interpretative course of Bible study, in one volume, from Genesis to Revelation.

GOING DEEPER
A series of devotional studies in knowing, loving and serving our Lord Jesus Christ.

HIS DEEPER WORK IN US
A further enquiry into New Testament teaching on the subject of Christian Holiness.

HIS PART AND OURS
Enriching exposition and devotional studies in the reciprocal union of Christ and His people.

MARK THESE MEN
Arresting studies in striking aspects of Bible characters with special relevances for our own times and the days ahead.

OUR HIGH CALLING
A series of devotional and practical studies in the New Testament doctrine of personal sanctification.

STRATEGIC GRASP OF THE BIBLE
Draws particular attention to critical factors, figures, pronouncements and turning points which have a pivotal or crucial relationship to the study of the Bible.

STUDIES IN PROBLEM TEXTS
The Word of God reaches the hearts of men by means of well-known, well-loved and well-comprehended texts, but the problem texts of the Bible discipline us in patience and painstaking investigation.

A NEW CALL TO HOLINESS

A Restudy and Restatement of New
Testament Teaching concerning
Christian Sanctification

J. SIDLOW BAXTER

ZONDERVAN
PUBLISHING HOUSE OF THE ZONDERVAN CORPORATION
GRAND RAPIDS, MICHIGAN 49506

DEDICATION

With heartfelt thankfulness to God these studies
in Christian holiness are dedicated to

ARTHUR H. CHAPPLE

for fifty years devotedly engaged in the vital
ministry of publishing Christian literature. A
wise counsellor to many authors, a businessman
of impeccable integrity, a publisher of highest
quality, a distributor of many outstanding Christian writings, whose influence in the propagating
of Christian truth is therefore incalculable.

FOREWORD

In these days, when so many loose and unworthy ideas of the Bible are fashionable, I am always glad to speak my own word of reverent testimony to it. I believe that the arguments for its divine inspiration are as sound as ever; and my own experience is, that the more I let the Bible speak to my heart, so the more does it *prove* itself to be the Word of God.

To me, the teachings of the Bible are not mere postulates of human philosophy, but "God-breathed" "testimonies" to truths divinely revealed, not humanly discovered. Overarching the whole wonderful revelation I see the inscription, "GIVE EAR, O EARTH, FOR THE LORD HATH SPOKEN" (Isaiah 1 : 2). Nor is that all; not only has God fixedly *spoken* in it. He is continually *speaking* through it, giving the written page an ever-living voice to all who have "ears to hear". Thus the Bible has an ever-contemporary originality; always springing new surprises, revealing new relevances for changing times, and new applications to successive generations of Christian believers.

In this connection, it is my persuasion that the Bible is trying to say something fresh to us again today on the deeply important, sacredly sensitive matter of Christian sanctification; and in these studies I ask the reader to *listen* with me—to catch the accents of *a new call to holiness* as that living voice from heaven speaks again through the written Word. Let our prayer be, "Speak, Lord, for Thy servant heareth".

J. S. B.

CONTENTS

SUPPLEMENTARY

THREE BIG QUESTIONS

WHY A NEW CALL?

"Within the hearts of a growing number of evangelicals in recent days there has arisen a new yearning after an above-average spiritual experience. Yet the greater number still shy away from it and raise objections which reveal misunderstanding or fear or plain unbelief. They point to the neurotic, the psychotic, the pseudo-Christian cultist and the intemperate fanatic, and lump them all together without discrimination as followers of the 'deeper life.' "

A. W. Tozer

WHY A NEW CALL?

TODAY, many peculiarly pressing issues are engrossing human attention around the earth; big political and ideological issues wrestle with each other in the international arena; and in the religious sphere big issues by way of the ecumenicity drive and its World Council of Churches. I am not underestimating any of these when I say that for the individual Christian believer none of them can be more challenging than the subject of this book ought to be.

In fact, no subject which ever engages the thought of Christian believers can be more sacredly commanding than that of our personal holiness, by which I mean an *inwrought* holiness of heart and life. Beyond contradiction, this is our "priority-number-one" concern. Admittedly, one would not infer so from the general appearance of things just now, but it *is* so, if the New Testament is true.

Although this deeper work of the Holy Spirit in the consecrated believer seems little expounded in the average church today, with the unhappy consequence that comparatively few Christians seem to know much about it in *experience*, it still remains true that this call to holiness is the *first* call of the New Testament to all Christians. For the moment, let just one text of Scripture represent the many to us: Ephesians 1: 4, staggering in its mystery and immensity:

"HE [GOD] HATH CHOSEN US IN HIM [CHRIST] BEFORE THE FOUNDATION OF THE WORLD, THAT WE SHOULD BE *HOLY* AND WITHOUT BLAME BEFORE HIM IN LOVE."

Yes, in the depthless mystery of that pre-mundane election the divine objective was our individual holiness, made possible for us in Christ, and effected within us by the renewing divine Spirit. Moreover, that holiness is an experiential sanctification meant to be known *in this present life*, as the context shows.

One of the saddest features of the present time is the lost emphasis on this inward and outward sanctification which purifies the soul in its deepest depths, and then transfigures the character. Yet all around us there are Christian believers wistfully longing to know the secret of inward cleansing, the way of deliverance from inward defeat, and the reality of

"A heart in every thought *renewed*,
And *filled* with love divine."

Many of us who are now no longer young cannot help feeling sorry that comparatively few younger believers in these days (so it appears) are hearing the New Testament doctrine of holiness opened up to them as *we* heard it in *our* early Christian life. It is not just that we are becoming fondly reminiscent of days which are now beyond recall, or that we think holiness teaching should be presented today in just the same attire as to a former generation. Our sigh is that the truth itself is largely choked, from a variety of causes. Thousands of young and eager disciples who are really "out of Egypt" are not being pointed on to the "Canaan" of sanctification and spiritual fulness which is the blood-bought present inheritance of the redeemed in Christ. Thousands who are really into "the blessing of Christ" are never pointed onward to "the *fulness* of the blessing" (Rom. 15: 29).

There is a Canaan rich and blest
    Which all in Christ may know,
By consecrated hearts possessed
    While here on earth below.

There is a vict'ry over sin,
    A rest from inward strife,
A richer sense of Christ within,
    A "more abundant" life.

Here rest and peace and love abound,
    And purest joys excel,
And heavenly fellowship is found—
    A lovely place to dwell!

Yes, besides regeneration there is *sanctification*. Besides righteousness imputed there is holiness *imparted*. Besides being "born of the Spirit" there is a being *"filled* with the Spirit". Besides "forgiveness of sins" there is deliverance from innate *sin*.

Rightly or wrongly, from John Wesley's time onward, this further, deeper, richer experience of inwrought holiness has by many been called the "second blessing", because of its usually being such a deep-going, post-conversion crisis-work of God in the soul as to differentiate it from all subsidiary "blessings". That name for it we certainly will not press here, since it has evoked much controversy. It is the truth itself with which we are concerned, rather than names for it. Our longing is that there may be a new revival of holiness teaching and experience in our evangelical churches; for apart from this "holiness without which no man shall see the Lord", our churches can never be the places of radiant fellowship and soul-converting power which they were meant to be. Not all the ecclesiastical machinery or newly-devised methods or ecumenical reunions which are now in vogue can be a substitute for "holiness unto the Lord." Truly did Spurgeon observe, "A holy church is an awful weapon in the hand of God"; but alas the opposite also is true: an *un*holy church God will forsake until "Ichabod" is written over its doors.

As an introduction to our exploration of the subject, it may be well worth while to spend a few minutes glancing back over the past eighty years or so, noting some of the developments which have a significant bearing upon it. I make no attempt at anything like a survey, but merely touch on certain salient features.

Wonderful indeed was the new emphasis on holiness which articulated itself among the churches of Britain and America during the latter half of the nineteenth century. Again and again, in the prefaces of well-known holiness books written during or soon after that time we find such rejoicings as these:

"One cannot but be profoundly thankful to God for the new emphasis on Scriptural holiness which is conspicuous among the churches in these days."

In U.S.A., well-known books by Dr. Asa Mahan, president of Oberlin College, Dr. Daniel Steele, professor of New Testament Greek at Boston University, editor Thomas K. Doty, and the eloquent Rev. A. M. Hills, all bear grateful witness to it. On the British side we find the saintly, wide-travelled Dr. F. B. Meyer rejoicing in "The great new conventions for the quickening of spiritual life on both sides the Atlantic", and the Rev. Evan

Hopkins, one of the founding fathers of the English Keswick Convention saying,

> "Perhaps there never was a time when God's Spirit was so wonderfully bringing home to the hearts of believers the glorious privileges which belong to them."

Such quotations might be multiplied. The older members of our churches can vividly recall how, in their young days, conferences and conventions and groups on the subject of Scriptural holiness were springing into being all over Britain and areas of America.

Holiness in New Apparel

Not that either the teaching of holiness or the emphasis upon it was then new. Nay, the call to Christian sanctity is as old as the New Testament itself. Yet I certainly do mean that the form, or doctrinal presentation, of the holiness message was new; and the joyfulness of the reawakened emphasis was new; and the pattern of holiness *experience* was new; and the development into a distinctive holiness *movement* was new. It would seem as though, beginning with John Wesley (1703–1791) there came nothing less than a *rediscovery* of New Testament doctrine concerning holiness. Others, who followed in the wake of that Methodist pathfinder, explored anew its exegetical aspects and its experiential practicalities. With a far more worthwhile eagerness than ever the Klondike or California gold-finds excited, the "rank and file" of Christian believers, thousands of them, pressed in to "know the doctrine", and to see "whether those things were so" (Acts 17: 11).

Just as the New Testament doctrine of our Lord's second advent and the cardinal truth of justification by faith, and the true doctrine of the Church, had all been buried for centuries beneath the sacerdotal draperies and superstitious perversions of Romanism, until the gigantic struggle of the Protestant Reformation began to uncover and free them again, so had it been with the true doctrine of Christian holiness. During the mediaeval centuries there were many holiness movements, but holiness had been thought of, all too often, in terms of monastic isolation, rigorous asceticism, and more-or-less morbid merit-works. Now, however, even as the true doctrine of salvation by faith, and the true doctrine of the Church, had been largely recovered for millions in Christendom, so the true New Testament doctrine of Christian holiness began to be rediscovered and re-explored.

By Wesley's time the concept of Christian sanctification had already been fairly rescued from the cloister and the sackcloth, from sentimental penance-mortifications, and from ascetic body-flogging. But now it became increasingly freed, also, from a sombre, Puritanical severity, from a stereotyped religious rigidity, and from the chains of a self-repressive negativeness. Flinging away those mediaeval graveclothes and strait-laced post-Reformation austerities which it was never meant to wear, Christian holiness now began to appear in beautiful raiment of gladness, and with songs of jubilant liberation. Wesley's insistence that entire sanctification is "perfect love" filling the heart and over-flowing through the life set the new urge in motion. On it moved, and out it spread, despite setbacks here and temporary recessions there. By and by, it could not be confined within Wesleyan boundaries. It was too big to be denominational. It was too badly needed by all, and too contagiously joyful, not to "catch fire" among the other Protestant churches.

New Distinctions and Accents

I doubt whether even yet we have fully "taken the measure" of what then happened, or, rather, *began* to happen. Most significant of all, perhaps, was the distinguishing between regeneration (or *newness* of life) and entire sanctification (or *fulness* of life); between justification (or righteousness *imputed*) and Christian perfection (or holiness *imparted*); between the *first* blessing (conversion) which does away with the legal *guilt* of sin, and the "*second* blessing" (entire sanctification) which deals with the inward *bent* to sin. These were the new accents which came with Wesley and then became increasingly current in holiness teaching.

The feature which should be noted thoughtfully is, that entire sanctification then became preached again as an inward transform-ation effected by direct, divine intervention, as a "second *work*" in those already regenerated, and therefore usually *later* than conversion. It is not something which can be achieved by mystical seclusion, or by supposedly meritorious religious exercises, or by any other contrivance of human effort; it is a post-conversion operation of God in the Christian believer. It cannot be *achieved*; it must be *received*. It is not a state which we *attain* by self-effort; it is an inwrought renovation which we *obtain* through Christ by the Holy Spirit.

Let it sink in: this was the crucial re-emphasis; true holiness is a radical renewing of the nature. Other religions may have their "holy men"; the Roman Church may have its monks and nuns and pilgrims; but all humanly contrived holiness is at best pathetically superficial; for despite all its outward devotement and self-denying rigours, it leaves human nature itself still unchanged, still sin-perverted and unsubjugated. Entire sanctification is a "second blessing" in which God Himself strikes a fundamental blow at sin in the very *nature* of the fully yielded believer, dealing with the basic evil itself, and renewing the innate proclivities of the soul by the Holy Spirit.

A Lasting Legacy and Impress

That teaching was so powerfully used of God, and so vividly implemented in the experience of multiplying thousands, that it left an indelible impress on Christian churches throughout the English-speaking world. When the Methodist revival as a whole had receded into the past, that was the "grand depositum" which it left for *all* the churches. A truer doctrine of Christian holiness had been recovered (for undoubtedly sanctification as a decisive "work of God" in the soul is what was preached long ago by the Apostles, and is fixedly deposited in the New Testament).

As time left the eighteenth century behind, competitive schools or theories emerged, with differing modifications or intensifications of the doctrine, some insisting that entire sanctification is nothing less than an unqualified eradication of the hereditary sin-principle, and others interpreting it as a less drastic deliverance through subjugation or counteraction by the Holy Spirit; yet all uniting in this, that the "second blessing" is a post-conversion, divine intervention which effects *inwrought* holiness. That was the teaching which, two or three generations after the Wesleyan beginnings, broke out *again* in the spreading holiness movement which reached its maximum extensiveness about the beginning of our twentieth century, or up to the First World War. Just here we neither commend nor condemn the phrase, "second blessing," or any theory linked with it. We are only looking back.

A decline: but why?

As we have lamented, the flood-tide of holiness enthusiasm has given place to a disappointing ebb. Where today is the spate of publications on holiness? Where are the crowded holiness meetings such as were widely in vogue fifty, sixty, seventy years ago? I concede gratefully that certain conferences which originated then are still largely attended. Yet even so, do we find the same specialized expounding of Scriptural holiness today as that of the earlier years, when the emphasis was distinctively upon the elucidation of holiness as a special *doctrine*, and as the inwrought *experience* of a distinct and deeper work of God in the Christian believer? It is no mere petulance which provokes our sigh of regret that today we are in the shallows of an ebb tide so far as holiness emphasis is concerned. This naturally raises the question: *Why?*

Eclipsed by bigger issue

There can be no doubt that the holiness movement became *eclipsed by a bigger issue*. That bigger issue was the grim battle to preserve the validity of Christianity *as a whole* against the deadly assaults of nineteenth and twentieth century rationalistic criticism. Many elderly Christians can still remember that first bewildering shock as the impact of the older "Modernism" shuddered through the Protestant churches in the earlier years of our century. Under the pseudo-aegis of "Modern Scholarship", rationalistic criticism, alias "Modernism", assaulted all the main citadels of Biblical revelation and traditional Christianity. With the Darwinian evolution theory riding high in the domain of science, and the "higher critical" schools capturing the intellectual aristocracy of Protestant Christendom, and the "New Psychology" hammering its way into our western educational institutions, evangelical Christianity was fighting a life-and-death battle. In all denominations, those holding to the evangelical faith were compelled to sink minor divergences and particular doctrinal emphases, such as those in the new holiness movement, and join hands in common cause against the one, common, deadly foe.

Harassed by Controversy

There is no doubt, either, that the decline is considerably due to the fact that the movement has been *harassed by controversy*.

When rival schools strongly contend for their competitive presentations of a doctrine, the doctrine itself is often brought into disrepute. I remember how perplexed I myself was, in the earlier years of my Christian life, by conflicting theories of the "Second Blessing." Some would say, "I am of Wesley", others "I am of Keswick". Some urged me to claim the complete annihilation of my sinful "old nature", while others, equally devout and dogmatic, warned me not to heed any such inanity, but to realize that innate sinfulness could only be suppressed. "Eradication" was the magic word of some. "Counteraction" was the watchword of others. Alas, I remember also the rasping *spirit* which all too often clove the differing groups. This was among the lesser personnel of the differing groups rather than among the leaders. It did not cancel all the lovely character-transfigurations in which the holiness fervour had authenticated itself; but it injected a poison which eventually caused wide discredit.

Divorce from Evangelism

Another reason for the waning of the holiness movement was its being *divorced from evangelism* in many places. After a glowing holiness meeting in our cotton-mill town of Ashton-under-Lyne, Lancashire, England, in the early nineteen hundreds, when I was but a boy, I overheard a lady exuberantly blurt out to a group of friends, "I've become so thrilled with this glorious holiness teaching that I seem quite beyond any interest in meetings just for the converting of sinners"! Many others, though not so frank, betrayed a similar enchantment with the one at the expense of the other. Beyond a doubt, the all-too-frequent diverting of the holiness movement from earnest evangelism became a definite factor in the ensuing deterioration.

Set-backs through Inconsistency

Still further, it cannot be denied that the holiness movement suffered increasing set-backs through *the inconsistencies of its adherents*. Just because the profession of practical sanctification involves the living of a blameless life, the holiness cause inevitably laid itself the more open to criticism when those professing the blessing exhibited demeanour which belied it. All too many such sham professors were allowed to hang round the holiness movement, and the doctrine became sarcastically stigmatized because of it.

Changeful Decades

But there has been one further factor in the decline of the holiness revival, which is second in influence only to the impact of theological radicalism. I refer to the changeful decades since the First World War. Never before, in so short a space, have the features and outlook of western society been so changed. Two world wars, staggering scientific discoveries and inventions, the rise of vast, anti-Christian ideologies, the splitting of the atom, and the repercussions from all these swift evolutions of our twentieth century, have had a distracting effect, most of all in relation to individual soul-culture. The individual has suddenly appeared so insignificant against the huge economic collectivisms and political totalitarianisms and international magnitudes of our day, that any specializing in the sanctification of the *individual* has seemed a religious luxury no longer tolerable. Despite the spate of revolutionary twentieth-century surprises, however, a saner attitude toward human individuality now seems to be emerging again; but in retrospect we can see only too clearly how the swiftly-unfolding peculiarities of the twentieth century have militated against the holiness re-call which was ringing through the churches as the old century gave place to the new.

Well, at a glance, such is the course things have taken. Beyond question the holiness movement brought a wonderful new exhilaration and enrichment to the evangelical churches. Therefore, despite certain very human blemishes which disfigured it, we may well regret its eclipse and diminishment.

WHAT ABOUT TODAY?

It seems to me that the hour is ripe and the need urgent for a rediscovery of the holiness message. Doubtless, the New Testament doctrine needs restudy and restatement; but beyond all "perhapses" there is an accentuated need today for a recall to Christian sanctification throughout our evangelical churches; and if there is to be a revival of the *experience*, there must be a new emphasis on the *teaching*.

Is not the present juncture opportune? Although the battle still drags on against theological "liberalism" in the Protestant denominations, the earlier shock-assaults have been contained, and successful counter-attacks in the fields of scholarly apologetic and archaeological testimony have ejected rationalistic criticism from the vantage-points which it used to hold under the name of "The New Theology." The theories of the "higher critics" went down one after another before the reply of unconquerable *facts*. The evangelical forces have regrouped and related themselves more confidently to the challenge. The "Liberals" of today simply dare not display the conceit of the earlier "Modernists" who swept in with their vaunted "assured results" which were supposedly going to demolish our "old-fashioned" ideas of the Bible once for all. Moses could not have written the Pentateuch, for writing was not known so far back in Hebrew history! The Messianic poem of Isaiah 40 to 66 simply could not have been written until long enough after the Babylonian exile! The "prophecies" of Daniel could only have been a "pseudepigraphon" from the time of Antiochus Epiphanes! Such brilliant blunders have been answered again and again, and none can deny the scholarly conclusiveness of the Evangelical replies or the confirmations supplied by archaeological findings.

Meanwhile, it still remains true that to people in general the most convincing apologetic of Christianity is its power to transform human lives. One Lazarus, raised, freed, radiant, proves far more to most folk than volumes of pen-and-ink discussions. As Acts 4: 14, says, "Beholding the man which was healed . . . they could say nothing against it." If the New Testament doctrine of holiness still works the lovely miracles of spiritual fulness and fruit-bearing which it wrought in Christian believers during the holiness revival of years ago, then the greatest blessing which could come to our evangelical churches today would be a "revised version" of it.

A Shift to the Experiential

At the present time, so it seems to me, we are needing the relief which comes of a new accent—something spiritually significant enough to turn our debate-wearied minds from the mere mechanics of religion to evidential Christian *experience* in the deeper things of the Spirit. Before all else, even before orthodox dogma, Christianity is a *life*. Holiness, according to the New Testament, is that life experienced and manifested in its purest, deepest, richest, gladdest, fullest qualities. Is it a *real* experience, or only imaginary? The holiness movement to which we have adverted proclaimed through a million eager voices, "Yes, praise God, it is real! It brings real victory over sin; real endue- ment of power from on high; real inward renewal of the propen- sities; real break-through in prayer; cloudless fellowship with Heaven, joy unspeakable, peace which passes understanding, and life more abundant!" Oh, we are needing that accent today, and a new revival of that *experience*!

A Shift from Superficiality

Another consideration which stresses the need for a new epi- demic of sound, Scriptural, holiness teaching is the superficiality of our average present-day Christian profession. There is an exuberant eagerness in modern Christian youth movements, but, in general, does the depth equal the noise? They are versatile, but are they also volatile? Oh, to see our Christian youth gripped by the deeper teachings of the Word concerning sanctification and the fulness of the Holy Spirit! Does someone object that the very words, "sanctification" and "holiness" are strange to the youth in our churches of today? That only confirms what we here say. The terms have dropped out of use, but they are still in the Bible. Does someone else say we need a new vocabulary by which to get the truth over to modern youth? No!—for others who have said so cannot invent a better. What we need is that the great old words shall "come alive" again today, under the power of the divine Spirit.

Of course, the whole pressure of our mechanised, urbanised, industrialised, congested, present-day world, with its wheels and propellers, its specialization and restless goads to go-getting, tends to beget spiritual superficiality; and in that we moderns all need sympathy. A thousand pities that our modern hurry- mania has been allowed to invade the churches! Instead of making the sanctuary and its services a haven of quiet retreat from the outside din and scramble, too many among us seem to deem it a necessary strategy to *copy* the outside world. So, instead of a relieving contrast there is an unrestful imitation, with "stream- lined" services, three-minute hymns, four-minute prayers, and fifteen-minute sermonettes. We know there are many exceptions, and we thank God for *all* those churches which have remained evangelical; but in the many, how skimpy the hymns, and what thin fare from the pulpit! Breeziness and singiness are no compensation for lack of depth and dignity! I believe that nothing could so restore quality to evangelism, and depth to our youth movements, and reverential dignity to our evangelical churches, as a revival of sound, sane, holiness teaching and holiness experience.

Wesley and Booth

That master mind, John Wesley, was quick to see how the revolutionary revival of which he and George Whitefield were the human progenitors would succumb to reaction unless the conversion of sinners was followed by the preaching of something *beyond* conversion. There was not only an Egypt of guilt and condemnation to be left behind, but a Canaan of Spirit-filled sanctification to be possessed! Wesley realised vividly enough that when the early exultations of soul-exodus had subsided, and the novelty of Christian discipleship had worn off, there might easily be a dangerous anti-climax, and a looking back to the flesh-pots of Egypt, unless there was a Canaan alluringly in prospect. Hence originated the widespreading Wesleyan holiness outreaches.

A century later, General Booth was quick to see the same thing in connection with his "Salvation Army". Booth's general-like genius revealed itself, not only in his naming and organising of the "Army", but also in his plan of campaign. He and his gifted wife foresaw that men and women who in their thousands had been saved from the foulest gutters of sin would easily fall prey to squalid reversions when once the excitement of their conversion had worn off, unless some soul-inspiring further goal were set before them. The upshot of this was the Salvation Army holiness movement. Catherine Booth and the early leaders of that sanctification crusade went like flaming seraphs up and down the land, preaching that message of twofold salvation through "blood and fire" for which the Army became famous—the removal of sin from the heart by the cleansing-power of the Saviour's precious blood, and the baptism of the Pentecostal fire.

And now, still another century later, are we not needing, even more poignantly, a further renaissance of New-Testament holiness testimony and experience? It need not articulate the self-same syllables of either the Wesley or the Booth presentation. *They* belonged to their own day and circumstances. *We* need a present-day version which will re-electrify the essentials while discarding out-of-date accidentals. Oh, that it might happen soon! There are many discouraged believers wistfully asking today, in Gideon's mournful words, "Where be all His miracles which our fathers told us of?" (Judges 6: 13). Some of us, at least, are convinced that a widespread new emphasis on sanctification, both doctrinally and practically, could be the answer.

Pray, where be all His miracles
    Of which our fathers told?
Say, were they genuine articles,
    Or fictions big and bold?
Nay, can we think our fathers lied,
    Or else were all deceived,
While impacts still today abide
    From what they then believed?

Say, where today the praying bands
    Which former days have known,
Upraising pleading, patient hands
    Toward the heavenly throne?
Say, if that praying holiness
    Infused *our* zeal to pray,
Would not the old-time miracles
    Break out afresh today?

A RIGHT APPROACH

A RIGHT APPROACH

WE are eager to get right into our subject with least delay. Yet I am persuaded that many of us, because of present-day influences upon our thinking, need the preparatory counsels of this chapter on a *right approach*, if we are readily to grasp the teaching of Scripture on the nature and possibility of personal holiness.

A Right Approach to Scripture

It is unlikely that those of unevangelical persuasion will peruse these pages; yet on the off-chance it may be wise to insist here that there must be a right attitude to *Scripture*. During the last quarter of the nineteenth century Albrecht Ritschl waved his beguiling wand over the intelligentsia of Germany. He was the apostle of a new Christian perfectionism; but it was a hypothetical perfectionism based on a naturalistic interpretation of Scripture. He was followed by Scholz, Karl, Holtzmann, Wernle, Clemen, Pfleiderer, Windisch, and others; all penmen of the "history-of-religion" school; all in open revolt against the nicknamed "miserable-sinner Christianity" of Lutheran and Reformation tradition; all tied to the apron-strings of a rationalistic "higher criticism"; and all having a de-supernaturalizing approach to the Bible.

Those men received or rejected the documents of the New Testament according to a literary detector-apparatus of their own invention for their own convenience. In dealing with Paul's teaching on sin and holiness they accepted as genuine or repudiated as spurious this or that epistle according to an arbitrary critical facility which wonderfully suited their own individual viewpoints but left them disagreeing among themselves.

There can be no true doctrine of Christian holiness going with a defective attitude to Holy Scripture. If Jesus is only a religious pathfinder, or a Christ emptied down to the level of human fallibility, and if Paul's doctrine is not the inerrantly communicated teaching of the Holy Spirit, what vital *reason* is there why I should listen to them? Their word has no more finality than any other which is merely human. On the other hand, if our Lord is the Divine Fulness incarnate, and if Paul is a controlled penman of the Holy Spirit, and if the Bible is the inspired Word of God, then there is certainty, authority, finality, and we may truly know what holiness is.

There is another reason, too, why we need to insist on a right attitude to Scripture. Even among those of us who glory in the Scriptures as the Word of God, it is easily possible to let a theory usurp the authority of the Word itself. There are those who think that if the Wesley school or some other format of holiness teaching be proved wrong, the holiness teaching of the Word itself falls to pieces. I thought so myself at one time, until I saw my theory had fitted me with coloured spectacles. If we are truly to learn God's way of holiness we *must* come to the Word with minds unfettered by merely human theory.

A True View of Sin

There must also be a right approach to the vexatious human malady known as *innate sin*, i.e. hereditary sin-tendency. A defective view of sin can only lead to some concept of holiness which is not truly Scriptural. In much of our holiness teaching today, hereditary "sin" is treated as a sort of separable entity within us, usually called the "old nature", or the "Adam nature", but that idea is a misleading error arising from the misconstruing of those Pauline phrases, "old man" and "body of sin" and "the flesh". The first two of those phrases (as we hope to show) should not be supposed to refer to an "old nature" within us; while "the flesh" equally definitely means a *disseminated* malfunctioning, not a concentrated growth or hard core which can be "eradicated", torn up by the root, or surgically excised by a "second blessing".

As I make these comments thus frankly and early, let me ask the kindly tolerance of gifted and beloved brethren in the ministry who preach (as I once did) what I am here disapproving. I know how much certain views of Romans 6: 6 and related passages mean to them (as they do to myself). Therefore I speak with the more respect. We shall be examining those Scriptures later. For the moment I simply urge that with unchained thinking we ponder these preliminary observations which I am convinced are necessary to a right approach.

That obstinate idea of our inherited sin-bias as an incumbent "old man", or "body of sin", or cankerous concentrate within us, must go. "Sin that dwelleth in me" is *not* to be thought of as a "something" which, although it is deep-seated within me, is not an actual ingredient of the present human ego, and which may therefore be "done away", or bound, gagged, and held down so that it cannot wriggle free. No, sin is an infection inhering *in* and diffused *throughout* our fallen human nature itself; a disease coextensive with our present being. We must rather think of sin, therefore, as blight in a tree, or a degenerative blood-disease in a human body. You cannot cut blight out of a tree, or anaemia out of a human body; yet the blight may be counteracted in the tree, and disease may be counteracted in the body, so that in proportion to the cure the tree produces good fruit, and the body regains healthful normality.

We repeat for emphasis (as it is vital): sin is a disease-condition co-extensive with our nature, and therefore not eradicable on a moral or spiritual operating table. I know that there are cases in which, through conversion to Christ, the drunkard's thirst for liquor, and the drug-addict's craving for narcotics, and the habit-slave's sickly perversity, have suddenly disappeared (as many a freed convert has testified and demonstrated); yet all such cases only serve to corroborate what we are saying. By way of parallel, malignant growths like cancer may be surgically removed from a human body, but the elimination of any one such local *expression* of a disease does not cure the general degenerative blood-condition which accompanied it. All the drunkards and drug-addicts and others who have been instantaneously freed by specific interventions of the Holy Spirit have later found themselves up against the same *general* disease-problem as all the rest of us—"sin that dwelleth in me" (Rom. 7: 17, 20, 23).

Regeneration and Renewal

That leads me to a further observation. Do some of us need corrected perspective as to the nature of *regeneration*? Even though there cannot be any such total "eradication" of sin as some earnest groups have taught, is it not Scriptural to say that *our human nature itself may be refined*? One becomes suspicious of such dogged platitudes as "God never improves the old nature; He gives us a *new* nature." Is not that distinction unscriptural? Where do we find our pre-conversion condition called the "old nature"? We certainly read about the "old leaven" (I Cor. 5: 7, 8) and the "old sins" (2 Peter I: 9); and "old things passed away" (2 Cor. 5: 17); but where do we read about the old *nature*? I am open to be informed. It is no use quoting Romans 6: 6, for in that verse the expression, "our old man", as we hope to show, is *not* a name for something inside us as individuals, but a Paulinism for the whole human race as it is in Adam.

It is the misunderstanding of Romans 6: 6 which is mainly responsible for this usual doctrine of "old" nature versus "new" nature, in the Christian believer. At my conversion to Christ, the Holy Spirit effected a new spiritual birth within me, thereby imparting a new spiritual life; but did that new life come to me in the form of a new *nature* having a distinguishable existence of its own, so that now, within the confines of my one human personality, two natures competitively subsist—an "old" nature and a "new" nature, neither of which is strictly identifiable as *myself*? If that idea of the "two natures" *is* true, then, of course, the hackneyed saying is valid: "When you sin, it is always the old nature, for the new nature cannot sin." But *is* that two-natures idea true? (See on that our companion volume, *His Deeper Work in Us*.) The real truth is, that when the Holy Spirit regenerated me, He regenerated *me*. He did not merely transfer to me, or create inside me, a new "nature"; He infused new and regenerating spiritual life into and through *my own human nature*, so that I became a spiritually renewed human being. And having been thus regenerated, I myself, in my own human nature, may become more and more refined by that same gracious Holy Spirit; for His first *infusion* of the new spiritual life is meant to become a *suffusion* of my whole personality.

Have we not all known consecrated and matured Christian believers whose moral nature itself in all its impulses and desires and affinities has been refined? Was the lovely difference in them merely that a "new" nature, a something not the real self, was now ascendent over an "old" nature, also a something not quite the real self? Then to my way of thinking, that is no real regeneration or sanctification of the *personality*. Just underneath the so-called "new" nature is the unchanged, evil thing, the so-called "old" nature, the pre-conversion ego still remaining. Conversion, regeneration, has only added something; it has changed nothing!

For myself, I cannot accept that; and I wish we could abandon some of our shibboleths which artificially defend it.

What about Ephesians 4: 23, "Be *renewed* in the spirit of your mind"? What about Romans 12, "Be ye transformed by the *renewing* of your mind"? Those texts urge a deep-going renovation in born-again Christian believers. But if already regenerated persons are to be still further "renewed", in what sense can they be? The usual idea of two distinct *natures* in the Christian—the "old" and the "new", cannot hold up against such texts. For according to that usual theory, when we sin, it is never the "new" nature, but the "old"; so the above-quoted texts about "renewal" cannot refer to the "new" nature, for that does not *need* renewal; yet neither can they refer to the "old" nature, for that (so the theory tells us) *cannot* be renewed. What then? Why, surely, those texts which we have quoted, like others which might be given, indicate that there may be, and should be, a renewal of *our human nature itself*.

That idea of the two mutually antagonistic "natures" needs to be discarded. The new life imparted to us by the Holy Spirit is not to be thought of as a "new nature" implanted within us, yet somehow distinct from what we actually *are*; it is rather to be thought of as a wonderful, new, blight-counteracting sap spreading throughout the tree, or as the transfusion of rich, new, health-bringing blood through the entire blood-stream of an ailing body, or better still as being, in actual fact, a vitalizing new *life* from the Holy Spirit, interpenetrating the whole of our mental and moral and spiritual nature. Let us recapture the great and precious truth that *human nature itself* may be sanctified and refined by the Holy Spirit. Have we not *all* sung and prayed with wistful longing many a couplet such as,

> "O Thou Spirit divine,
> *All* my nature refine"?

I believe, with the older theologians, in "total depravity" and "original sin", yet both those scowling phrases can be misread. When we aver the "total depravity" of our Adamic human nature, we dare not mean that our humanhood is *totally* bad. If it were, we would be demons, not humans. From beginning to end the Bible recognises the good as well as the evil in our fallen nature.

Acts 10: 35 is representative when it says, "In every nation he that feareth God and worketh righteousness is acceptable to Him." Everywhere in Scripture, and quite apart from our Christian doctrine of regeneration, men are exhorted to righteousness, nobility, virtue, charity, goodness.

By "total depravity" we mean, not a complete moral rottenness, but that *every part* of our nature, as members of Adam's fallen race, is *infected and damaged* by hereditary sin-effects. The Bible view of our tripartite human nature: spirit, soul, body, is that spiritually we are dead; morally we are corrupt; physically we are weakened and mortal.

When we speak of "original sin" we must distinguish between commission and condition. There is no *commission* of sin in an infant. There is no more a committing of sin in the ungrown infant than there is in a bird or a squirrel. Sin, in the sense of *committing* it in thought, word, act, only comes with the dawn of moral consciousness. I remember the shock it gave me when, as a young believer, I read a printed sermon on "Infant Salvation", by my great preacher-hero, C. H. Spurgeon, in which he speaks of "infant *guilt*". Spurgeon was strongly Calvinist, yet how such a clear-brained prophet as he could ever espouse such a freak idea as infant *guilt* still puzzles me. "Guilt" is a *legal* term, and refers exclusively to *transgression*. There is no guilt where there is no transgression; so, as there simply cannot be moral transgression in a babe, neither can there be guilt. By "original sin", then, we mean only an inherited *condition*; a condition, alas, which comes into this world with fresh repetition every time there is a human birth.

Ever since Pelagius, in the fifth century, there have been sporadic rebellions against the doctrine of "original sin". Never was there a more cultured repudiation of it than by the German scholar, Ritschl, as the last century slipped away. He was not content even with the Pelagian conceit of a will originally poised without bias. No, we each come into the world with a bias for the *good*. According to him, we all sin, as we grow, because immaturity is no match for environment. We sin because we are born into a "*kingdom* of sin". But in the language of logic, that argument is hysteron-proteron, a reversing of the true order; for that universal sinfulness or "kingdom of sin" into which we are born is itself a *product* of original sin.

Yet there was one aspect of truth then emphasized which maybe needed new notice, namely, that besides "original sin" there is original *goodness*. Let none of us who hold the doctrine of "original sin" think it treasonous to believe also in the inheritance of propensities for *good*, for this does not mean that unregenerate man has any goodness which can contribute to his regeneration or salvation. Unless we recognize that besides innate proneness to evil there is innate good, we provoke confusion and become other than truly Scriptural. All the way through, Scripture assumes and appeals to this presence of a remaining good in our hereditary humanhood, and it does this without in the slightest degree diminishing its exposure of our constitutional perversity. Unregenerate man is spiritually dead, but he is not *morally* dead, even though perverted. Conscience bears witness to that (Rom. 2:15). We shall not gain a fully Scriptural idea of our intended sanctification unless we recognize *both* of these two hereditary aspects—"original *sin*" and original *good*. Because there is "original sin" holiness must be divinely *INWROUGHT*. Because there is original good, our nature may be divinely *REFINED*. Yes, regeneration regenerates *ME*. It does not merely attach to the "me" a supposed "new nature." It is I myself who have become spiritually reborn; and the new life is meant to renew *my whole moral nature*.

Christian Standing and Privilege

Also, the more I reflect upon it, the surer I become that we cannot have a true disposition toward the New Testament teaching on holiness unless we have a discerning appreciation of *our standing and privilege in Christ*. Nobody thanks God more than I for the Protestant Reformation. Nobody glories more than I in its triumphal arch of the "doctrines of grace", with its shining keystone "justification by faith". Nobody marches more positively than I under the aegis of Luther and Calvin. Yet do not some of us who march under that honoured banner need to rethink this matter of our standing and privilege in Christ?

Let me explain. I am not saying that the so-called "miserable sinner" emphasis of the Reformers is wrong. More than ever, in these days of hurried living and harried thinking, we need jolting out of our undisturbing psychiatric euphemisms for sin, and our palliating views of human corruptness. More than ever, despite our twentieth-century science and culture, we need the Reformation emphasis on sin.

Yet, even so, the "miserable sinner" emphasis may be overdone to the point where it actually *incapacitates* our response to the New Testament message of inwrought holiness. The Christian life was never meant to be an everlasting "penitent form"; a continual returning of the prodigal from the far country; an incessant repetition of the publican's groan, "God be merciful to me, a sinner." We Christian believers, alas, are still sinners; but we are no longer merely perpetual petitioners for pardon. We have found the "everlasting mercy" and the blood-bought "forgiveness" which covers all our sin! Although, alas, we still grieve our Father, we are no longer prodigals; we are *at home*, restored to true sonship, and in filial fellowship with Him! We are no longer "standing afar off", like the publican, and distantly begging, "God be merciful (literally, be *propitiated*)"; for the one all-inclusive, eternally-final propitiation has now been made on our behalf, and we have entered into it!

All the New Testament epistles were written to Christian recipients, and they all alike assume that the new Christian standing has fundamentally changed all the relationships of those who are "in Christ Jesus". The standpoint is, not that we are fervently *seeking* forgiveness but that we are *already* forgiven in a way which puts us on a new footing—"Even as God also in Christ *forgave* you" (Eph. 4:32). We are not just *seeking* peace with God, but "being justified by faith we *have* peace with God" (Rom. 5:1). We are *already* "delivered out of the power of darkness, and translated into the kingdom of God's dear Son" (Col. 1:13). We are *already* the restored, regenerated "children of God" (1 John 3:2). We are *already* "sealed with the Holy Spirit" as the "earnest of our inheritance" (Eph. 1:13, 14).

All the many such New Testament references add up to a magnificent certitude of *ASSURANCE*—an assurance of eternal salvation in Christ, and of unlimited welcome *as sons of God* at the throne of "the Majesty on high". Therefore we no longer limp there in prodigal's rags, or uncertainly beg as abject aliens. We draw near with filial confidence, gratefully to appropriate what has already been guaranteed. To do so is not presumption; it is God-honouring faith with a blood-sealed warrant. The whole Hebrews epistle is written to show us that it is doubt, not faith, which is God-dishonouring. We are to "come *BOLDLY* to the Throne".

Such, I insist, is the true attitude of the born-again in Christ ; and it alone is the approach which prepares Christian hearts to receive, through consecration and faith, the promised blessing of inwrought holiness. Yet although that attitude undoubtedly concurs with the New Testament epistles, you would scarcely think so, according to much of the "miserable-sinner" emphasis which is supposed to glorify God the more by dwelling with mournful constrictedness on our ugly sinfulness and destitute wretchedness.

Perhaps I can best exemplify by a quotation. It comes from a renowned and saintly preacher who in every dimension was a bigger and better man than I; and, therefore, simply out of ardent admiration I quote without naming him.

"Our guilt is so great that we dare not think of it. . . . It crushes our minds with a perfect stupor of horror, when for a moment we try to imagine a day of judgment when we shall be judged for all the deeds that we have done in the body. Heart-beat after heart-beat, breath after breath, hour after hour, day after day, year after year, and all full of sin; all nothing but sin, from our mother's womb to our grave."

But is that the true language of the cleansed and regenerated Christian heart? "Our *guilt*"—but has not all our guilt been borne and removed by the great Sin-bearer? Must we keep speaking of it as though it still hangs over our heads? Is *that* honouring to God?

"*A day of judgment. . . .*"—but does not the Word say that the Christian believer "shall not come into the judgment"? Could any guarantee be clearer than John 5: 24 or Romans 8: 1?

"*All nothing but sin, from our mother's womb to our grave!*" What life-long hopelessness. What starless blackness of night! Even David, in his *Miserere*, does not indulge such dolorous extremism. Amid his bitterest gush of self-reproach he still believes, not only that a pitying Heaven will "blot out all his iniquities", but that a "clean heart" and a "right spirit" may be divinely wrought within him. Is it not a morbid mistake to think that Christian godliness is made still godlier by traipsing it round in perpetual sackcloth and ashes? Is that true to New Testament emphasis?

"All nothing but sin, from our mother's womb to our grave!" In this depressing obsession with our vileness is there not (even though unintended) a depreciation of our Lord's saviour-hood? Does He not *"save* His people from their *sins"*? Has He not done a saving work *within* us, "purifying our *hearts* by faith"? Alas, we are still sinners, still unworthy, and we realize it more keenly than ever; but blessed be His Name, we are "new creatures in Christ"; He has led us in many a triumph, and His "precious blood" continually "cleanseth from all sin".

"All nothing but sin, from our mother's womb to our grave!" My deepest Christian sensibilities cry out against it, for it reflects cruelly on the dear Saviour who has transformed this heart of mine from a hovel into His sanctified shrine, and has shed the love of God within it by His Holy Spirit. Again and again my heart has been a temple of holy worship. From the very centre of my being I have loved and adored Him. From the inbreathing of His own life my soul has ascended to Him in longings and prayers and motives and intercessions and grateful responses which I *know* were unfeignedly sincere. But I must call them all "nothing but sin"! Unless we break free from such erring extravaganzas of "miserable sinnerism" how can we be in a fit state to hear the New Testament voices which call us, as "sons of God", to the experience of inwrought holiness?

Not long ago, a very Calvinistic friend of mine strove to per-suade us that this lopsided drag of "miserable sinnerism" is a "precious doctrine" inasmuch as, by continually jagging us into a hurting sense of our shameful wickedness, it "magnifies the abounding grace of God" and begets within us "more dependence on Christ." But which of the two, in reality, "magnifies the abounding grace of God" the more—my continued floundering *in* sins, or my being saved *out* of them? Which of the two makes me the more grateful to the "abounding grace of God"—repeated pardon for hapless defeats, or imparted power bringing victories? Which of the two increases my "dependence on Christ"—"the precious doctrine" of my ugly sinnership and abasing unworthi-ness, or the truly Apostolic doctrine of my new sonship in Christ, and my *union* with Him in moral conquest?

There is a right and wrong "miserable sinner" attitude. It is the *wrong* which we here sincerely disapprove. May we never forget the New Testament emphasis, that the Christian belongs to the new, in Christ, rather than to the old, in Adam. It has been truly said, "The Christian belongs to what he is to *become*; not to what he has left behind." The same New Testament which humbles us to the dust as sinners, also calls us *"saints"*. It says that we already *are* saints, positionally, in Christ, and that we are to *become* saints of His in our *character*.

Fascination with Theory

Let me add a final caveat against slavery to holiness *theory*. A review of the successive holiness schools and schemes during the past two hundred years shows with disturbing repetition the almost mesmeric effect which a captivating tangent can exercise over the mind. Men have mistaken theories for theorems, and novelties for certainties, sometimes with dire consequences.

During the last quarter of the nineteenth century there developed in Germany a remarkable movement which became known as *Die Heiligungsbewegung*, that is, "The Sanctification Movement." There was no German-Evangelical National church into which it did not penetrate. In the space of one generation it became a movement of such influence and scope as the German Protestant churches had never seen since the Reformation. In its spiritual aspects it was a German counterpart of convention movements in England. Indeed, it grew from the same origin as they did, i.e. the meteoric holiness campaign of Robert Pearsall Smith, and W. E. Boardman's book, *The Higher Christian Life*.

More than any other, Theodor Jellinghaus gave complexion and safeguard to the main movement in Germany. His "Higher Life" doctrine was derived from Pearsall Smith and Boardman's book. He himself wrote a number of books, but that which set forth the standard theology of the "Higher Life" was his massive volume, *The Complete, Present Salvation Through Christ*. For nearly forty years he was the earnest, gifted, trusted leader of the movement. Never did a man more diligently persevere in advocating the "higher life" doctrine after the Smith and Boardman distinctive pattern, with the usual teaching as to Romans 6, and the crucifixion of "our old man", and the reckoning of oneself to be "dead indeed unto sin".

Eventually, in grievous disillusionment, he felt conscience-bound publicly to renounce the teaching which he had championed so faithfully through the years. In 1912 he issued a book, *Avowals About My Doctrinal Errors*. What it cost him thus openly to demolish that which had been the most precious and conspicuous emphasis of his long and revered leadership, few can realise; but he had at last concluded that the fond theory was not true either to Scripture or experience. His book came as a shock to the Christian public, the more so because it was the honest recantation of such an one as Jellinghaus. How far he was right or wrong, of course, is a matter of individual opinion; but Jellinghaus himself remains a sad monument to the heart-rending disillusionments which come through hallucination with specious theory.

There is an old proverb which says that some people "cannot see wood for trees". It is equally true, in this sacred concern of individual holiness, that some of us may hardly see Scripture for theories. I believe our usual theories of holiness have gone seriously astray in their particular teaching as to Romans 6, and their concept of "two natures" in the believer, and the supposed destroying or rendering "inoperative" of the so-called "old nature" by an inward crucifixion with Christ. My conviction is, that until we disentangle holiness teaching from those popular errors we shall never recover the glad simplicities of sanctification as taught by the New Testament. Into those matters we shall probe later. Meanwhile, I do not ask that my own views be accepted on any aspect, but that we come to the teaching of Scripture with open mind, so as to learn the real *meaning* and know the real *blessing* of holiness.

Let me recapitulate: for in these days of shaken foundations and theological chaos this matter of a right approach needs all the more emphasis. There *must* be a right approach to the Bible as the authentic Word of God. There *must* be a right approach to the hereditary sin-bent in human nature—for if we are wrong as to the malady we shall be wrong as to the remedy. There *must* be a right approach to the meaning of regeneration, and a clear-sighted appreciation of our true Christian standing. Also, as we have just added, we must free our thinking, as far as possible, from bondage to stereotyped theory which we may hitherto have accepted and assumed to be Scriptural merely because it is conventional or associated with imposing names.

Among those who travel with us through these chapters it is

not unlikely that some will be Eradicationists after the thorough-going Wesley pattern. Perhaps others may be Counteractionists after the earlier or present-day Keswick form of presentation. Others may be Pentecostalists holding the now characteristic concept of complete sin-expurgation through the so-named "baptism of the Holy Spirit". Other readers may be full-time Christian ministers—which I sincerely hope may be the case, for one of my saddest retrospects as I now look back over the past eighteen years of continuous travel in U.S.A., Canada, Britain, and elsewhere, is the number of earnest evangelical ministers who shy away from the subject of holiness because of the unsatisfactory theories and controversy connected with it. I ask of one and all a prayerful open-mindedness as we now get into these studies; for this matter of Christian holiness is sacred and vital above all other spiritual concerns.

> Teach me, O Lord, as only Thou canst teach;
>   Tutor my erring mind, illume my eyes,
> That I, with prayerful, guided upward reach,
>   May grasp the vital truth which sanctifies.
>
> Come to me through the Paraclete divine;
>   Teach me my heavenly birthright to possess;
> My mind, my brain, my will, my *all* be Thine,
>   And Thy suffusing life my holiness.

THEORY VERSUS EXPERIENCE

NOTE

As we move further into these reflections on holiness we cannot avoid encountering a certain "strife of theories"; and our fear is lest to some readers (particularly younger believers) the precious subject should seem too tangled for further pursuance. We would gladly have over-leapt the next three chapters, except that they really are necessary if we are to *guard* as well as *guide*. Furthermore, in many an instance, one of the surest ways of showing how right the truth is, is to show how wrong error is.

I have some concern, also, lest these earlier chapters should give the impression that this book is designed to counter *wrong* theories rather than expound the *right* one! I am only too anxious to get on with the latter; but our eventual emphasis on the *true* will be all the more intelligent if we have first unshackled our thinking from error, knowing *why* it is error.

THEORY VERSUS EXPERIENCE

COULD anything be more wonderful than the New Testament message of a present heart-holiness provided in Christ for His redeemed people? To all who read these pages we say: Seek this heart-holiness above all else. The more out of keeping it seems with the flimsy moral standards of the day and the poor spiritual average in the churches, the more needful it is. Enquire carefully what the New Testament actually teaches about it. Then wait on God for it until you have the inward witness that the reality is yours. So will you find the "joy unspeakable", and become indeed a channel of divine grace to others.

Never was that advice more eagerly given; but, alas, no sooner do we give it than we encounter a problem. There are sharply contradictory views as to how this inward sanctification is *effected*, and as to what extent it deals with indwelling *sin*. Because of this, in its doctrinal aspects, holiness has been made to look like "a house divided against itself". In fact, rival theories and seemingly irreconcilable cleavages of interpretation have gradually inflicted such seeming complexity on the subject that thousands of holiness-hungry hearts have turned away discouraged.

Yet what the Bible teaches on personal holiness is not only vital, it is *simple*. As in other connections, so here, it is human theory, not divine truth, which is complicated. Is anything simpler than the Lord's Supper, as enjoined in the Scriptures? Yet see how ecclesiastical systems have complicated *that*! Dear reader, read on: if this and the next two chapters seem controversial it is only because we are hacking through theories which obfuscate the truth. Remember, often the truth itself is clearer and dearer to us when we have to cut our way to it through entanglements of human theory.

Of holiness theories there are especially *two* which have long held sway; and still today, wherever the holiness emphasis remains, either one or the other is preached as the true "way of holiness"—

not perhaps with the same dogmatism as formerly, yet just as decidedly. I am convinced that *both* theories are wrong. Both of them have brought wonderful promise of deliverance from indwelling sin, and both have brought thousands into later bondage. If we are again to see a revival of Christian believers rejoicing in the authentic experience of inward sanctification, the New Testament message (so I believe) must be rescued from these two impressive but subversive theories.

One of them is known as the *"eradication* theory"; the other as the *"counteraction* theory". Maybe many younger Christians today are unfamiliar with those expressions. None the less, all need to know what is represented by them, so as to be guarded from error and guided to the real truth. This is the more needful because both these theories are associated with honoured Christian leaders and movements. Therefore, reluctant though we are to interrupt the direct line of our present studies, we must turn aside awhile to counter these attractive errors.

The Eradication Theory

Take the first of them; that which we call the *eradication* theory. Ever since the venerable John Wesley formulated it, this doctrine has been widely promulgated all over the Christian world, and still is. The teaching is, that in "entire sanctification", which comes by way of the "second blessing", there is complete eradication of "inbred sin", of the sinful "old man" or "old nature" or "the flesh", or the "carnal nature" which still lingers in the believer after conversion. The teaching is based on texts such as Romans 6: 6, which, in our Authorized Version reads, "Our old man is crucified with Him [Christ] that the body of sin might be destroyed." Here are representative quotations from John Wesley.

"Inward sin is then totally destroyed; the root of pride, self-will, anger, love of the world, is then taken out of the heart. . . . The carnal mind, and the heart bent to backsliding, are entirely extirpated."
(*Sermons*, vol. 1, p. 124.)

" 'I am crucified with Christ; nevertheless I live; yet not I, but Christ liveth in me'—words that manifestly describe a deliverance from inward as well as outward sin . . . 'I live not' (my evil nature, the body of sin, is *destroyed*)."
(*Sermons*, vol. 2, p. 19.)

"The body of sin, the carnal mind, must be *destroyed*; the old man must be *slain*, or we cannot put on the new man, which is created . . . in righteousness and true holiness."

Journal of Hester Ann Rogers.

The same eradication doctrine floats to us in unhesitating overtones from the famous Methodist Hymnbook of 1780. For instance:

> Enter my soul, *extirpate* sin,
> Cast out the cursed seed.
>
> Speak the second time: Be clean!
> Take away my *inbred* sin.

Did Wesley and the hymnbook really *mean* "eradication"?—or was it poetic hyperbole? There can be no doubt that real eradication was meant, for it effected (supposedly) a complete *"extinction"* of innate sin. Alluding to Romans 6: 6, Wesley wrote, "I use the word 'destroyed' because St. Paul does. 'Suspended' I cannot find in my Bible." (*Letters* 4: 203.) Tyerman, in his *Life of John Wesley*, says that at the first Methodist Conference, in 1744, Christian perfection was thus defined:

"A renewal in the image of God, in righteousness and true holiness. To be a perfect Christian is to love the Lord our God with all our heart, soul, mind and strength, *implying the destruction of all inward sin*; and faith is the condition and instrument by which such a state of grace is obtained" (italics ours).

Representative Others

So has it been from then until now: the eradicationists have not only taught it, but have triumphantly gloried in it as a "going the whole way with the word of God". Here are a few representative quotations from influential teachers.

"In regeneration sin does not *reign*; in sanctification it does not *exist*. In regeneration sin is *suspended*; in sanctification it is *destroyed*. In regeneration irregular desires are *subdued*; in sanctification they are *removed*."

W. Macdonald, *Perfect Love.*

"Justification saves from sinning, but not from the *tendency* to sin, improperly called sin because it lacks the voluntary element essential to guilt. But in those proclivities to sin, though repressed, there is peril and cause of inward strife, the flesh warring against the spirit, and the spirit against the flesh. When this war ends by the *extinction and annihilation* of the flesh as the lurking-place of the sin-principle, there is deliverance from *sin*, also, as well as from *sinning*."

Daniel Steele, Love Enthroned.

"Entire sanctification is an act of God's grace by which inbred sin is removed and the heart made holy. Inbred sin or inherited depravity is the inward cause of which our outward sins are the effects. . . . It exists in every human being that comes into the world, as a bias or proclivity to evil. It is called, in the New Testament, 'the flesh,' the 'body of sin,' our 'old man,' 'sin that dwelleth in me,' and the simple term 'sin' in the singular number." "Now all Christian denominations are agreed as to the real existence of this inbred sin and also as to the fact that it is not removed at conversion. . . . But God has in every age required His children to be holy. And to be holy signifies the *destruction or removal* of inbred sin, nothing more and nothing less and nothing else than that."

Dougan Clark, Theology of Holiness, pp. 27–29.

Present-day Voices

It may be asked, however, if the eradication of inbred sin is taught by responsible thinkers and teachers today. Yes, it is, and by excellent brethren too. One of the most respected evangelical Bible teachers in U.S.A., and a much valued friend of mine, published a writing shortly before his heavenly home-going, and said:

"In the purpose of God, at Calvary, every Christian died when Christ died. 'We who died to sin' is our description (Rom. 6: 2) because of this fact. 'Knowing that our old man'—our natural self, 'was crucified with Christ' (Rom. 6: 6). . . . So we are to reckon ourselves 'dead unto sin' (Rom. 6: 11).

"Now for the practical value of this for daily living. Instead of leaving me to struggle with my sinful nature and its promptings, Christ took that nature with Him to be crucified, 'that the body of sin might be done away'—made inoperative, put out of business—'that so we should no longer be in bondage to sin' (Rom. 6: 6, E.R.V.). Thus Christ made it unnecessary and unreasonable for me to sin.

"Knowing that the self in me which gets angry died with Christ, was put out of business, I am free not to get angry; and I never do. I used to be subject to the movings of envy and jealousy; but no longer, since I count myself dead to all such. I used to worry, but the 'I' that worries, Christ included in His death. I used to be impatient, but the self in me which would get impatient, died with Christ, and I am free."

I recently read a useful holiness study by a contemporary author who is a gracious and gifted speaker at Conferences on the deeper spiritual life. He says,

"Some declare that sin must remain in the heart of the believer until death, but in Romans, chapter 6, verse 6, we read that our corrupt, sinful nature can be *destroyed*, that henceforth we should not serve sin. Three times in that chapter we are told that we are made 'free from sin'. Note that the word is 'sin' and not 'sins'. It therefore refers to our sinful nature which can be put off (Eph. 4: 22), and cleansed away (1 John 1: 7). We must hold to this clear teaching of God's Word, though we will not argue with those who differ in their interpretation of it. ..."

So the eradication theory is: that having yielded all to Christ we are by faith to identify ourselves with Him in His death, believing that our "old nature" is "crucified with Him" and "destroyed." Thenceforth we are to "*reckon*" ourselves "dead indeed unto sin"; and if we do, then the "reckoning" of ourselves dead to sin will become actual *experience* of it.

Recently the Manual of a well-known evangelical denomination gave the viewpoint of that body thus:

"We believe that original sin, or depravity, is that corruption of the nature of all the offspring of Adam by reason of which everyone is very far gone from original righteousness or the pure state of our first parents at the time of their creation, is averse to God, is without spiritual life, and is inclined to evil, and that continually. We further believe that original sin continues to exist with the new life of the regenerate, *until eradication by the baptism with the Holy Spirit*." (Italics ours.)

The Big Contradiction

Is the eradication theory right or wrong? We purpose a little later, to examine it exegetically (the written Word always being our decisive court of appeal). But before one word of exegetical criticism of it is submitted let me pay tribute to the many loyal servants of our Lord who have preached it. Some of the most illustrious names in the Church's history of the last two hundred years are associated with it, from that saintly giant, John Wesley, onwards. Let all those dear brethren in the Christian ministry who still teach it be assured that my frank animadversions on the *theory* are expressed with cordial Christian love to *them*, among whom I cherish valued friends, and could wish I were half as devout as they. So, if they chance on these pages, let me ask their *brotherly* scrutiny. If what I submit can be refuted I will welcome correction. In this present chapter I touch on eradication only in relation to the hard facts of *experience*, and I do so by quoted testimony from one whom all of us have admired.

Dr. H. A. Ironside, in his trenchant little work, *Holiness; the False and the True*, paints a sorry picture of his own inner torture, and that of other Christian workers, brought up during earlier years in the eradication doctrine. If ever a young man sincerely handed himself over to Christ, and reverently "claimed the blessing", and intensively persevered to experience the eradication of inbred sin, he did. Yet at last, exhausted after years of painful trial and re-trial he knew that any further pretence was sheer hypocrisy: and at the same time he discovered that others around him who professed "the blessing" were similarly heart-sick with secret agony of disillusionment.

After his conversion in early youth, he linked up with the Salvation Army, which at that time, to quote his own words, was at "the zenith of its energy as an organization devoted to going out after the lost". Young Harry soon enjoyed the Army "Holiness Meetings". Substantially, the teaching was this: "When converted, God graciously forgives all sins committed up to the time when one repents. But the believer is then placed in a lifelong probation, during which he may at any time forfeit his justification and peace with God if he falls into sin from which he does not at once repent. In order, therefore, to maintain himself in a saved condition, he needs a further work of grace called sanctification. This work has to do with sin the root, as justification had to do with sin the fruit. The steps leading up to this second blessing are, firstly, conviction as to the need of holiness (just as in the beginning there was conviction of the need of salvation); secondly, a full surrender to God, or the laying of every hope, prospect and possession on the altar of consecration; thirdly, to claim in faith the incoming of the Holy Spirit as a refining fire to burn out all inbred sin, thus destroying *in toto* every lust and passion, leaving the soul perfect in love and pure as unfallen Adam."

Dr. Ironside tells how he continually sought the blessing, until: "At last, one Saturday night . . . I determined to go out into the country and wait on God, not returning till I had received the blessing of perfect love. I took a train at eleven o'clock, and went to a lonely station twelve miles from Los Angeles. There I alighted, and, leaving the highway, descended into an empty *arroyo*, or water-course. Falling on my knees beneath a sycamore tree, I prayed in an agony for hours, beseeching God to show me anything that hindered my reception of the blessing. Various matters of too private and sacred a nature to be here related came to my mind. I struggled against conviction, but finally ended by crying, 'Lord, I give up *all*—everything, every person, every enjoyment, that would hinder my living alone for Thee. Now give me, I pray Thee, the blessing.'

"As I look back, I believe I was fully surrendered to the will of God at that moment, so far as I understood it. But my brain and nerves were unstrung by the long midnight vigil and the intense anxiety of previous months, and I fell almost fainting to the ground. Then a holy ecstasy seemed to thrill all my being. This I thought was the coming into my heart of the Comforter. I cried out in confidence, 'Lord, I believe Thou dost come in. Thou dost cleanse and purify me from all sin. I claim it now. The work is done. I am sanctified by Thy blood. Thou dost make me holy. I believe! I believe!' I was unspeakably happy. I felt that all my struggles were ended.

"With a heart filled with praise, I rose from the ground and began to sing aloud. Consulting my watch, I saw it was about half-past three in the morning. I felt I must hasten to town so as to be in time for the seven o'clock prayer-meeting, there to testify to my experience."

From then onwards, young Ironside was an earnest testimonial and advocate of the doctrine. The wilderness was past; he was in Canaan; he was "entirely sanctified"; inward sin-bias was now "destroyed"; or so he thought. But as time went on, evil desires began to reassert themselves. He was nonplussed. However, a leading teacher assured him that these were only "temptations", not actual sin: so that pacified him for a time. Later he became a cadet, then a lieutenant, then a captain, in the Salvation Army. During those years there were tormenting relapses, all-nights of prayer, renewed struggles after self-crucifixion, with inescapable evidence that the supposed eradication of his "sinful nature" was a delusive sophism. He writes: "And now I began to see what a string of derelicts this holiness teaching left in its train. I could count scores of persons who had gone into utter infidelity because of it. They always gave the same reason: 'I tried it all. I found it a failure. So I concluded the Bible teaching was all a delusion, and religion was a mere matter of the emotions.' Many more (and I knew several· such intimately) lapsed into insanity after floundering in the morass of this emotional religion for years—and people said that studying the Bible had driven them crazy. How little they knew that it was lack of Bible knowledge that was accountable for their wretched mental state —an absolutely unscriptural use of isolated passages of Scripture!

"At last I became so troubled I could not go on with my work. ... Finally, I could bear it no longer, so I asked to be relieved from all active service, and at my own request was sent to the Beulah Home of Rest, near Oakland. . . . In the Rest Home I found about fourteen officers, broken in health, seeking recuperation. I watched the ways and conversation of all most carefully, intending to confide in those who gave the best evidence of entire sanctification. There were some choice souls among them, and some arrant hypocrites. But holiness in the absolute sense I saw in none. Some were very godly and devoted. Their conscientiousness I could not doubt. But those who talked the loudest were plainly the least spiritual. They seldom read their Bibles, they rarely conversed together of Christ. An air of carelessness pervaded the whole place. Three sisters, most devoted women, were apparently more godly than any others; but two of them admitted to me that they were not *sure* about being perfectly holy. The other was non-committal though seeking to help me. Some were positively quarrelsome and boorish, and this I could not reconcile with their profession of freedom from inbred sin. . . . At last I found myself becoming cold and cynical."

Dr. Ironside tells how he struggled free at last from this specious perfectionism which had so flogged and foiled him. Then he adds: "Since turning aside from the perfectionist societies, I have often been asked if I find as high a standard maintained among Christians generally who do not profess to have the 'second blessing' as I have seen among those who do. My answer is, that after carefully, and I trust without prejudice, considering both, I have found a far higher standard maintained by believers who intelligently reject the eradication theory than among those who accept it. Quiet, unassuming Christians, who know their Bibles and their own hearts too well to permit their lips to talk of sinlessness and perfection in the flesh, nevertheless are characterized by intense devotion to the Lord Jesus Christ, love for the Word of God, and holiness of life and walk."

Dr. Ironside later became one of the best-known evangelical leaders of our time; a powerful preacher and a judicious Bible expositor. We have given our quotations from him for three reasons: (1) In those early years, not only was he open-minded to the eradication theory, he was fervently disposed in its favour. (2) He not only sought and claimed "the blessing" with intense sincerity, but persevered protractedly, "hoping against hope" that it might yet prove real. (3) His eventual verdict is one of honest conscience, from first-hand evidence, not from prejudice. My own testimony is, that what *he* found, in himself and others, I too have found, in basically similar experience, and also through interchange with trustworthy Christian brethren who at first gloried in the teaching, then later found themselves mocked by it.

We respect the sincere desire of eradicationist teachers to "go all the way" with the wording of Romans 6, but (even if their interpretation of the wording in verse 6 were permissible) the theory is disproved by experience. I have yet to meet even an eradicationist who would seriously maintain that his or her supposedly once-for-all eradication-surgery had left an *utter* absence of all thoughts or desires less than the absolutely holy.

The only way that our eradicationist brethren can make their experience even approximately measure up to their theory is by insisting (as some indeed do) on an easier doctrine of sin. Only is there sin (so they aver) where there is voluntary activity of the will. Yet even if we concede that such is true of sinful acts (i.e. transgression in thought, word, deed), what about those subtle stirrings, desires, inclinations, outside the domain of the will, and deeper than immediate consciousness itself, which with deadly repetition *originate* sin? The eradication theory, in loyalty to the wording of passages like Romans 6, teaches that all such proclivities are *extirpated*: but can we find such absolute and continuing extinction *any*where, even in saintliest experience?

Long before Harry Ironside floundered in his quagmire of eradicationist problems, John Wesley found his feet in similar bogs. Writing to Miss Jane Hilton in 1769, he lamented, "Although many taste of that heavenly gift, deliverance from inbred sin, yet so few, so exceeding few, retain it one year; hardly one in ten; nay, one in thirty." Similar regrets are jotted intermittently up and down his Journal. Again, in his *Sermons* (vol. 2, p. 247) he sadly observes, concerning certain persons who were once sanctified (in the eradicationist sense), "Nevertheless, we have seen some of the strongest of them, after a time, moved from their steadfastness. Sometimes suddenly, but oftener by slow degrees, they have yielded to temptation; and pride or anger, or foolish desires, have again sprung up in their hearts. Nay, sometimes they have utterly lost the life of God, and sin hath regained dominion over them."

All such instances of lapse pose a problem—a problem which, in the aggregate, becomes one of deadly acuteness for the eradication theory. It is this: if, in the entirely sanctified, the "*old* nature" has become extinct (as the eradicationists claim) and the new nature (as they say) *cannot* sin, being a direct divine impartation, then when entirely sanctified persons *lapse* into sin, which part is it which sins? It cannot be the "*old* nature", for that is gone; yet it cannot be the "new" for that is the inbreathed life of the Holy Spirit. Which other territory is there within the human personality? Is it altogether to be wondered at, that a perplexed John Wesley, in a letter to his brother Charles (see *Works*, vol. 12, pp. 135, 136) once wrote, "I am at my wit's end with regard to . . . Christian perfection." "Shall we go on asserting perfection against all the world? Or shall we quietly let it drop?"

What, then, of the words, "crucified" and "destroyed", in Romans 6: 6? It will be our endeavour, a few pages hence, to prove that the eradicationist theory radically misinterprets not only that verse but the whole context in which it occurs. Meanwhile, according to our light, we counsel all those pilgrims who are enquiring after "the way of holiness" not to follow the eradicationist signpost. In saying this we do not forget esteem for those brethren who with highest motive have preached it as truly Scriptural. The eradication theory is one of those well-meant but misleading formulations that have made holiness seem strange and complicated to many. When once we free our minds from such misunderstandings, and get to the unencumbered teaching of the Word, we shall see how radiantly positive and *simple* the New Testament doctrine of holiness is. But if some still cling to the eradication theory we shall charitably defend their right to differ, and still "esteem them very highly, in love, for their work's sake" (1 Thes. 5: 13).

A WELL-MEANT ALTERNATIVE

Error is least of all pleasant to disapprove when it is utterly sincere and clothes itself in the theories of saintly men whose aim is altogether the honour of our Lord. Therefore, unorthodox though our procedure may be, we have decided to leave our quotations anonymous where we make adverse comment. This completely removes all personal flavour and restricts attention to the subject alone. Some of the brethren quoted are no longer with us, but we are resolved not to let our reasonings on such a sacredly spiritual subject as Christian holiness seem at any point to reflect even in the faintest degree upon dear men of God the memory of whom is as "precious ointment poured forth".

J.S.B.

A WELL-MEANT ALTERNATIVE

IN our preceding chapter Dr. Harry Ironside shone his red lamp of warning on the eradication theory. Yet neither he nor we could ever leave unspoken our genuine esteem for the many outstanding servants of our Lord who have taught it. Some of them have been such saints, and have walked so closely with God, that although we diverge from their theory, we may well covet their *experience*.

Our attitude is equally warm as we now touch on that other theory which we mentioned, i.e. the teaching that inward sanctification is effected, not by an eradication of our inherited sin-bias, but by a powerful *counteraction* of it. The counteraction theory is meant as an alternative to that of eradication.

There is little difference, really, between the "counteraction" theory and what used to be called the *"suppression"* theory (i.e. that although the sin-bias cannot be eradicated it can be thoroughly suppressed). The "counteraction" form of presentation is an exegetical amplification of the other, and has often been referred to as the *Keswick* theory.

Let this be clearly grasped: the "counteraction" theory *denies* eradication, and teaches victory *over* our hereditary sinfulness rather than complete freedom *from* it. It holds that the way of sanctification is by the counteraction-effect of an *inward joint-crucifixion with Christ*, and by "the law of the Spirit of life in Christ Jesus". Through the years, this theory has become firmly associated with certain well-known movements which are highly thought of by very many.

In this chapter we give representative quotations. Let it first be understood, however, that wherever we make disapproving comment it is always with cordial esteem for men whom we regard as consecrated servants of the Lord, and in some cases as uniquely gifted scholars of the Word. Our purpose is to show that this peculiar teaching of sanctification by counteraction misin-

terprets Scripture and engenders bondage in Christian believers;
but the pure motive and high aspiration of many who have taught
it will never once be in question.

Frankly, criticism here is most distasteful to us, even though
it is purely exegetical, never personal. On such a subject as holiness
we would fain shun the controversial. Yet if we are most effectively
to open up what we believe to be the true New Testament teaching
we cannot evade prior encounter here with this further theory
which in our judgment *deforms* the truth. So, if these earlier pages
seem rather argumentative may I point out that there is a big
difference between exercising one's critical *faculty*, and indulging
a critical *spirit*. For the former we thank God and pray to use it
reverently. From the latter may our dear Lord save us and give
us instead a gracious sympathy.

The fairest method we can think of is to give actual quotations,
so as to let the theory talk to us in its own words, and then append
our comment. The quotations are kept to a minimum, yet such is
my concern not to cast reflection on any of the excellent brethren
who are quoted that I leave all the quotations anonymous (see
fly-leaf note). Most of them are taken from a composite publication
issued a few years ago, containing expositions by different contributors from about fifty years ago up to the present. The theory
is taught as definitely today as it was fifty years ago, though there
may be some shift in incidental form or phrase of presentation.

For the sake of some who may be new readers in the subject
let me emphasize that the polemic centre-point of cleavage
between the two theories, i.e. Eradication and Counteraction,
has always been Romans 6:6 which, in our King James Version,
reads:

> Knowing this, that our old man is crucified with Him [Christ]
> that the body of sin might be destroyed.

There are other texts and passages involved, but beyond
question the centre-point has always been Romans 6. For confirmation of this see our fly-leaf quotation from Steven Barabas,
on page 72. Both the Eradication and Counteraction theories
take Paul's two expressions, "our old man" and "the body of
sin," as meaning a (so-called) "*old nature*" which (theoretically)
inheres in born-again Christian believers. On the basis of
Romans 6:6 the Eradicationist argument is, that this sinful

"old nature" may be completely excised, so as to exist no more in the fully sanctified believer. Over against that, our Counteractionist interpreters modify the meaning of Romans 6:6 in line with their earnest insistence that the evil "old nature" must remain within us to our last day in mortal flesh. We ourselves believe that *both* theories are just as wrong as they are sincere —as we shall respectfully endeavor to show.

If I may momentarily anticipate our later chapters, let me state here, without waiting, our central thesis in these studies. It may be concentrated thus:

> *The inwrought santification of Christian*
> *believers is effected, not by a (supposed)*
> *inward union with our Lord Jesus in His*
> *crucifixion*-death, *but by full union with*
> *Him in His resurrection*-life.

I mention this in advance because, from these earlier chapters where we seek to show that our New Testament does *not* teach any such inward identification of believers with our Lord in His Calvary death, some reader might possibly get the impression that we are "pulling down" without "building up." We are sorry there is any *need* for the former; but our *positive* proposition will be all the clearer afterward. It is our conviction that Romans 6 and certain other Scriptures (e.g. Galatians 2:20) while unspeakably precious in themselves, do *not* refer, as is generally taught, to the believer's inward sanctification. If we can *prove* that such is the case, then the sooner we cease to allow fallacious misapplications of those passages to keep complicating this sacred subject of Christian sanctification, the better.

And now, as we come to our representative quotations from spokesmen of the Counteractionist theory, perhaps we may usefully fore-mention its three salient features. (1) Experiential sanctification comes by an inward co-crucifixion with Christ. (2) That inward crucifixion is, in particular, a crucifixion of the so-called "old nature"—or, as some call it, our "former self." (3) But although the "old nature" or evil "self" may be thus crucified, its crucifixion does *not* mean its eradication, but only its being (as is said) "rendered inoperative," or thereby counteracted. (4) The "old nature" must inhere within us to the end

of our life on earth. This last-mentioned is iterated emphatically, as the first of our few quotations will show.

> "Though God does not remove that *indwelling principle*, or
> corrupt thing we call sin, yet He does by His infinite mercy
> give us a perfect, perpetual, and enjoyable deliverance from
> the activities, from the power, from the domination of sin,
> moment by moment, so long as we trust Him and acknowl-
> edge ourselves to be *guilty* sinners at every instant of our
> lives. I pause at that word, and reiterate it: while we acknowl-
> edge ourselves to be *guilty* sinners every moment . . ." (Italics
> ours.)

> "One said to me, 'If Christ was revealed to destroy the works
> of the devil, how can there be any sin left? I replied, 'Dear
> brother, do wait a bit; Christ's day is coming' . . . *When God
> sees fit to take us away from this poor, corrupt, mortal flesh,*
> corruption shall give place to glory." (Italics ours.)

So deliverance comes only by our being ridded of the physical
body—as though the body itself ("this poor, *corrupt* mortal
flesh") were sinful!

> "Notwithstanding that indwelling corruption does, as I hold,
> necessarily stain every thought and word and deed of life . . . the
> Lord Jesus Christ is only thereby made more and more beautiful. . . ."

Yet however anxious the preacher may have been to convince
us that the "evil nature" remains in us "to the last", staining
"every thought, word, deed", it strangely jars on our spiritual
sensibilities to be told that our Lord Jesus is *"thereby* made more
and more beautiful." The Word of God recognizes no such use-
fulness of indwelling sin! On the contrary, it is indwelling sin
which *dulls* our perception of His beauty.

> "Thanks be to God—let us announce it very clearly—though sin
> does remain to the very last, we believe, both in the being of the man,
> and also in the outcome from the man, yet there is no necessity what-
> ever for a child of God ever to commit one single known sin."

So, by bold pronouncement, there is no deliverance "to the
very last" from this evil nature, this "indwelling corruption",
yet there is "no necessity whatever" to commit "one single known
sin"! The physician says, in effect, to the patient, "You are a

cripple; you will always be a cripple; yet there is 'no necessity whatever' for you ever to take one crippled step again!" Or, "You are a withered consumptive; you will always be a consumptive; yet there is 'no necessity whatever' for you ever to breathe one consumptive breath again"!

"The great teaching . . . is that there is a delivering Lord, a mighty Jesus, who by His infinite love has made provision . . . for the preservation of every child of God from any one known sin; and *to pass through us* such thoughts, such words, and such deeds as shall be always acceptable to God the Father when they are rightly presented to Him through Christ Jesus our Lord."

So there is *no* changing of our nature; but Christ causes "acceptable" thoughts, words, deeds to *pass through us*. Those thoughts are not strictly our own, arising from a renewed human nature; they originate with God and come *through* us. As the preacher adds, "The thoughts of God . . . are passed into the child of God through the brain; and then they are coming out into words and works." Alas, even then we can have no personal holiness; for the preacher pathetically explains that although the "thought" is passed to us from God, and "comes to us absolutely perfect", it passes out of us "tainted, as water passing through a pipe would necessarily be tainted if the pipe were in some degree defiled in its composition". So, not only does our nature remain uncleansed, but even the holy thoughts of God through us are "tainted" in transmission! The speaker himself must have perceived that in supposedly preaching holiness he was denying the possibility of it, for he finalizes the point thus:

"Then you say: Where is this peace and this blessed rest of soul? Why, it is in this: As the thing [i.e. the thought from God] comes forth from me, as it were through a [defiled] fountain, *the blood of Christ is ever dripping upon it as it emanates.*"

Is not that a strange picture of holiness! My sinful nature cannot be changed; indwelling corruption must remain "to the last". There is never "a single thought, word, or deed" that is not "tainted by sin". No holy thoughts originate in myself, they are *God's* thoughts "passed *through* me", and even those are "tainted" in transit through me and the blood of Christ must be "ever dripping" upon them as they "emanate" from me. What good is it that the dear preacher forgets himself in one place, and says, "I can begin to think the thoughts of God"? Nay, he has made such holy thought impossible by insisting that the "I" is incurably corrupt. But what a comforting contradiction he slips into when he says, "That taste . . . that appetite . . . may, by the grace of God, be subdued and *removed*!" Perhaps that word, "removed" was a slip, but it breaks like a sunshaft through drab clouds! And, of course, we are prompted to ask, quite naturally: If *one* "appetite" may be "removed", as the preacher remarks, then why not *others*?—and why not *all*?

Other Slants and Aspects

I pass by other addresses, with recurrent expressions such as "empty of self", "dead to self", "the death of the self", all of which are unscriptural as well as psychological impossibilities, and halt at an address upon *Threefold Deliverance*, i.e. deliverance from sin (1) as defilement, (2) as a habit, (3) as a law or tendency. Bound up with the counteraction idea, certain peculiar distinctions are drawn. Here is one:

"But let me now very earnestly entreat you to mark the distinction between the *heart* and the *nature*. The evil heart is not the evil nature. It is in this connection that thousands of people are making a great mistake. No wonder they get confused in the matter of sanctification. The heart is capable of passing through varying conditions. The nature remains unchanged. The heart may be cleansed, sanctified, and made the dwelling-place of God. But you cannot sanctify the evil nature. Therefore let us not confuse the heart, the evil heart, with the evil nature."

Now surely this distinction here between the "heart" and the "nature" is artificial and misleading. We have looked up the 958 instances where our Authorised Version has the word "heart", in its singular, plural, and compound forms, also the Hebrew and Greek usage; and if one thing stands out it is this: that when used in its figurative sense the heart represents, more often than anything else, either the whole mental and moral being, or the centre-point of thought, desire, will, and feeling. In a representative sense, the "heart" *is* the "nature", the living, self-aware human person. In a moral sense, what I am in my heart, that I am in my nature. Yet we are told that the heart may be cleansed, but not the nature![1]

The speaker rightly defines the heart as "the place within you where three things are focused—your thoughts, your desires, and your will". On another line he calls it the inner world of intellect, emotion, volition. Now if all our thought, desire, will, intellect, emotion, volition, are the "heart" (as he himself says) but not the "nature", then what can the "nature" possibly *be*? What *else* is there in our mental and moral being beside intellect, emotion, volition, desire, and conscience? If the "nature" is some vagary outside all these, is it worth even noticing? And if "you cannot sanctify" the nature, then why do we let audiences sing such prayers as,

"O Thou Spirit divine,
All my *nature* refine"?

Of course, we need to realize that in these intricate distinctions and in the ensuing references to inward crucifixion with Christ, the aim is to rescue holiness doctrine from the "eradication" idea that the evil "old nature" may be *removed*. But, as we shall increasingly see, the self-contradictory "counteraction" theory is a wrong reply.

"If you are regenerate, you can never become unregenerate, but you can have an evil heart."

Nay! If the "heart" means thoughts, desires, and will (as the speaker says), and if all *that* can be evil ("an evil heart"), and if (as he says) the "nature" *cannot* be changed, then what *is* regeneration?—and what part *does* it regenerate?

This superfine distinction, however, between "heart" and "nature", is followed by another which, to my own mind, seems just as strangely factitious.

"Now here let me again very earnestly emphasize the necessity of making another distinction, between the 'old man' and 'the flesh'. They are not the same. . . . The 'old man' is not the *flesh*."

[1] I may usefully appropriate the comment of Dr. Chester K. Lehman on the Scriptural use of the word "heart". He says, "Guided by Old Testament usage, we would say that to David *heart* meant the whole inner man. It was variously used for the mind and understanding, for the will, for the affections, for the conscience, for the motives, for the whole soul." (*The Holy Spirit.*)

He tells us that the "old man" is "the *unconverted* self", or "the unconverted man", or "your old self". Then, referring to Romans 6: 6, he continues:

"What does that mean? It means that not only were your sins laid upon Christ, but you yourself, as an unconverted person, were nailed on the Cross with Christ; your old self was crucified with Him. Let us bear in mind, then, that the old man (your 'old self') is *not* the old *nature.*"

So the "old self" was crucified with Christ, but the "old nature" was *not!*—part of me hanging there, and part not! Paul indulges no such exegetical vivisection. When Romans 6: 2 says, *"We* died to sin,"* it allows no such dissection as the speaker makes. Similarly, Galatians 2: 20, "I have been crucified with Christ," means the whole "I".

How complicating are all these artificial distinctions!—the "heart" is not the "nature". The "evil heart" is not the "evil nature". The "old man" is not the "old nature". The "old self" is not "the flesh", nor is it the "old nature". The "evil heart" may be "cleansed"; but the "evil nature" *cannot* be cleansed. The "old man" alias the "self" or "yourself" (i.e. the *you*) was "nailed to the Cross" and "crucified", but the "old nature" apparently was *not!*

But why do such gifted and well-meaning teachers trip themselves into such contradictions and ambiguities as we have noted? It is because neither they nor any other can possibly fit Romans 6 into their "counteraction" theory. They are obliged somehow to dispose of that awkward sixth verse so as to answer the forthright interpretation of the eradicationists who take the words, "crucified" and "destroyed", in their plain meaning. Romans 6: 6, however, remains obstinately there: a "thorn in the side" of the counteraction theory; and none of the doctors can remove it. I myself believe entirely in counteraction, in the sense that the believer's inward sin-condition is counteracted by "the law of the Spirit of life in Christ Jesus" (who could *dis*believe it when it is so clearly Scriptural?) but the struggle to wring it from Romans 6: 6 is about as successful as squeezing blood out of a stone or growing figs on a thistle.

It is pathetic to see how, again and again, counteraction exponents will drag Romans 6: 6 into their reasonings when it is not even germane, and only causes them to take risks with the wording of Scripture.

"Now we too have a nature which in itself is absolutely sinless, a new 'divine nature' (2 Peter 1: 4); but although we dare not say, even when in the most glorious enjoyment of full salvation, that *sin is dead*, yet we can truthfully say (and we dare not say otherwise) that when abiding in Christ, and fully believing in Romans 6, *we are dead*, dead to sin, dead with Christ."

So, according to that speaker, we must not say that "*sin* is dead" in us, but we can say that "*we* are dead" to sin. Yet in downright reality, what is the *practical* difference between the two? What matters it in *experience*, whether we say that sin is inwardly dead to *me*, or that *I* am inwardly dead to *it*? If either is true, then both are; and if either is *un*true, then both are.

"If the Bible tells me that it is one of God's facts that the 'flesh' is to be incorrigibly bad, even to the very end (Rom. 8: 7), I do not grieve over the fact, although it is very humbling; but I fix my eye on God's provision against it, a provision so glorious that I cry out of joy—Jesus Himself, a Saviour, who not only took my sins to the Cross and paid my debt, but took me to the Cross, and nailed up my 'old man' to the accursed tree; who has power to keep that 'old man' from coming down from the Cross; yea power to enable me to reckon myself as 'crucified, dead, and buried' with Himself, and to make the reckoning good. This 'having died unto sins' (1 Peter 2: 24 R.V.) is practically *cleansing by blood*."

Is not that a further confection of contradictions? The "old man", the "me", is nailed to the Cross, yet is not dead, but Christ "has power" to prevent his "coming down from the Cross". Simultaneously our Lord enables me to reckon that same "old man", or "me", to be "*dead and buried*", and He "makes the reckoning good" in my experience! I am fastened on the Cross, yet dead in the grave, both at the same time!

Well, both cannot be true? so which is? If you say (with *some* counteractionists) that the "old self" is pinioned there, in continuous crucifixion but not actually dead, then not only do you make the sanctified life one of continuous inward torture, but you destroy the believer's *real* identification with Calvary; for our Lord's crucifixion (like every other crucifixion) ended in real death, without any such prolongation of crucifixion. On the other hand, if you say that the sinful self has actually *died* with Christ, and that He makes *this* good in experience, you have become an eradicationist!

Counteractionist Dilemma

I refrain from giving more quotations lest this more negative part of these studies may seem unkind after all. Wherever I turn, I find these or similar contradictions tied up with the counteraction theory. The plain fact is that Romans 6: 6 ("Our old man is crucified with Him, that the body of sin might be destroyed") is an awkward spoke which simply will not fit into the wheel of the counteraction theory. So long as its exponents keep to counteraction as taught in Romans 8, i.e. the counteraction of "sin" and of "the flesh" by the "law of the Spirit of life in Christ Jesus", all is well; but as soon as they try to force it from Romans 6: 6 they stumble into unavoidable self-contradiction; for Romans 6: 6 does not teach counteraction; it teaches *destruction through crucifixion*, as anyone can see.

One after another counteractionist preachers will "explain" to us that the word "destroyed", in Romans 6: 6, does not really mean destroyed, but only "rendered inoperative" or (according to viewpoint) "done away". Those among them who say that "the body of sin" means our "sinful old *nature*" insist on "rendered inoperative". Those among them who say that "the body of sin" means our "unregenerate *former self*" prefer to read it "done away". But these superfine distinctions are mere hair-splitting; for in Romans 6: 6, as any straight-thinking mind must see, the word, "destroyed", is the completive counterpart of the verb, "was crucified"—

> "Our old man was *CRUCIFIED* with Him, that
> the body of sin might be *DESTROYED*."

Therefore, "destroyed" here cannot mean anything less than what crucifixion brings about. Or, more pointedly, Romans 6: 6 teaches *DESTRUCTION BY CRUCIFIXION*.

Does this mean then, that Scripture teaches a destruction-by-crucifixion of "inborn sin" or the so-called "old nature" in a Christian? We hope to show that Paul's expressions, "the old man" and "the body of sin" have no reference whatever to a suppositionary "old *nature*" inside the believer. All I am concerned with here is to show the contradictoriness of the counteraction theory as it is still often presented.

So long as they stay with Romans 7 and 8, its exponents are on safe ground; but as soon as they start "explaining" chapter 6, especially verses 6 and 11, they put themselves in a barbed-wire entanglement. Then why do they not leave chapter 6 alone? Simply because they *must somehow* lessen the force of that word, "destroyed", which means so much to the eradication theory. Thus a curious antithesis arises between the eradicationists and the counteractionists. The eradicationists are always struggling to level *experience* up to the wording of the *text* while the counteractionists are always trying to weaken the wording of the text down to the level of *experience*!

That word, "destroyed"

One only needs to dig a little into the Greek behind our English translation to see how tenuous, how exparte, is the counteractionist argument against that rendering, "destroyed". The Greek word, *katargeo*, which our King James Version translates "destroyed", is made up of the verb, *argeo*, which means to render idle or inactive, and the particle *kata*, which is prefixed to intensify it; so that the combined form, *katargeo*, has the sense of utterly so. It means, put *utterly* out of action. It occurs 27 times in our New Testament. No less than fourteen English words are used to represent it in our Authorised Version. (For an analysis of these see our postscript to this chapter, on the word, "Destroyed".)

One has only to glance through those 27 occurrences to know what is the basic meaning of *katargeo*. It is to "bring to nought" or to "do away". In itself it does not necessarily mean to destroy in the sense of effecting non-existence, but neither does it necessarily *not* mean that. In each instance the usage and context must decide. In some cases it obviously *does* mean utter cessation (I Cor. 13: 8, 15, 26, etc.). In others it scarcely can (Rom. 7: 6, Luke 13: 7).

In Romans 6: 6, where *katargeo* is translated as "destroyed" (A.V.) and "done away" (E.R.V. and A.S.V.), it goes with "was crucified". When a body is "destroyed" or "done away" by crucifixion, what is meant? Nothing less than the utter end of life in it. To insist, as some of our counteractionist brethren do, on translating *katargeo* as "rendered inoperative" may possibly be allowable in some places; but to force it to mean *only* that in

Romans 6: 6 is scarcely a justifiable delimitation from an exegetical point of view.

Yet even if we do thus delimit the translation, it does not lend support to their form of the counteraction theory; for if the so-called "old nature" or "former self" is "done away", or "rendered inoperative", why is there any further *need* to counteract it? Peculiar inconsistency!—"done away" yet with us to our dying day!—"rendered inoperative" yet always needing counteraction!

We refrain from further animadversions here, and would emphasize again that those already ventured are made in a cordial spirit. In our next pages we shall endeavour to prove by frontal attack that both those theories are fundamentally wrong. Then, having cleared our way through those long-persisting misinterpretations, we shall set forth what we believe to be the *true* message of inwrought holiness, or "the *fulness* of the blessing".

Yet while we firmly believe that both of the above-mentioned theories are untenable Scripturally, we do not forget all the many precious truths concerning consecration and holiness which have gathered *round* them, and have focussed *in* them, and have been preached *along* with them. All the way through these studies our longing prayer and earnest purpose—far from any mere refuting of theories—is to get at the real truth of Scripture, and point the way to a true experience of Christian holiness.

> With all my heart I long to know
> The way, the one true way to go
> Wherein to tread with eager feet
> In God's all-holy will complete;
> And on my pilgrim journey press
> With songs of heart-deep holiness.
>
> How many signs, the way along,
> Can look so right but be so wrong!
> How oft do errors still beguile,
> And lead astray by many a mile!
> How many pilgrims, lured aside,
> In devious by-paths wander wide!
>
> Yet in the Book of Truth divine
> How steadily the way-marks shine,
> To make those pilgrims truly wise
> Who read with heav'n-anointed eyes!
> And since the way is writ so clear
> Why need we further doubt or fear?

Dear Spirit, clear my inward eyes
To see the truth which sanctifies—
God's way of holiness, wherein
Is true, full vict'ry over sin;
That holy walk with God to know—
The bliss of heav'n begun below!

POSTSCRIPT ON THE WORD, "DESTROYED" IN ROMANS 6:6

As stated, the Greek word, *katargeo*, rendered as "destroyed" in Romans 6:6 occurs 27 times in the New Testament. No less than 14 English words are used to translate it in our Authorized Version. Its 27 occurrences are as follows, given in the Authorized (or King James) Version, the English Revised Version, and the American Standard Version, which in my own judgment are together, the best in our English tongue.

	A.V.	E.R.V.	A.S.V.
2 Cor. 3:13	"abolished"	"passing away"	"passing away"
Eph. 2:15	"abolished"	"abolished"	"abolished"
2 Tim. 1:10	"abolished"	"abolished"	"abolished"
Gal. 5:11	"ceased"	"done away"	"done away"
Luke 13:7	"cumbereth"	"cumber"	"cumber"
Rom. 7:6	"delivered"	"discharged"	"discharged"
1 Cor. 6:13	"destroy"	"bring to nought"	"bring to nought"
2 Thess. 2:8	"destroy"	"bring to nought"	"bring to nought"
Heb. 2:14	"destroy"	"bring to nought"	"bring to nought"
Rom. 6:6	"destroyed"	"done away"	"done away"
1 Cor. 15:26	"destroyed"	"abolished"	"abolished"
1 Cor. 13:10	"done away"	"done away"	"done away"
2 Cor. 3:7	"done away"	"passing away"	"passing away"
2 Cor. 3:11	"done away"	"passeth away"	"passeth away"
2 Cor. 3:14	"done away"	"done away"	"done away"
Rom. 4:14	"of none effect"	"of none effect"	"of none effect"
Gal. 5:4	"of no effect"	"severed from"	"severed from"
Gal. 3:17	"of none effect"	"disannul"	"disannul"
Rom. 3:3	"without effect"	"of none effect"	"of none effect"
Rom. 3:31	"make void"	"of none effect"	"of none effect"
1 Cor. 13:8	"shall fail"	"done away"	"done away"
Rom. 7:2	"is loosed from"	"discharged"	"discharged"
1 Cor. 1:28	"bring to nought"	"bring to nought"	"bring to nought"
1 Cor. 2:6	"come to nought"	"coming to nought"	"coming to nought"
1 Cor. 13:11	"put away"	"put away"	"put away"
1 Cor. 15:24	"put down"	"abolished"	"abolished"
1 Cor. 13:8	"vanish away"	"done away"	"done away"

Is it not clear beyond misunderstanding that the basic meaning of *katargeo* is to bring to nought; to do away. How can it mean *less* in Romans 6:6?

WHAT ABOUT ROMANS 6: 6?

"The most important passage in the New Testament on this aspect of Keswick teaching is Romans 6. Evan Hopkins once said that in the early days of Keswick there was no passage of Scripture which was more frequently to the front than this chapter. That is true, but it is just as frequently used today. It is doubtful whether a Keswick Convention has ever been held in which one or more speakers did not deal with this chapter. Because of its extreme importance, more than once it has been called the Magna Charta of the Christian. There is no understanding of Keswick without an appreciation of the place accorded by it to this chapter in its whole scheme of sanctification. One of the key verses in the chapter is the sixth: 'Knowing this, that our old man is crucified with Him, that the body of sin might be destroyed, that henceforth we should not serve sin'."

Steven Barabas.

WHAT ABOUT ROMANS 6: 6?

UNDOUBTEDLY Romans 6: 6 has been the main battle-centre in
the disagreement of holiness theories. What is its true meaning?
That question is of decisive importance; for once we see its true
meaning, any seeming complicatedness about holiness begins to
clear away like mist before a bright sunrise, and we see the whole
landscape. in an alluring new light. Look carefully at the text
again:

"Knowing this, that our old man is crucified with Him [Christ]
that the body of sin might be destroyed, that henceforth we should not
serve sin."

As we have seen, this is said by some to teach a complete
eradication of the so-called "old nature" or "body of sin" in the
believer. By others it is limited to the lesser meaning that this
hereditary sin-proneness is rendered more or less "powerless" or
"inoperative". Yet strangely enough it would seem that when
rightly understood, Romans 6:6 does not refer to inward sanctification at all, as the following pages will endeavour to show.

First, then, this text has been continually misinterpreted
through failure to appreciate rightly its *location* in the total
structure of the Romans epistle. We must learn, at long last, to
interpret it in agreement with its occurrence in the progressive
argument of the whole. It is always good to take a new survey
of Romans. Perhaps, as Professor J. A. Findlay said, "For the
purpose of systematic theology it is the most important book of
the Bible". The epistle has a triform lay-out. (1) The first eight
chapters are doctrinal, and their subject is, *how the Gospel saves
the sinner*. (2) The next three chapters are dispensational, and
their subject is, *how the Gospel relates to Israel*. (3) The remaining
chapters are mainly practical, and their subject is, *how the Gospel
bears on conduct*. This threefold structure is emphasized by the
feature that Paul ends each of the three movements with a

culminative climax. If I may be allowed to transplant a page from volume 6 of my own work, *Explore the Book*, here is the epistle in flat analysis (see across).

Now it is with part one, of course, that we are concerned here, because that is where chapter 6: 6, our focus-point, occurs. Observe carefully, then, how chapters one to eight unfold. After a short introduction (1: 1–15) Paul proceeds to elucidate *how the Gospel saves the sinner*.

How would we expect a Gospel manifesto such as Romans to begin? Would we not expect Paul first to show the deep and urgent *need* for this Gospel? That is precisely what he does. First he shows us why the *Gentiles* need it (1: 18–32). They need it for two reasons: (1) they are transgressors, which makes them legally *guilty*; (2) they are sinners in their very nature, which makes them morally *corrupt*. Then he shows why the *Jews* need it (2: 1–3: 20). They need it for the same two reasons: (1) they are legally guilty—for the very law of Moses in which they boast is that which most condemns them; (2) they are morally corrupt, for their own prophets and psalmists say so—"all gone out of the way", "none that doeth good" (3: 12). Note carefully, then, that with both Gentiles and Jews the plight is twofold:

Both Gentiles and Jews have "sinned"—acts of transgression.
Both Gentiles and Jews are "in sin"—an internal condition.

Transgression is the *legal* aspect. The inward condition is the *moral* aspect. As to his transgressions, man is legally guilty and therefore under *condemnation*. As to his inward condition, man is morally corrupt and therefore *perishing*. This, let me underscore again, is the human plight: "*SINS*" (plural) and "*SIN*" (singular).

But now, from chapter 3: 21 to the climax at the end of chapter 8, Paul shows how the Gospel *answers* this double problem of "sins" (transgressions) and of "sin" (inward condition).

The Gospel answer as to "sins" (plural) is given in chapters 3: 21 to 5: 11.

The Gospel answer as to "sin" (singular) is given in chapters 5: 12 to 8: 39.

This can easily be verified. Up to that break at chapter 5: 12 the word, "sin", occurs only three times, whereas after it, to the end of chapter 8, it occurs no less than 39 times. E. W. Bullinger wrote, "No exposition is worthy of the slightest attention which

THE EPISTLE TO THE ROMANS
The Gospel, the power of God to Salvation.

Introductory 1: 1–15.

1. DOCTRINAL: HOW THE GOSPEL SAVES THE SINNER
(1: 16–8: 39).

THE RACIAL PLIGHT—"SINS" AND "SIN" (1: 18–3: 20).
The Gentile guilty and sinful (1: 18–32).
The Jew guilty and sinful (2: 1–3: 20).

THE GOSPEL ANSWER—(*a*) AS TO "SINS" (3: 21–5: 11).
Judicially (3: 21–4: 25).
In experience (5: 1–11).

THE GOSPEL ANSWER—(*b*) AS TO "SIN" (5: 12–8: 39).
Judicially (5: 12–7: 6).
In experience (7: 7–8: 39).

2. NATIONAL: HOW THE GOSPEL RELATES TO ISRAEL
(9: 1–11: 36).

DOES NOT ANNUL THE PURPOSE WITH ISRAEL (9).
Because not all Israel true Israel (vs. 7–13).
And an elect remnant being saved (vs. 27–29).

RATHER, IT FULFILS THE PROMISE TO ISRAEL (10).
But Israel bent on salvation by works (vs. 1–4).
And stumbles (9: 32) *through unbelief* (vs. 18–21).

AND CONFIRMS THE PROSPECT BEFORE ISRAEL (11).
Israel's fall made to bless Gentiles (vs. 1–24).
And all Israel shall yet be saved (vs. 25–29).

3. PRACTICAL: HOW THE GOSPEL BEARS ON CONDUCT
(12: 1–15: 13).

THE CHRISTIAN LIFE AS TO SOCIAL ASPECTS (12).
The root—consecration and renewal (vs. 1–2).
The fruit—service and love to others (vs. 3–21).

THE CHRISTIAN LIFE AS TO CIVIL ASPECTS (13).
Its expression—conscientious submission (vs. 1–7).
Its foundation—love to one's neighbour (vs. 8–14).

THE CHRISTIAN LIFE AS TO MUTUAL ASPECTS (14: 15).
The principle—mutual considerateness (vs. 1–23).
The incentive—the example of Christ (15: 1–13).

Supplementary: chapters 15 & 16.

does not mark this division between verses 11 and 12". His comment, perhaps, is rather severe, but there is no doubt that the sharp "divide" is really there, and is crucially important to our understanding of the apostle's argument. Probably most of us have already sensed the switch-over to a new aspect at that twelfth verse of chapter 5—"Wherefore, as by one man *sin* entered into the world . . ."

Now significantly enough, in both these sections, i.e. on *"sins"* (3: 21–5: 11) and on "sin" (5: 12–8: 39) the apostle follows the same procedure. In both he shows the Gospel answer first *judicially*, and then the answer *experientially*.

Take the earlier of the two sections—on "sins", in chapters 3: 21 to 5: 11. Paul shows first how God deals with the problem of "sins" *judicially* (3: 21–4: 25). Then he shows how God deals with the problem of "sins" *experientially*, i.e. in our human consciousness (5: 1–11). This is how the section runs:

THE GOSPEL ANSWER AS TO "SINS" (3: 21–5: 11)

Judicially (3: 21–4: 25)
    (a) Justification, or imputed righteousness now comes through faith in Christ "set forth as a propitiation" (3: 21–31).
    (b) Justification by faith as a principle of divine operation may be seen in Old Testament: David and Abraham (chapter 4).

Experientially (5: 1–11).
    (a) "Therefore being justified by faith, *we have* . . . we have . . . we stand . . . we rejoice . . . we glory . . ." (5: 1–4).
    (b) "The love of God is shed abroad *in our hearts* by the Holy Spirit which is given unto us" (5) "We joy in God" (11).

If we now move on to the further section (5: 12, to the end of chapter 8) in which Paul gives the Gospel answer to the problem of *"sin"* (singular) we find the same procedure. First the apostle shows us how God deals with the problem of sin *judicially* (5: 12–7: 6). Then he shows us how the Gospel deals with this same problem of sin *experientially*, that is, in our subjective, human experience (7: 7–8: 39).

THE GOSPEL ANSWER AS TO "SIN" (5: 12–8: 39)

Judicially (5: 12–7: 6)
    (a) Deliverance from sin as a racial involvement in Adam comes

by a similarly *inclusive new headship in Christ*: "As by one ... sin and death; so by One ... many righteous (5: 12–21).

(b) Deliverance from sin as racial slave-master who hands us over to law and death, is by *judicial identification with Christ* in His once-for-all death to sin and the law (6: 1–7: 6).

Experientially (7: 7–8: 39).

(a) "Sin which dwelleth in me" (7: 17, 20, 23) is now counteracted and overcome by the new "law of the Spirit of life in Christ Jesus" (7: 24–8: 4).

(b) The indwelling Holy Spirit now imparts victory over the flesh and the body, restores sonship, gives guidance, and all needed teaching, making us "more than conquerors" (8: 5–39).

Now the fact which immediately stands out when we thus see Romans 6 where it occurs in the progress of the apostle's argument is, that it does not occur in the *experiential* section at all, but in the *judicial*! The much-controverted sixth verse about the crucifixion of the "old man" has hitherto been misapprehended by each of the contending theories through failure to appreciate its connection structurally in the epistle, i.e. *not* with the experiential, but with the judicial. In Romans 6 Paul is not discussing how God sanctifies you and me *inwardly* or experientially, but how God dealt once for all *judicially* with sin as an hereditary evil in man, by putting away the whole Adam humanity representatively on the Cross.

Once this structural location of the text is appreciated as indicating a *judicial*, not an experiential reference, various other features immediately rally in confirmation of it. One of these is, that in this passage (5: 12–7: 6) all the *verb tenses* which relate to our Lord's death and the believer's association with it are either *aorists* or (in one or two cases) *perfects*. The Greek "aorist" denotes an act at a definite point in the *past*, and excludes all idea of present continuousness. The Greek "perfect" denotes an act already done, completely *ended*, and therefore non-continuing.[1] It is much to be regretted that these verb tenses are not carefully reproduced in our King James Version. Their being loosely misrepresented by our English present tense in Romans 6 has undoubtedly given rise to much erroneous thinking.

Glance back, then, through the passage (chapter 6: 1 to 7: 6)

---

[1] The Bagster *Analytical Greek Lexicon* defines the aorist tense as "strictly the expression of a momentary or transient single action"; and the perfect tense as an act already "terminated in past time" with a resultant "effect in the present".

and see how true it is that all the verb tenses pertaining to our Lord's death and our identification with it are aorists or perfects. To save tediousness here we give them all at the end of the chapter. Examine them later there, to verify the accuracy of what we are stating here. Think carefully what it means. Not one of the references to the believer's union with the death of Christ indicates a death to be died in the present. They all refer to a death away back *then*. Not one of them speaks of a *dying* with Him. They all speak of a death completed and over.

What are we to conclude from all this? Let us reflect carefully. Romans 6: 6 does *not* say that "our old man *is* crucified." Our King James Version has misled us. What Paul says is, that "our old man *was* crucified", in the sense of a·completed and final act of the past. Nowhere in the passage is death to sin, or the death of "our old man", a death which the believer is to die *now*, but always a past act which took place at the death of Christ; something completely enacted *then* and *there*. Therefore, since Paul is thus clearly thinking of it as one completed act of the past, it is obvious that he must be thinking of it as one completed *judicial* act, quite apart from anything which God does here and *now* within the believer. Why, even verse II, which has caused many wistful seekers after sanctification to believe that they could inwardly die to sin, and then *"reckon"* themselves dead in the sense of a continuing *condition*, guards us against that very thing; for its first word says that we are to reckon ourselves dead to sin ·"likewise" (ὄντως) that is, in *the very same* once-for-all *judicial* sense of the preceding verse.

None of us would dare to argue seriously that his or her "old nature" was *actually* crucified with Christ on the cross of Calvary, nineteen hundred and more years ago; for those of us now on earth were not then alive. It is common, however, to hear it argued: "I may not have been actually alive then, but I died to sin then and there in the reckoning of God; and what happened *positionally* there, God will now make real in my *experience*, if I will let Him." But this fond idea that God will "make it real" in present experience is mere wishful presumption; for if Romans 6: 6 does not teach it (and it does not) where else in the Word do we find it? Some of us have been so thoroughly brought up on that illusory theory that it is hard for us now to think in any other way. Yet where, I ask again, does the Word teach it? The answer is *nowhere*.

But next, having seen how all the relevant verb-tenses in Romans 6, as well as its structural location, betoken a *judicial* viewpoint, notice how the same judicial aspect is indicated by *recurrent words and phrases*. The full passage covers chapter 5: 12 to 7: 6. Observe the recurrence of the word, "law", meaning usually the law of Moses.

Chap. 5: 13 "For until the *law* sin was in the world, but sin is not imputed where there is no *law*."

5: 20 "Moreover, the *law* came in that the trespass might abound. . . ."

6: 14 "For sin shall not have dominion over you, for ye are not under the *law*, but under grace."

6: 15 "What then? shall we sin because we are not under the *law* but under grace?"

7: 1 "Know ye not, brethren (for I speak to them that know the *law*), how that the *law* hath dominion over a man as long as he liveth?"

7: 2 "For the woman which hath an husband is bound by the *law* to her husband as long as he liveth; but if the husband shall have died, she has become discharged from the *law* of the husband."

7: 3 "She is free from the *law*. . . ."

7: 4 "Wherefore, my brethren, ye also were made dead to the *law*. . . ."

7: 5 "For when we were in the flesh, the motions of sins which were through the *law*. . . ."

7: 6 "But now we have been discharged from the *law*, having died to that wherein we were held."

Does not this repeated reference to the *law* add further evidence that the main drive of the context is legal, or *judicial*?

Added to this is the feature that all the characteristic words of the passage are those which have to do with the *judicial* aspect of salvation.

Chap. 5: 13 "Sin is not *imputed* where there is no law."

5: 14 "After the likeness of Adam's *transgression*. . . ."

5: 15 "If by the *trespass* of one. . . ."

5: 16 "For the *judgment* came of one unto *condemnation*; but the free gift came of many trespasses unto *justification*."

5: 17 "They which receive the gift of righteousness. . . ."

5: 18 "So then, as through one *trespass* the judgment came unto all men to *condemnation*; even so by one act of *righteousness* the free gift came unto all men to *justification*."

5: 19   "Through the obedience of the One shall the many be accounted *righteous.*"

5: 21   "Even so might grace reign through *righteousness. . . .*"

6: 7   "For he [the Christian] that hath died is *justified. . . .*" (not "sanctified"!)

6: 14   "For sin shall not have dominion over you, for ye are not *under the law*, but under grace."

6: 15   "What then? Shall we sin because we are not *under the law. . . .?*"

6: 23   "For the *wages of sin* is death, but the free gift of God is eternal life."

7: 1   "The *law* hath dominion over a man. . . ."

7: 2   "*Discharged* from the *law. . . .*"

7: 4   "Wherefore, my brethren, ye also were made *dead to the law.*"

7: 6   "But now we have been *discharged from the law. . . .*"

If all this does not denote that Paul has the objective, *judicial* aspects of salvation predominantly in mind, then indeed we are strangely mistaken.

But again, if (as is usually supposed) Romans 6 teaches a subjective treatment of the "sinful nature" in the individual believer, then the chapter contains *strange incongruities of phraseology*. Take verse 14, for instance. It says, "For sin shall not have dominion over you, for ye are not under the law, but under grace." Now if verse 6 teaches the crucifixion of the "old man" (as a supposed something inside us) and the destruction of a "body of sin" in the believer; and if verse 11 means that we are to "reckon" ourselves "dead to sin" in the sense of an *inward* death to it (as is usually taught) then surely verse 14 would have said, "For sin shall not have dominion over you, for the body of sin within you has been done away, and ye are now inwardly dead to sin." How weak and disappointing (apparently) is what Paul actually does say, i.e., "For sin shall not have dominion over you, for ye are *not under the law*"! If, however, we see that the reference is racial and judicial, not individual and internal, the words, "for ye are not under the law" are exactly in keeping. Is it not plain that the "dominion" of sin to which Paul here refers is *legal* dominion, not inward and moral?

Or again, take verse 12: "Let not sin therefore *reign* in your mortal body, that ye should obey it in the *lusts* thereof." How strange is this in verse 12, if verses 6 and 11 teach that the evil "nature" within has been done away, and that the believer is now inwardly "dead" to sin! How *could* sin "reign" if it is "done away"? How *could* there be "lusts thereof" in one who is "dead" to it? If verses 6 and 11 do indeed teach such a doing away of indwelling evil, and such a death to it, then that twelfth verse is an anti-climactic exhortation to maintain something far *less* than that!

Or, refer to verse 7 again: how extraneous, how disappointing it seems (if Paul is thinking of inward, individual sanctification) that he should say, "For he who has died [i.e. to sin] is *justified* from sin"! Surely, one would have expected something such as, "For he who has died is freed from indwelling sin and its tyranny."

Or further, in verse 13, does not the injunction, "Neither yield ye your members as instruments of unrighteousness *unto sin*", seem contradictorily feeble after the assertion (as is supposed) that sin, with all its desires, has been completely "done away" from the heart?

Why, even verse 13, "Yield yourselves unto God", seems a strange injunction to be addressed to those who (supposedly) were now inwardly *dead* to sin. If inward death to sin had truly taken place in those Roman believers, how could they be any *less* than already "yielded" utterly to God?

Or, just once more, if the theme of Romans 6 is inward sanctification through eradication or counteraction of sin in the heart, does not the last verse of the chapter seem lamely off the track?— "For the wages of sin is death, but the gift of God is eternal life through Jesus Christ Our Lord." Think carefully: this last verse is an interim culmination-point to which the foregoing verses lead. To what, then, has the (supposed) teaching of inward death to sin now led? It has led merely to a statement of salvation in its *judicial* aspect, as a deliverance from *penalty* (the "wages of sin"), and *not* to some triumphant statement of salvation in the *inward* sense of death to "sin that dwelleth in me". (Of course, the last verse of chapter 6 is precious *in itself*. What we are pointing out is, that if Romans 6 teaches an *inward* spiritual surgery of sanctification, as is commonly held, then that last verse is a strange anticlimax.)

Is it not already clear, from its structural location, and from its punctiliar verb-tenses and from its terminology, that Romans 6, when it speaks of our union with Christ in his death, refers *not* to a subjective, present-tense experience, as is usually assumed, but to something objectively enacted in the past, with a *once-for-all judicial finality?*

We might take many more pages proving that Romans 6 does not refer to our inward sanctification, but perhaps it will suffice if we submit just four more confirmatory factors.

Non-mention of the Holy Spirit

A noticeable feature of the New Testament is that our Lord's atoning work *for* us is uniformly associated with the Cross, while His sanctifying work *in* us is just as definitely attributed to the Holy Spirit. This Romans epistle itself illustrates it. Where is its first reference to the Holy Spirit? It is chapter 5: 5, which is the epistle's first reference to salvation inwardly *experienced*. All the objective aspects of our salvation centre in the Cross. All the subjective and inward is the work of the Holy Spirit. Chapters 6 and 7 and 8 conform to that. In chapter 6, as we have shown, there is salvation in a judicial sense. Then chapter 7 shows a further problem—"sin that dwelleth *in* me." Then chapter 8 tells the great deliverance—the Holy Spirit being mentioned no less than nineteen times. Let the *non*-mention of the Holy Spirit in Romans 6, therefore, confirm what we have said as to its objective and judicial nature.

Contradicted by Experience

Again, if Romans 6 teaches, as many suppose, a present, *inward* crucifixion and death to sin, then how strange it is that not one of those who so interpret the chapter can honestly measure up to its actual wording! Look again at verse 10, which is the pivotal declaration of the chapter concerning our Lord's death on Calvary.

"For in that He died, He died unto sin once (Gr. ἐφάπαξ, *once for all*) but in that He liveth, He liveth unto God."

How, then, can a believer's union with Christ in *that* "once-for-all", judicial death to Sin as an external Exactor, two thousand years ago, be a present-day *inward* crucifixion and death to sin in the believer's nature? Who would dare to say that he had died to inward sin in *that* once-for-all way? We respectfully challenge *any* man, whether eradicationist or counteractionist: If you claim that your union with Calvary is one of present experience, then your inward death to sin must be a *ONCE-FOR-ALL* death, as *His* was; but is it? Can you honestly say that even the slightest sinward tendency once-for-all expired, with never a fleck remaining?

A Significant Illustration

There is reason to regret the break between chapters 6 and 7. We must not allow it to blur the continuity of Paul's reasoning. The fact is, that what he *states* in chapter 6 he *illustrates* in the early verses of chapter 7; and the illustration is meant to picture the *kind* of death which we died with Christ.

"Are ye ignorant brethren, how that *THE LAW* hath dominion over a man so long as he liveth? For the woman that hath a husband is *BOUND BY LAW* to the husband while he liveth; but if the husband die, she is *DISCHARGED FROM THE LAW* of a husband. . . . Wherefore, my brethren, *YE ALSO WERE MADE DEAD TO THE LAW* through the body of Christ; that ye should be joined to another, even to Him who was raised from the dead . . ." (7: 1–4).

Surely, that illustration is enough to show how erroneous is the theory that Romans 6 teaches a present, *inward* crucifixion and death to sin. See how Paul himself *applies* it in his final comment on it (verse 6).

"We were discharged [aorist] from the *LAW*, having died [in the past: aorist] to that wherein we were held."

The Baptismal Burial

Another factor which indicates that the death to sin which Paul teaches in Romans 6 is *not* an inward, experiential death, but solely a *positional* death, is that he links it back, in the past tense, with the initiatory rite of *baptism*. It is not a death effected *now*, but a death professed *then*. See again the opening verses of the chapter, which I quote from the A.S.V. because the King James Version blurs the aorist tenses:—

"What shall we say then? Shall we continue in sin, that grace may abound? God forbid. We who *DIED* to sin, how shall we any longer live therein? Or are ye ignorant that all we who *WERE BAP-TIZED* into Christ Jesus *WERE BAPTIZED* into His death? We *WERE BURIED* therefore with Him through baptism into death: that like as Christ was raised from the dead through the glory of the Father, so we also might walk in newness of life."

How decisive, then, are those past tenses: "We who *DIED* to sin . . . we who were *BAPTIZED* . . . into His DEATH. We were *BURIED* with Him through baptism into *DEATH*". Surely it is plain that the believer's death in Romans 6 is *not* a death which has yet to be effected inside the believer. Even less can it be a continuous *dying*. It is a death as completely past and done with as our Lord's own crucifixion. Therefore it *must* be a judicial death, and cannot be a present-tense *experience*. (On this see Professor William Barclay's enlightening annotation in Appendix, p. 245).

A Contradictory Misfit

Still another significant pointer to the real meaning of Romans 6 is that "wretched man" at the end of chapter 7. If the *sixth* chapter teaches, as is supposed, either the eradication or the "rendering inoperative" of the "old nature" or "old man", why do we find forlornly *following* it that "wretched man" groaning over unrelieved bondage to "sin that dwelleth in me", and crying, "Oh, wretched man that I am! who shall deliver me?" The fact is, that the "wretched man" passage is an inexplicable misfit, an enigmatical contradiction of all that Paul has just said—if chapter *six* teaches *inward* death to sin. (For a full discussion of this see our companion volume, *His Deeper Work in Us*).

New Testament Testimony

Another factor which has a decisive bearing on our interpretation of Romans 6 is that not once, anywhere in the New Testament, is the believer's death with Christ, or death to sin, spoken of as taking place in the present, or as being a continuous dying. Here are all the references, with the truer rendering of the verb-tenses in the E.R.V. and A.S.V. (I have not included 1 Cor. 15: 30, 31, or 2 Cor. 4: 9, 10, as the reference there is solely to *physical* dying.)

Authorized Version	*The Truer Rendering*
Rom. 6 : 2 "How shall we that are dead to sin live any longer therein?"	"We who *DIED* to sin, how shall we any longer live therein?"
6 : 4 "Therefore we are buried with Him by baptism unto death."	"We *WERE* buried therefore with Him through baptism into death."
6 : 7 "For he that is dead is freed from sin."	"For he that *DIED* has been justified from sin."
6 : 8 "Now if we be dead with Christ . . ."	"But if we *DIED* with Christ. . . ."
6 : 10, 11 "For in that He died, He died unto sin once. . . . Likewise reckon ye also yourselves to be dead indeed unto sin."	"He died unto sin *once for all* . . Even so [i.e. once-for-all] reckon ye also yourselves dead unto sin."
7 : 4 "Wherefore, my brethren, ye also are become dead to the law. . . ."	"Wherefore, my brethren, ye also *WERE MADE* dead to the law."
2 Cor. 5 : 14 "We thus judge, that if One died for all, then were all dead."	"We thus judge that One died for all, therefore all *DIED*."
Gal. 2 : 19 "For I through the law am dead to the law."	"For I through the law *DIED* to the law."
Col. 2 : 20 "Wherefore if ye be dead with Christ from the rudiments of the world . . ."	"If ye *DIED* with Christ from the rudiments of the world . . ."
3 : 3 "For ye are dead, and your life is hid with Christ in God."	"For ye *DIED*, and your life is hid with Christ in God."
2 Tim. 2 : 11 "For if we be dead with Him, we shall also live with Him."	"For if we *DIED* with Him, we shall also live with Him."
1 Pet. 2 : 24 "That we being dead to sins, should live unto righteousness."	"That we, having *DIED* unto sins might live unto righteousness."

Well, so far as I know, there we have all the data; and what must we deduce? Is it not provenly clear that Romans 6 does *not* teach a present, experiential death or dying to sin in the believer? Is it not equally clear that the usual holiness formulas based upon that chapter are wrong and harmful?

Perhaps, to some readers, eager for more positive light on the way into holiness, this critical examination of Romans 6: 6 and its context may seem an impeding delay. Others of us, however, will by now be seeing how misleading are those usual misinterpretations, and how necessary it is to disentangle our thinking from such fallacies if we are ever to grasp with unhesitating hand the true promise of holiness.

It is a regret, let me say again, that our earlier chapters in this book have to be occupied with this demolition of *error* on the subject of sanctification. The enchanting hopes, however, which the eradication and counteraction theories have held before enquirers, only to leave them eventually disillusioned and bewildered, have necessitated it. We are quick to appreciate all that Wesley and others have meant for good in so many ways; yet that cannot blind us to these seriously aberrant teachings on Christian holiness. All of us, indeed, have reason enough to ask continually for guidance direct from our Lord through the Holy Spirit who *inspired* the sacred Scriptures.

> Lord, lead me into truth, I pray,
>   Anoint my eyes to see;
> Lest into error's maze I stray,
>   And somehow, Lord, miss *Thee*.
>
> For Thou Thyself hast plainly said,
>   "The truth shall make you free";
> Yea, more, Thy very blood was shed
>   To bring that truth to me.
>
> Oh, teach me from Thy written Word
>   The truth, the truth indeed;
> Until, from sin and error, Lord,
>   My heart is wholly freed.

ADDENDUM

It may be objected that despite all we say about the *judicial* character of Romans 6, the chapter surely is teaching us something which pertains to present *experience*. It certainly is. We readily agree. From its opening verse onwards it argues that because of what God has done for us in Christ there should be an inward response to it on our part. If, in the judicial reckoning of God, we "died with Christ" can we presume to "continue in sin" that grace may "abound"? If we have been spiritually "raised" with Him, how can we behave as though still spiritually dead? Must we not now "walk in newness of life"? Yes, of course Romans 6 bears on our inward experience and outward behaviour. All we are saying is, that it does not teach an inwrought eradication of sin, or the impaling of a so-called "old nature" within us, by an inwardly enacted co-crucifixion with Christ.

But there are others who say: Even though Romans 6 is to be taken in the judicial sense, is it not meant to have a *counterpart* in our inner experience? The answer to that is: No, not unless it can be shown from Romans 6 or from some other New Testament passage. But for a fuller reference to that please read our excursus at the end of this book: DOES ROMANS 6:6 HAVE A COUNTERPART IN OUR PRESENT EXPERIENCE?

AORIST AND PERFECT TENSES IN ROMANS 6

Verse 2   "How shall we who died to sin [$ἀπεθάνομεν$: first person plural aorist = at a point of time now past] live any longer therein?"

Verse 3   "Know ye not that all we who were baptised into Jesus Christ [$ἐβαπτίσθημεν$: first person plural aorist = baptised at that point of time now past] were baptised [same aorist] into His death?"

Verse 4   "Therefore we were buried with Him [$συνετάφημεν$: first person plural aorist = in that one act now past] through baptism into death."

Verse 5   "For if we have become [$γεγόναμεν$: first person plural perfect = have already become by a completed act] conjoined in the similitude of His death. . . ."

Verse 6   "Knowing this, that our old man *was* conjointly crucified [$συνεσταυρώθη$: third person singular aorist = in that one concluded act, away in the past] that the body of sin might be destroyed [$καταργηθῇ$: third person singular aorist subjunctive = in one completed act destroyed] that we should not be in bondage to sin".

Verse 7   "For he who died [$ἀποθανὼν$: aorist participle = the one having died in a past completed act] is justified from sin".

Verse 8   "Now if we died [$ἀπεθάνομεν$: first person plural aorist = then and there in the past] with Christ. . . ."

Verse 10 "For the death that He died [$ἀπέθανεν$: third person singular aorist = died in a completed past act] He died unto sin once [$ἐφάπαξ$: adverb = once for all] . . . ."

Verse 11 "Likewise [$ὄντως$ = in that very same way, i.e. in that once-for-all way] reckon yourselves dead indeed unto sin. . . ."

Verse 17 "But thanks be to God, though ye were the bondservants of sin, ye obeyed [$ὑπηκούσατε$: second person plural aorist = in one completed act of saving obedience] from the heart that form of teaching to which you became committed [παρεδόθητε: second person plural aorist passive =became committed in one complete act, i.e. at conversion to Christ].

Verse 18   "And being freed [ἐλευθερωθέντες: nominative plural participle aorist=having become then completely freed] from sin. . . ."

Verse 22   "But now, being freed [ἐλευθερωθέντες: nominative plural participle aorist=having become then completely freed] from sin. . . ."

Chap. 7: 4   "Wherefore, my brethren, ye also were made dead [ἐθανατώθητε: second person plural aorist = ye were made dead in one completed act] to the law, through the body of Christ, that ye should become [γενέσθαι: aorist infinitive =to have become so in one completed act] joined to Another, even to Him who was raised from the dead".

Chap. 7: 6   "But now we were discharged [κατηργήθημεν: first person plural aorist=discharged in one definite act of the past] from the law, having died [ἀποθανόντες: aorist participle =having in one completed past act died] to that wherein we were being held".

This use of either the aorist or the perfect in every reference to our Lord's death and our association with it is the more striking because of the *continuous* tenses used in other appropriate connections (see "walk" and "serve" and "live" and "reign" and "obey" and "held", in 6: 4, 6, 8, 12, 16—7: 6, respectively; and other verses).

THE "OLD MAN" CRUCIFIED

"Nay, with regard to the holy Scriptures themselves, as careful as they are to avoid it, the best of men are liable to mistake, and do mistake day by day; especially with respect to those parts thereof which less immediately relate to practice. Hence, even the children of God are not agreed as to the interpretation of many places in holy writ; nor is their difference of opinion any proof that they are not the children of God, on either side; but it is a proof that we are no more to expect any living man to be infallible, than to be omniscient."

John Wesley.

THE "OLD MAN" CRUCIFIED

WHAT, then, does Romans 6: 6 really teach? Paul says it was *"our old man"* which was crucified with Christ. Does that expression mean an "old nature", or "inbred sin" within you and me, as is usually taught? It does not. It is a Paulinism meaning *the whole human race in Adam.* This can be certified by reference to the other places where the expression occurs. Take Ephesians 4: 22–24.

"That ye put off, concerning your former manner of life, *the old man,* which is corrupt according to the deceitful lusts . . . and that ye put on the new man, which after God is created in righteousness and true holiness."

Obviously that "old man" cannot be our innate corruption or "inborn tendency to sin", for it is something which *we* can "put off"—as we certainly *cannot* do with our "inborn tendency to sin"!

As a matter of fact, Ephesians 4: 22 is not strictly an *exhortation* to "put off" as in our King James Version. The Greek verb is another aorist (infinitive): "Ye *have* (or did) put off the old man [in one completed act] . . . ye *have* put on the new man." How then can the expression, "our old man", mean our "inborn tendency to sin"? *We* cannot "put off" *that* in one completed act!

Or turn to Colossians 3: 9, 10.

"Lie not one to another, having put off [aorist: a past transaction] *the old man* with his deeds, and having put on [aorist again] the new man, which is being renewed into knowledge after the image of Him who created him."

So, there again, it is *we* who have "put off", in one completed act, the "old man"; which proves conclusively that the "old man" simply cannot mean our inherited "corrupt nature", for that is an hereditary condition which we ourselves simply cannot "put off", as all of us know only too helplessly. W. H. Griffith Thomas rightly says, "An exhortation to 'put off the old man' would be tantamount to an exhortation to become regenerate"—and we certainly cannot regenerate ourselves!

Let us say it again emphatically: our "old man" is not a name for a so-called "old nature" or "inbred sin". It is a Paulinism for *THE WHOLE HUMAN RACE IN ADAM*. Just as the "new man" is the whole body of believers, the whole "new creation", the whole new relationship in Christ, so the "old man" is the "*old*" creation, the whole of the old relationship in Adam. In *that* sense, Paul's exhorting his readers on the ground of their already having put off the "old man", and having put on the "new man" (as professed in their baptism) is at once transparently pertinent. He is telling them that inasmuch as the "old man" in Adam was now "done away" in the judicial reckoning of God, and as attested in their own baptismal testimony, they should now cast off the *graveclothes* of the old, and wear the resurrection raiment of the "new" in Christ. The exhortation has nothing whatever to do with our "*inborn* tendency to sin", or a so-called "old nature".

That the phrase, "our old man", is indeed a figuration of the whole human race in Adam, is further confirmed by reference to other Pauline passages. In 1 Corinthians 15: 45, the apostle speaks of "the first Adam", and in verse 47 calls him "the first *man*" (same Greek word as in Romans 6: 6). To Paul, the first Adam is the old Adam, or the "old man". He sees all men as either in the old or in the new (2 Cor. 5: 17). Indeed, the very passage (Rom. 5: 12—21) which leads to the "old man" of Romans 6: 6 is all about the "one man" (Adam) through whom comes death, versus the "one man" (Christ) through whom comes life. This in itself should have guided and guarded all of us in interpreting Romans 6: 6. Glance again through chapter 5.

The Old	*The New*
"Through *one man* sin entered into the world" (12)	"Adam is a type of Him [the One] who was to come" (14)
"By the trespass of *one* the many died" (15)	"Grace, by the *one man*, Jesus Christ" (15)
"By the trespass of the *one* death reigned" (17)	"They shall reign in life through the *One*" (17)
"Through the disobedience of the *one man* the many were made sinners" (19)	"Through the obedience of the *One* shall the many be made righteous" (19)

Chapter 6, remember, is a continuation and *application* of these contrastive parallels. What, then, is more soundly contextual than to identify the "old man" (*anthropos*) of chapter 6: 6 with the recurrent "one man" (*anthropos*) of chapter 5?

Apparently, one small grammatical peculiarity in Romans 6: 6 is responsible mainly, though needlessly, for the orthodox misinterpretation. It is the change from "the" to "our"—that is, "*our* old man". Yet this very word which has been supposed to refer to a so-called "old *nature*" in each Christian believer points us *away* from that. The plural, "our", goes with the singular, "man", indicating, not an "old man" in *each* of us, but one "old man" including *all*. If Paul had meant his phrase to be used distributively of individuals, would he not have used the plural? Or, if he had meant an old *nature* in each of us, would he not have used the actual word for "nature" (*phusis*), which he uses elsewhere thirteen times in his epistles? The expression, "our old man", simply cannot mean a so-called "old nature" in each of us, for in the rest of the New Testament it has corroboration nowhere, and contradiction everywhere. Scripture does not say anywhere that only a *part* of us was crucified with Christ—whether we call it "our old man", or our "old nature" or anything else, but it does teach a judicial joint-crucifixion of each individual *totally*, along with the whole Adam race *collectively*.

If further argument is required to refute the common misinterpretation of the phrase, "old man", in the three texts where it occurs (Rom. 6: 6, Eph. 4: 22, Col. 3: 9) let me here call attention particularly to the Greek word which is translated as "man". In all three texts it is the same Greek word, *anthropos*. It occurs in the New Testament 344 times in the singular; 192 in the plural; 10 in the possessive; making a total of 546. From beginning to end of the New Testament, in the Authorized Version, and in the English Revised Version, and in the American Standard Version, the uniform translation of it is "man" or "men" or "man's". In only three instances out of the 546 have the E.R.V. and A.S.V. even slightly diverged from the A.V. (i.e. Mk. 12: 14, "any one" instead of "any man"; and John 6: 14, "people" instead of "men"). With that quite trivial difference, our three greatest versions unite in demonstrating that the only exact translation of *anthropos* is "*MAN*", and that the one meaning is "man" in his totality, not some imagined sub-area such as an "old *nature*", or some such specific concentrate as a so-called "sinful *self*."

What about more recent translations? Their testimony is just as solid that the true translation of *anthropos* is "man". Not one of them translates it as "nature" (for details see appendix on *Anthropos*).

So, let it be settled, according to the Greek *anthropos*, the phrase, "our old man", in Romans 6: 6 does *not* mean an "old *nature*" inside us; nor does it mean so when we relate it to its context; nor when we compare Romans 6: 6 with kindred Pauline comments elsewhere. Etymology, context, and cross-reference are all against it. As we have said, "our old man" is an expressive Paulinism for *THE WHOLE HUMAN RACE IN ADAM*.

The "Body of Sin"

But now, what is meant by those further words, "that the *body of sin* might be destroyed"? (The verb is another aorist meaning destroyed in a completed past act).

The "body of sin" cannot be the *physical* body which each of us has, for *that* body has never been "destroyed", or "done away" in one completed act! Whether we render the Greek as "destroyed", or "nullified", or "done away" is immaterial. When a man has been crucified, in one completed past act, does it matter much whether we say he has been "destroyed", or "nullified", or "done away"? The effect is the same anyway! No such destruction through joint-crucifixion has occurred to our physical body. Furthermore, such an expression as "the body of *sin*" could scarcely refer to the *physical* body, for it would suggest that the body itself is sinful, an idea contradicted by the whole force of New Testament teaching.

Admittedly, some of those who teach that the "body of sin" is our physical body *deny* that this makes the physical body itself sinful. Paul's meaning (they say) is, that our flesh-and-blood organism is the "instrument" or "vehicle" or "slave" of sin. But no; we cannot allow any such attempted outflankings of Paul's clear meaning. If the "body of sin" is the physical body, yet the physical body is not itself sinful, then why had it to be "destroyed", "rendered inoperative", "done away"? Or again, if the body itself is not sinful, how can it be, in any *peculiar* way, the stronghold or accomplice of sin?

Let it be settled once for all; this flesh-and-blood body is morally *neutral*. There can be no such quality as sin-proneness in a merely physical organism. This natural body of mine is non-sentient matter. It cannot, in itself, think or know or choose or even feel. I may say that there is a pain in my arm, but the pain is not really felt *by* the arm; for if the arm be severed from the body, it has no feeling whatever in itself. What is true of the arm is true of the whole body. It is the *occupant* of the body who thinks, knows, chooses, feels, inclines. So far as human *moral* patterns are concerned, the body reacts exactly, good or bad, according to the mind which is living in and moving through it. My own experience, after observant introspection, is, that this flesh-and-blood mechanism of mine, so far as moral drive goes, is just as ready to serve one way or the other. It is just as ready to be the servant of righteousness as the servant of sin. Is not that why Paul says, in this same sixth chapter of Romans: "As ye presented your members servants to uncleanness, even so now present your members servants to righteousness" (19)? I am not forgetting that in chapter 7: 23 Paul speaks about "the law of sin which is in my *members*." Let it be observed, however, that even there it is not the bodily "members" themselves which are sinful, but the "law of sin" which operates through them.

Away with any such idea as that the body itself is sinful, or that it is the "seat" of sin, or that it is a Judas continually betraying us! That is the distorted idea which lay behind much of the monasticism of the Middle Ages. It is the error which set many an agonised ascetic thrashing and disfiguring the poor body in a forlorn hope of beating sin out of it. It is the error which gave a spurious extra virtue to celibacy, and to cloistered aloofness from the vulgar crowd outside. It gave a deadly wrong turn to the concept of holiness, and sent it flogging bodies instead of saving souls. It cannot be repeated too emphatically that the body is neither moral nor immoral. Being non-sentient it is *a*-moral. It is good or bad according to the mind which indwells it.

Certainly, the body needs to be disciplined—as Paul himself says. So does a horse, a dog, a physical muscle. So does all co-ordinated activity. But in no instance does the discipline imply *sin* in that which is to be disciplined.

Nor can "the body of sin" mean a supposed lump-mass or *aggregate* of sin in our nature, as though sin were a "foreign body" (as doctors would say) in the system. Some of those who suppose that the "old man" and the "body of sin" mean an evil "self nature" prefer the rendering, "that the body of sin might be *rendered inoperative*." They would fain adapt the verse to teach that the suppositionary "old nature" is fastened to the Cross, as it were, wriggling a bit maybe, not quite dead, but in a state of crucifixion, and thereby "rendered inoperative". A thrilling picture of sanctification!

Such an interpretation, however, stands self-condemned. The text no more teaches a prolongation of crucifixion or a protracted dying than yesterday can be extended into tomorrow. It teaches crucifixion as a past and completed act. The very *figure* of crucifixion shows that finality is meant. When a man has been crucified, he is not merely dying, he is *dead*. Therefore the verse cannot refer to our "corrupt self", for in no Christian's experience has there been such an absolute death to sin.

Whatever else Romans 6: 6 may or may not teach, it certainly teaches a past and completed crucifixion with a correspondingly complete *effect* expressed in that word "destroyed". So, if some of our brethren insist that it refers to our "inborn tendency to evil" (see Scofield note on verse), they simply *must* accept the teaching of a completed crucifixion and *death* of it. But if that inborn old "Adam" is completely "done away" or "destroyed" and "dead", what about those who (as it is put) "fall away from the blessing", or who, even after their supposed "death to sin" find subtle risings of wrong within? One naïve eradicationist explained it to me as the evidence of a new "old nature" growing within! So where are we? Instead of one, final crucifixion, a crop of *new* "old natures" and a multiple-crucifixion doctrine!

Pauline Usage of the Word

But if the "body of sin" is neither the physical body nor inbred sin, what is it? Why, surely Paul uses the word "body" figuratively to mean the whole Adam humanity in its corporate totality. The sense is,

"Our old man [the old humanity in Adam] was crucified with Him [in a completed past act] that the body of sin [the whole physical part through which the sin of the old humanity expresses itself] might be done away."

There is coming a time when the whole physical creation in Adam will be "done away" *actually*, but even now, it is done away *judicially*. Speaking of His Cross, our Lord said, *"Now* is the judgment of this world." Up to that time Adamic humanity had been tested in various ways; it was on probation; but now it was to be tested no more; it was to be judged. When the Adam race nailed the Son of God to that Cross it demonstrated beyond need of further proof its final failure. It was on probation no longer; it was judged and judicially done away. Romans 6: 6 echoes and amplifies that; the whole Adam race is judicially done away in Christ, who now brings in the *new* humanity. Therefore to be living for this mortal body is to be living for that which is judicially (even though not *actually*) dead; which is why Paul writes in Romans 8: 10, "If Christ be in you, *the body is dead* because of sin [in Adam]; but the Spirit is life because of righteousness [through Christ]."

Guidance from Context

The more we reflect, the more evident it becomes that "the body of sin" refers to the whole Adam race. Does not the context, once again, guide us to this? The section leading up to Romans 6: 6 begins at chapter 5: 12. From that verse, to the end of chapter 5, all swings round, "As by one man [Adam] . . . so by one man [Christ]." The one man is the old; the other is the new. The characteristic of the old is *sin*.

"By one man *SIN* . . . and death" (12)
"By the *OFFENCE* of the one [man] . . . many died" (15)
"By one that *SINNED* . . . condemnation" (16)
"By the *TRESPASS* of the one death reigned" (17)
"By one man's *DISOBEDIENCE* many were made sinners" (19).

In the *new* "man" (Christ) there is righteousness and life. In the *old* "man" (Adam) there is sinfulness and death. As the members of the new humanity in Christ are said to be *His* "body" (12: 5), so here, in a similarly figurative way, all the members of the old humanity in Adam are *his* "body". The "body of *sin*", then, is the whole Adam humanity as viewed in its guilt before God.

Guidance from the Wording

That such is the purport of the context is clinched by the discriminative wording in the text itself. The two expressions, "our old man" and "the body of sin", *must* mean practically one and the same thing, or at least two *aspects* of the same thing, because the one was crucified that the other might be destroyed—which could only be if the two were practically identical. To nail culprit A to a cross would not destroy culprit B there, unless A and B were one. Just so, "our old man" and "the body of sin" are two aspects of the same reality. Notice that although Paul speaks of "our old man", he does not say, "*our* body of sin". Why the careful discrimination between "our" and "the"? Because "*our* old man" means all that *we* were by connection with the Adam humanity, whereas "*the* body of sin" is not ours but *Adam's*. The body is always that which *belongs*. The "body of sin" is Adam's. Thus the force of Romans 6: 6 is,

"OUR OLD MAN	—all that we were by position and relation in Adam, with all our culpability and condemnation;
"WAS CRUCIFIED WITH HIM	—was judged and executed in the One-for-all death of Christ;
"THAT THE BODY OF SIN	—the whole Adam humanity as guilty before God;
"MIGHT BE DESTROYED	—completely done away in the judicial reckoning of God;
"THAT WE SHOULD NO LONGER BE IN BONDAGE TO SIN"	—that is, no longer in *legal* bondage through *judicial* guilt.

Endorsement by Parallel

Now there are some of us who have been so thoroughly brought up on *other* "interpretations", namely, that "our old man" is an old self-life, and that the "body of sin" is either the physical body or a lump-mass of sin within us, that we still may not be wholly convinced by the corrective exposition of it which I have here submitted. So let me try to clinch the verdict by referring to yet another Pauline passage which parallels with Romans 6: 6, and unmistakably endorses what we have said of it. The passage is 2 Corinthians 5: 14–17.

Rom. 6: 6.	2 *Cor.* 5: 14, 15 (*E.R.V.*)
"Knowing this, that our old man was crucified with Him, that the body of sin might be done away, that we should no longer be in bondage to sin."	"One died for all, therefore *all died* [in Him] and He died for all, that they which live should no longer live unto themselves, but unto Him."

"*All died*" in Him! Surely the parallel is clear enough to be conclusive. Furthermore, when we thus understand Romans 6: 6, it immediately harmonises with the opening question of the chapter (which it does *not*, if "our old man" and the "body of sin" are made to mean something inside the individual). The opening question is, "Shall we continue in sin, that grace may abound?" —and the chapter answers *that* by arguing that since the old Adam humanity was judicially done away we should no longer live for the old, but for the new, in Christ. The chapter is *not* an answer to such questions as, "How shall we get victory over indwelling sin?" or "How shall we find deliverance from an Adam-nature within us?"

Another circumstance, also, which corroborates our corrective interpretation of Romans 6: 6 is the non-mention of "the flesh". Mark it well: the struggle between the Holy Spirit and "the flesh", that inner evil in our nature, does not come into view until chapter 7. The Holy Spirit is never even mentioned in connection with "our old man" and "the body of sin". Why? Because, as we keep saying, "our old man" and "the body of sin" are *not* names for something *inside* us as human individuals, they point to something which was done *outside* us, once for all, on that Cross of long ago.

Galatians 2: 20

But we are sure to be asked: "What about *other* texts which apparently *do* teach that our self-life was crucified with Christ? Where are they? Does someone refer us to Galatians 2: 20?

"I am crucified with Christ: nevertheless I live, yet not I, but Christ liveth in me; and the life which I now live in the flesh I live by the faith of the Son of God, who loved me, and gave Himself for me."

To translate the verb-tense strictly here, Paul does not say "I am", but "I *have been* crucified with Christ". Paul means, not a present experience of *being* crucified, but a joint-crucifixion already completed. The preceding verse should be enough at once to settle that.

Verse 19	*Verse* 20
"I *died* [aorist] to the Law, that I might *live* unto God."	"I *have been* crucified with Christ nevertheless I live . . ."

But what about the context? It has nothing to do with the inward; it is all about *justification*. See the verses which precede Galatians 2:20.

"Knowing that a man is *NOT JUSTIFIED* by the works of the Law, but through faith in Jesus Christ, even we [i.e. we Jews] have believed in Jesus Christ, that we might be *JUSTIFIED* by the faith of Christ, and not by the works of the Law; for by *THE WORKS OF THE LAW* shall no flesh be *JUSTIFIED*. But if while we seek to be *JUSTIFIED* by Christ, we ourselves are found sinners, is therefore Christ the minister of sin? God forbid. For if I build again the things which I destroyed, I make myself [again] a *TRANSGRESSOR*. For I through the Law *DIED TO THE LAW* that I might live unto God."

Yes, that is what leads right up to Galatians 2: 20. It is all about justification and the Law, not about inward sanctification. Then, as soon as Paul says, "I *have been crucified* with Christ," he completes the paragraph by adding,

"I do not frustrate the grace of God; for if *RIGHTEOUSNESS* come by *THE LAW*, then Christ died in vain."

Is it not as plain as can be that the context is concerned with *justification*, not with an inward crucifixion of self? Is it not equally clear that when Paul says, "I *died* to the law. . . . I *have been* crucified with Christ," he is thinking of the Cross in its *judicial* sense not of some supposed *internal* dying in ourselves? Why, when we reflect on it, what is Galatians 2: 20, but Romans 6: 6 in the singular?

Do we need add more? Galatians 2: 20 does *not* teach joint-crucifixion of a so-called self-life in present experience. Why do preachers of the inward-crucifixion theory keep treating Galatians 2: 20 as though Paul said, "My *old nature* is crucified with Christ"? He said no such thing. He said, *"I"* (the total man), meaning, of course, his *judicial* identification with the Christ of the Cross.

Galatians 5: 24

What about Galatians 5: 24?—"They that are Christ's have *crucified the flesh* with the affections and lusts." It may be said that "the flesh" here surely *does* refer to our inborn depravity. I agree that it does. What is more, it speaks of "the flesh" as being "crucified". But *that* crucifixion simply cannot be a joint-crucifixion with Christ, for very cogent reasons. In Romans 6: 6, the joint-crucifixion of "our old man" (the old humanity in Adam) with Christ, was a judicial act effected by *God*; whereas here, in Galatians 5: 24, the crucifixion is something which believers themselves do. It is a *self*-crucifixion.

Moreover, note the apostle's use of the aorist tense again here: "They that are Christ's *crucified* the flesh. . . ." His thought is not that of a continuing crucifixion, but rather of something which those Galatians had already *done* in their conversion to Christ and by their brave public avowal of Christ in baptism. In those days, to profess Jesus as Saviour, as Christ, as God, was in most places to court serious trouble, if not martyrdom. In that sense it certainly had been a crucifying of the flesh; but Paul wants them to realise, also, that it was a self-crucifixion in a deeper way, i.e. that it implied a crucifying of *all* fleshly appetites and ways.

That such is his meaning, and *not* a supposed joint-crucifixion with Christ, is confirmed by his later exclamation in chapter 6: 14, "But God forbid that I should glory, save in the Cross of our Lord Jesus Christ, by whom the world is crucified unto me, and I unto the world." Once again our Authorised Version blurs the tense of the verb. What Paul says is ". . . by whom the world *has been* crucified unto me, and I unto the world". He is not thinking of a present, continuous, inward crucifixion of the "self", but of a crucifixion *completed*. In what sense, then, had that completed crucifixion occurred? Surely no one will contend that Paul meant his analogy here to be literalized. Not with literal actuality had either the "world" or Paul been transfixed to our Lord's Cross outside the city wall. No; but once Paul had grasped the meaning of that awful yet glorious Cross (which was indeed "the judgment of this world": John 12: 31), it had become *representative* of the ended relationship between himself and the "world". As for the "world", it was to him a thing crucified and done away. As for himself, every desire he formerly had for the deceptive glamours of the "world" was crucified and done away. That is what he meant; neither more nor less. It was a crucifixion complete and over, as the aorist and perfect tenses both indicate. He is *not* teaching a present, continuing crucifixion of a so-called "carnal nature" by some supposed "identification" of it with our Lord on Calvary.

So far as I know, those are the only verses in the New Testament which speak of the believer as being "crucified"; and not one of them teaches a present, experiential joint-crucifixion of the believer's old "self-life" with our crucified Lord. How could they? If they did, they would be teaching a palpable impossibility.[1]

Wrong Applications!

How often wrong *explanation* of Romans 6: 6 leads to wrong *application* of it! We give just one instance. In a compilation of addresses recently published one of the able contributors has an address on "Our Old Man Crucified" in which he tells us that "the body of sin" is not the totality of sin, nor the substance or essence of sin, but *our natural body* as used and claimed by sin. All believers were judicially identified with Christ in His death to sin, the *result* of which is (so he says) that our bodies are now free from sin's claim, and need no longer serve sin. Then (the usual fallacy) this must be individually appropriated by faith if this liberation is to become real in our *experience*. He lucidly illustrates this as follows:

"In America the Deed of Emancipation which set free millions of slaves was first executed before a single slave could know practically what freedom meant. We come to the Cross and see that we are free, that in virtue of our identification with Christ, *the body of sin, as such, is emancipated*—'being now made free from sin'. Go and claim it; this is faith's function. It is done. It is just what a slave had to do in America. The news comes to him that the Deed of Emancipation has been executed. But he is still in bondage, he is under the power of a cruel master. It is not a question of struggling out of his power, but of simply claiming his right. He is legally set free. By faith he claims that privilege. Then comes the practical experience. . . . Your old master, sin, has no legal claims upon you. . . . *Claim your legal freedom, and you will know experimental freedom*" (italics ours).

How apt! Yet how wrong! for it brings the speaker into flat contradiction of Paul. All we need to do is to put Paul's words side by side with those of the theory:

Paul	Theory
"Our old man was crucified with Him, that the body of sin might be *DESTROYED*."	"In virtue of our identification with Christ, the body of sin, as such, is *EMANCIPATED*."

[1] That our emended interpretation of Romans 6: 6 is true is also shown by the contradictoriness of suggested alternatives. See appendix on this (page 251).

That which Paul says is "destroyed" the theory says is "emancipated". Why such a contradiction? Simply because the speaker has misinterpreted "the body of sin". What he strangely fails to notice is, that in Romans 6: 6 it is *"WE"* who are liberated (not the "body of sin"!); "that *WE* should no longer be in bondage to sin."

Unfortunately, that is not all. Through his wrongly using "the body of sin" to mean "our natural body", the speaker trips into further error:

"Claim your legal freedom, and you will know experimental freedom."

Such are well-meaning statements which, instead of leading to freedom, betray believers into bondage. Being made free *"legally"* from sin does *not* free my body or its members in an experiential way from indwelling sin-activities, any more than it freed Paul's "wretched man" who (*after* coming through Romans 6: 6) was still wailing, "Sin which is *in my members'* (7: 23).

"Claim your *legal* freedom," the theory exhorts us. Yet our "legal freedom" from sin is not something which is to be "claimed" at all. It is *already* ours if we are "in Christ". It is not one of those *spiritual* provisions which may be claimed in the way, for instance, that a truly consecrated heart may reverently claim the enduing of the Holy Spirit. No; my *legal* freedom in Christ is a status absolute and final which became fully mine the moment I became united to Him at my conversion. There are no degrees in justification. *All* the righteousness of Christ became judicially mine, by imputation, *then*.

The patent fallacy in the Emancipation illustration is its confusing of the legal with the moral. When those slaves were freed, did their being freed *legally* change their nature *morally*? No; neither, in Romans 6, does the *judicial* emancipation of the believer from Sin (as a cruel slave-master) bring any such *inward* deliverance from sin in the "natural body" as the theory would have us "claim". However, as it is distasteful to criticize such beloved experts as that speaker, we relegate further comments to Appendix on *"The Body of Sin"*. We do not wish to add anything but what is strictly necessary to prove that the usual interpretations of Romans 6: 6 are wrong.

Of course, in leading us through this masterly explication of our *judicial* emancipation, in chapter 6, Paul is eagerly on his way to the completive master-strokes of chapter 8, where he expounds our *inward* liberation from sin, through the "law of the Spirit of life in Christ Jesus"; but (as we have said) when holiness teachers try to argue such inward deliverance on the basis of our *judicial* identification with Christ in chapter 6, they outrun Paul; they throw his dissertation "out of gear"; and then find themselves flung back again by the "wretched man" of chapter 7, who, despite having come through chapter 6 has *not* yet found deliverance. Such misapplying of the *judicial* to the experiential is as evidently wrong as saying that two and two make five, or that a triangle has four sides.

Frankly, when we hear holiness preachers didactically instructing their audiences to "take God at His word" in Romans 6; to "reckon" themselves *inwardly* "dead indeed unto sin" by a supposed joint-crucifixion and death of a supposed inner "old man" on the Cross of Christ two thousand years ago, we can only deplore the doctrinaire pedagogy of the *schema*, and, despite the acclaim, feel sincerely sorry for the earnest people who are being well-meaningly deluded by it.

However, let me add (much to my own relief) we are now quite through the more argumentative and somewhat negative chapters of this series. They have been a necessary clearing of the ground from exotic misgrowths of complicating theory. Beginning with our next chapter we emerge from these entangling copices into an open meadow with unimpeded footway. We shall employ ourselves in interpreting the positive New Testament message concerning the sanctification of Christian believers. We shall seek to arrive at a new understanding and definition of holiness. May God grant that these succeeding chapters will prove to be the gateway into new blessing for at least some of those who may chance to read them.

> Open my inward eyes,
>   Teacher divine,
> Spirit of glad surprise,
>   Within me shine;
> Quicken my inward sight,
>   So that I see
> Shining in clearest light
>   Thy word to me.

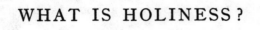

WHAT IS HOLINESS?

"Man's moral nature and God's are essentially one. God is light, and in Him is no darkness at all. The man of pure heart is light also . . . True it is that of no Christian can it be said, as of God, that in him is no darkness at all. The pure in heart all have defects. Nevertheless their purity is real, and so highly valued of God that in Scripture dialect the man of pure heart is called 'perfect', his infirmities notwithstanding."

A. B. Bruce.

"God created man in His own image"— Gen. 1: 27.
"Being renewed after the image of Him that created him"—Col. 3: 10.
"We . . . are being changed into the same image"—2 Cor. 3: 18.

WHAT IS HOLINESS?

The centre-point of these studies is the question: *What is holiness?* or, more particularly, what is the holiness to which the New Testament calls Christian believers? That is the enquiry which is before us in this present chapter.

Holiness, however, like many other intangibles, is not easy to define so as to bring a vivid image of it before the eyes of the mind. It is easier to describe than to define. Some, perhaps, might define it negatively as absence of sin, or positively as absolute virtue. Or maybe some would define it ethically as impeccable righteousness, or more spiritually as moral perfection. Yet all such definitions are abstract and unpictorial and therefore elusive. We need somehow to apprehend holiness photographically; and with this in mind I do not hesitate to affirm that the truest preliminary description is,

HOLINESS IS LIKENESS TO GOD,

or, more precisely, likeness to the *moral character* of God.

This, so I believe, in both Old and New Testaments, is the centric idea in the call to holiness. Away back in Leviticus, there we see it, gleaming over the vestibule of the Israel theocracy, as the first and supreme requirement: "*Ye shall be holy; for I JEHOVAH YOUR GOD AM HOLY*" (Lev. 19: 2). It was this which first gave coherence and sanction to all the Levitical enjoinments and prohibitions, ceremonial, sacrificial, hygienic, social, moral and spiritual. The Ten Commandments are simply an amplification of it in ten aspects: "*Ye shall be holy, for I JEHOVAH YOUR GOD AM HOLY.*"

This challenge: "*Ye shall be holy, for I JEHOVAH YOUR GOD AM HOLY,*" surely rebuts those teachings which would persuade us that in most of the Old Testament the idea of holiness does not have an ethical content. Disappointingly enough, some of our ablest scholarship seems to be still captivated by this misconception that in the Old Testament, especially its earlier parts, holiness is merely *religious separation*, tribal, ritual, sanitary, dietary, and non-ethical.[1]

The truth is, that *all* the Mosaic regulations, whether concerning clean versus unclean animals, physical defilements and purifications, or abstention from the licentious customs of surrounding nations—*all* have a reflex reference to holiness of *character*. Not one whit less than that is implied in the words, *"Ye shall be holy, for I JEHOVAH YOUR GOD AM HOLY."* Would anyone have the temerity to tell us that when God said, "I Jehovah your God am holy," He intended no more than "I, Jehovah your God, distinguish between clean and unclean animals; between the hygienic and the unhygienic"?—or some other such meaning? Nay, He meant no less than this: "There shall be in *your* character that which corresponds to *Mine*." That nothing less was meant is confirmed by the New Testament quotation of it in 1 Peter 1: 14–16.

So, as a beginning, we say that the holiness to which we are called, as Christians, is *moral likeness to God*. What, then, is such God-likeness? In the New Testament there are three verses which tells us what God *"is"*—

> God is spirit —John 4: 24
> God is light —1 John 1: 5
> God is love —1 John 4: 8

Those three definitions remarkably concentrate the teaching of the Bible, and at the same time give a first answer to our question, What is holiness?

"God is Spirit"

Take the first of them: "God is *spirit*." Throughout Scripture, "spirit" and "matter" are contrastively distinguished. They are not

---

[1] It will be understood, of course, that I wholly reject the higher critical late-dating of Leviticus, or any other part of the Pentateuch. I believe that archaeological, historical and New Testament testimony are all against it. Those suppositionary penmen of the Pentateuch, *E* and *J* and *D*, and their anonymous redactors, are to me the furtive phantoms of a misguided scholarship. Nor need we shrink from claiming, with the four Gospels open before us, that in speaking thus "we have the mind of Christ"— for our Lord's testimony to the Old Testament, and to the Pentateuch in particular, is not only clear, but ample, and should be accepted as final.

merely rarity and density of the same substance; they are different in nature. Spirit is not rarefied matter. Our Lord did not say, "God is matter in its most refined form." Nor does the Bible anywhere countenance the Communist dictum that the human soul is merely "matter in motion". The old notion, modernly sponsored by Communism, that "spirit" is simply matter thinned out in subtle attenuation, is a convenient philosophy for atheists, but it is not science, for it has no basis whatever in ascertained fact. It becomes clearer than ever that the material universe was created by a vast Mind, and that therefore mind cannot be mere extenuation of matter. Nay, since mind *controls* matter, how can it be a *product* of matter? It is even more difficult to see how mental states such as hope, fear, anger, desire, or other such abstract realities can be merely refined matter!

But why labour the point speculatively when we are solely concerned with it *Scripturally*? The Word teaches that spirit and matter are essentially different; and that the God who created all things is Himself *spirit*. This means that God views everything in an essentially spiritual way, inasmuch as matter, even in its largest dimension and longest duration, is not permanent reality. One God-conscious, non-material, human soul is of bigger significance than Orion and Pleiades and all the stellar myriads of the Milky Way. That is why the incarnate Son of God once bled on this tiny pebble of a planet to save us.

Now just as God himself, before anything else, is essentially spiritual, so the first mark of holiness in any of ourselves is a corresponding *spirituality* in outlook, attitude, desire, and sense of values. With opened eyes we perceive that it is the intangibles which are the imperishables. In the words of 2 Corinthians 4: 18, "we look not at the things which are seen, but at the things which are not seen; for the things which are seen are temporal, but the things which are not seen are eternal." This spirituality is the first prerequisite of holiness.

There is a "holiness" which is "of the flesh"—a sanctimony of "touch not; taste not; handle not"; but it is a counterfeit; and Paul's indictment of it is: "Which things have indeed a show of wisdom in will-worship and humility, and severity to the body; yet not in any honour [to God], but only for the gratifying of the flesh"—i.e. by a reputation for superior sanctity (Col. 2: 23). Any of us can verify by observation that the unvarying signature of genuine holiness is *spiritual-mindedness*. All the Enochs who have "walked with God" have revealed so. It has been their choice of the spiritual in preference to the material, and their disenchantment with the things of this present world, which have made them an exasperating enigma to the loud men of earth's "Vanity Fair".

Yet this spirituality is never self-advertising. It is seen in the set of the sails, rather than heard through the skipper's megaphone. It expresses itself through the soul's reactions, rather than by oral announcements. It sounds no horn; on the contrary, it is a silent diffusion, as the fragrance of a rose. Even more, what atmosphere is to the lungs, this spiritual-mindedness is to holiness.

"God is Light"

Halt now at the second of those three New Testament concentrates: *"God is light."* John's full word runs, "God is light, and in Him is *no darkness at all"*—light sheer and shadowless.

"God is light." This is definition by parallel. What light is to the natural world, God is in the spiritual. Only in light can we see; yet light itself cannot be seen; it is transparent. It may be prismatically broken up into its primary and secondary spectra, but light itself is invisible.

John has in mind the two main properties of light, as his references show. (1) Light is *manifestant*; it reveals the things which are, making them visible to natural sight. (2) Light is *transparent*; which further means that where there is light with "no darkness at all", the transparency is utter.

Light is the opposite of "darkness", which conceals and deceives and which therefore represents moral *evil*. "For everyone that doeth evil hateth the light, neither cometh to the light lest his deeds should be exposed" (John 3: 20). The deepest darkness is *hate*. Twice over it is written, "He that hateth his brother is in the darkness" (1 John 2: 9, 11). By the same parallel, also, *truth* is the light, and error is darkness. "He that doeth truth cometh to the light, that his deeds may be made manifest" (John 3: 21).

So, then, the analogy, "God is light," means that holiness, or moral likeness to God, is (1) such purity of mind as exposes in sharp distinguishment the beauty of goodness and the ugliness of evil; (2) a sheer transparency—of motive, purpose, and desire.

Yes, holiness (moral likeness to God) is transparent purity and sincerity of the mind.

"God is Love"

Thirdly, "God is love."[1] What this means can be known only by observing how John in particular and the New Testament in general refer to the love of God. Some of us may be rather surprised to learn that in every instance where the divine love is described, it is not a passive, inward emotion, but an active, outreaching benevolence; not a self-contained complacence, but a self-emptying *otherism*; not a contemplative sublimity of feeling, but a redeeming compassion toward the unworthy and unlovely, the defiled and deformed; a love which gives and gives and gives again.

Here are a few of the texts which represent the New Testament teaching: "God so loved the world that He *gave*. . . ." (John 3: 16); "The kindness of God our Saviour, and His love toward man, appeared . . . according to His mercy He saved us" (Titus 3: 4); "Herein is love, not that we loved God, but that He loved us, and sent His Son to be the propitiation for our sins" (1 John 4: 10).

I suspect that many of us, in our quest after holiness, have imagined that being filled with the love of God would flood our consciousness with a kind of contemplative rapture, or a sense of infinite satisfaction. That is why many have developed a "holiness" turned inward instead of outward; mystical instead of practical; self-centred rather than God-centred; sentimental rather than evangelistic; and egoistic rather than altruistic. The love which John means when he writes, "God is love," is the most self-forgetting otherism in the universe, and when it is indeed "shed" within us (Rom. 5: 5) it lifts us right out of ourselves into a magnanimous solicitude for the wellbeing of others.

Moral God-likeness

What we are saying, then, is that Christian holiness, in its first aspect, is moral likeness to the Holy One who calls us. In fact,

---

[1] In a preceding chapter we stressed the need for a right approach to the Bible. How important is our attitude to revelation and inspiration when we encounter such an assertion as, "God is love"! If inspiration is no more than "religious genius", or "extra-sensory perception", or "mystical insight", or anything else less than direct divine communication, then the statement that "God is love" is no more, even at best, than a speculative deduction. If, however, it is the utterance of authentic divine inspiration, it is the profoundest and sublimest "*multum in parvo*" ever penned.

that is word-for-word what First Peter 1: 15 says it is, according to the A.S.V. margin: *"Like the Holy One who called you,* be ye yourselves also holy in all manner of living." What is God like? "God is spirit." "God is light." "God is love." What, then, is Christian holiness? It is (1) spiritual-mindedness of outlook, appraisal, desire, and choice; (2) transparent purity of aim and motive; (3) self-forgetting outreach to bless others. Thus described how much (or how little) genuine, practical, Christian holiness is there?

DIVINE HOLINESS INCARNATED

Yet although holiness may be introductorily described as moral likeness to God, do we not all feel that if we are truly to know it, we need somehow to *see* it? We need not only to have it described, but to see it revealed. The mysterious wonder of New Testament revelation is, that we can and do see it, lived out before our watching eyes, in One who comes to us clothed in our own humanity yet saying, "He that hath seen Me hath seen the Father." In Him the divine holiness "comes alive" to us, not merely as some new definition, but in visible incarnation.

In Him, in His humanhood, in His deeds and words, in His passive reactions and active responses, in His miracles and parables, in His public and private behaviour, in His sympathies and aversions, in the way He lived and the way He died; in Him, from His Jordan baptism in water to His Calvary baptism in blood, we see the holiness of heaven expressed in human form on earth. Would we know what true likeness to God is? Then we must look and learn of Him who said, "He that hath seen Me hath seen the Father."

What, then, is it that we see in Jesus? He was often in secret prayer, but He was no mystic. He was fond of periodic solitude, but He was no monastic. He was abstemious, but He was no ascetic. He had nothing in common with the religious "Zealots" and their contentious violence; yet neither did He ever once visit the nonpartisan "Essenes" in their cloistered isolationism. There was moral apartness, yet no social aloofness. There was sanctity, but no frigidity. He abhorred hypocrisy, but was overflowingly sympathetic where there was contrition. He neither fawned on the rich nor despised the poor. He neither coveted wealth nor condoned poverty. He never compromised principle a hair's breadth, yet He was a congenial mixer with a keen aliveness toward people and things. He had boundless compassion, friendship, understanding, for boys and girls, for the aged, for the sick, for the suffering, for the bad who wanted to be different, and the good who wanted to be better. He saw God everywhere and in everything; and His master-passion was to do the Father's will. He was utterly guileless in His self-abnegating outreach of heart to heal and mend and bless others. He was the sublimest embodiment of gracious otherism ever known: and, most significant of all, in revealing the one true Godhead, He revealed also the one ideal *manhood*. There is no mistaking Him, except by the blind: He is "God manifest in the flesh"; sinless in essence, stainless in conduct, guileless in motive, quenchless in love.

In Jesus the ideal and the actual are one. He is the superb *norm* of true humanhood, that is, humanhood as originally created and divinely intended. As Professor Henry Drummond said, with a permissible touch of refined colloquialism, "Jesus is the perfect Gentleman"—the exquisite blend of "gentle" and "man", of tenderness and virile heroism; "meek and lowly in heart," but with an awesome flash of ire in His eyes before which the temple money-traffickers cowered and slunk away.

Years ago, at a large gathering in Manchester, England, a minister prayed a prayer which has had a decided influence on my thinking ever since: "O God, make us *intensely spiritual*, but keep us *perfectly natural*, and always *thoroughly practical*—even as Jesus was." That prayer was finely photographic. It captured the dominant lineaments of our Lord's holy manhood: "intensely spiritual"; "perfectly natural"; "thoroughly practical"; the living expression of "God is *spirit*," "God is *light*," "God is *love*." Yes, that was Jesus; and that was the divine holiness incarnate. So then, holiness, which we have preliminarily described as moral likeness to God, may now be more concretely represented *as likeness in heart and life to Christ*.

HOLINESS INWROUGHT

The crowning-point of New Testament revelation on this subject is reached in its doctrine of the Holy Spirit. That holiness which is likeness to God, and is exhibited in Christ, is now *inwrought* by the Holy Spirit within the fully possessed Christian believer. With what reverent awe ought we to worship in the presence of such a divine mystery! How glibly we sometimes talk about the supernatural operations of the Holy Spirit in regeneration and sanctification! Let us "put off our shoes", for the place whereon we stand is "holy ground".

There may be *inwrought* in you and me, a real heart-holiness from God, through Christ, by the Holy Spirit. That is not just a nostrum or theory; it is the truth of the Word. In the Old Testament holiness is *demanded*. In the Lord Jesus it is *provided*. By the Holy Spirit it is *imparted*. Of course, that which is absolute in God can be only relative in ourselves. Yet just as ethical righteousness is basically the same whether in God or the creature, so is it with holiness (see flyleaf quotation).

Not Wholly Instantaneous

Yes, holiness may be inwrought; but how? Can we accept that it is inwrought *instantaneously* as a "second blessing"?

Those who teach that the sin-bias in human nature can be "eradicated" have maintained that at the "second blessing" there is an instantaneous extinction of "indwelling sin", and a consequent full restoration into the image of Christ. Others have preached a moderated version of this; yet they too have held that in response to consecration and faith there comes an instantaneous "rendering inoperative" of the "old man", and an inward renewal into holiness. Such teachings are astray, for they are based on the usual misinterpretation of Romans 6: 6, that our "old man" is a supposed "old *nature*", separable from the basic human ego, and treatable as an entity in itself.

The eradicationist idea creates a comic-serious predicament. With the so-called "old nature" extirpated, and the unable-to-sin "new nature" left completely unopposed, the believer (at least theoretically) is less able to sin than Adam and Eve before the Fall! In desperate sincerity, many have *claimed* to live sinlessly; though even they could only claim so by resorting (as Wesley did) to an accommodated view of sin, i.e. that there is no sin apart from volition.

Others, who hold that the so-called "old nature" cannot be "eradicated" but only "counteracted" or "rendered inoperative" through an inward co-crucifixion with Christ, precipitate an even stranger problem. In fact, so it appears to me, their theory becomes a circus in which our "old man" is the sleekest acrobat who ever performed. According to some, he is on the Cross, but still wriggling and never quite dead. According to others, he can be off and on the Cross again and again. According to still others, he is not only "crucified", but "dead" and "buried", yet like Bram Stoker's vampire, Count Dracula, he keeps coming back to life, in different forms, working evil, and then sneaking back to his coffin again! According to others, he is "dead indeed", but only so long as we keep "reckoning" so. Such makeshifts are self-evidently wrong, and (let me re-emphasize) it is because sin is viewed as a kind of foreign "body" or separable evil "nature" in us.

Complete Possession

Then *what* is the instantaneous something in the deeper work of sanctification to which many have testified? It is COMPLETE POSSESSION BY THE HOLY SPIRIT, in answer to the believer's complete self-yielding. There can be *degrees* of yieldedness to Christ. The instant we reach the final point of *utter*-yieldedness, there is a correspondingly *instantaneous possession* by the Spirit—though not always with accompanying emotional transports (for instantaneousness is not synonymous with tumultuousness).

Various aspects of this infilling we shall consider later. Here we are concerned with only one aspect, namely, how *holiness* is inwrought by it. Many who have known this infilling as a sudden pervasion have experienced such inward rapture that they have supposed it to be a complete deliverance from inbred sin; but they have been mistaken, as many of them have later admitted.

The all-important point is, that although this oft-called "second blessing", this infilling by the Holy Spirit, is itself instantaneous, it does *not* effect an all-at-once *holiness*; it is only the *starting*-point of inwrought holiness. From then onwards the Holy Spirit has unobstructed opportunity to develop His deeper work of holiness in the now fully-possessed believer.

To ask anyone (as used to be often asked): "Have you *had* the second blessing?"—as though it were an all-in-one operation, is quite off-line. That is because, as we keep saying, our hereditary sin-disease is not a local growth or foreign "body" which can be dealt with in one isolated crisis; neither must we think of it as an *aggregate* of evil which can be heaved overboard like contraband cargo from a freighter. Sin is a diffused infection of thought, desire, motive, impulse, inclination, and even of instinct, right through our moral nature. But from the moment the Holy Spirit fully possesses us, He begins to correct, purify, refine, inbreathe and renovate all the qualities, tempers, urges, propensities, and functionings of the mind, the emotions, and the will. *That* is how holiness begins and continues to be inwrought. Alas, the very explaining of it tends to make it sound complicated. Yet it is only in analysis that it is so: the *experience* of it is simple when the Holy Spirit is given a wide-open door.

This, we must add, of course, that although inwrought holiness is a *progressive* renewal, there is a wonderful introductory experiencing of holiness as soon as the Holy Spirit really infills us. Think who He is! He is the unutterably Holy Spirit of *God*. That He should transfuse *His* life into ours is itself a precious mystery which may well subdue us to adoring worship; and that He should completely suffuse the consecrated heart cannot but bring rich foretaste of heaven. As soon as He fills us, His very presence inwardly atmospheres us in holiness, so that our whole consciousness is elevated, illumined, and spiritually expanded.

But still, that is *His* holiness, not ours. The deeper miracle is that He comes to effect holiness in *me*. Sublimating as His infilling presence may be, that by itself does not effect holiness in my own nature, any more than flushing a room with fresh air cures it of dry-rot in its walls. There are grain warehouses today in which a new device is being used against night-time raiding by rats. Strong ultra-violet-ray lamps are turned on, the light from which is such torture to rats that they will not expose themselves to it. Perhaps that is not the pleasantest of illustrations, but by parallel it vivifies the distinction which we are here making. When the Holy Spirit infills the yielded mind, evil thoughts, desires, motives, cannot openly endure the pure light of His transfused holiness, yet they still lurk deep in the human nature. I need not only the infilling presence of *His* holiness, but holiness *inwrought* by Him in my own being; and such inwrought holiness is what He graciously intends. He comes not only to infill me, but to *renew* me.

A Misleading Deviation

At this point we cannot speak too earnestly about an aberration which has had quite extensive vogue, especially during the past hundred years; an error the more deceiving because it seems puristically spiritual and jealously honouring to Christ. Its banners are "Christ our holiness", "Christ our life", "Christ our all", "Christ our victory". Its New Testament coupling-links are such texts as 1 Corinthians 1: 30, "Christ . . . is made unto us . . . sanctification"; Galatians 2: 20, "I live, yet not I, but Christ liveth in me"; Colossians 3: 4, 11, "Christ . . . is our life"; "Christ is all."

Its special accent is, that Christian holiness is Christ Himself infilling the believer. I cannot be holy in myself; interior holiness is *Christ in me*. For instance, the excellent Mrs. Hannah Whitall Smith[1] writes in good Quaker style to her son, in 1873,

"But do not expect, dear boy, ever to find thy old nature any better or any nearer thy ideal; for thee never, never will. Thee thyself, that is, thy old nature, will always be utterly vile, and ignorant, and corrupt; but Jesus is thy life now. It is with thee, 'No more I,' but Christ who liveth in thee. And is not this glorious—to lose thy own life, and find Christ's diviner life put in its place?" (*Record of a Happy Life*, p. 88).

It will be noted that Mrs. Smith's comments here are based on the usual hand-down, that there are "two natures" in the believer, one of which, although incorrigibly vile, inheres ineradicably until life's last hour on earth.

The letter also identifies that corrupt nature as the real human person, in the words, *"thee thyself, that is, thy old nature,"* which incidentally provokes the reply query: How then did that utterly evil self of mine receive Christ as Saviour *before* I had the new nature? There was nothing else in me (according to the theory) which could have received Him, unless I already had two natures *before* my conversion (a naughty little knot for certain holiness expositors to untie!). Or could it have been that the Holy Spirit worked upon that imperviously evil "thee thyself" to receive Christ and be converted? No; for we are warned again and again (in theory) that the only thing which God can do with that evil old nature is to condemn it and finally destroy it!

[1] Author of the famous little book, *The Christian's Secret of a Happy Life*.

And next, Mrs. Smith, with a strange blend of mysticism and literalism, actually substitutes Christ for the human personality, making Paul's words, "No more I," mean, "to lose thy own life; and find Christ's divine life *put in its place*." That is an ultra-spiritual over-straining of Paul's words, to the neglect of the "me" and the "I" which complete the text. Indeed it makes Christian holiness to be so exclusively "in Christ", that it is altogether *not* a renewal of our own nature into holiness.

"Victorious Life"

This well-known form of "Higher Life" teaching reaches intensification in the "Victorious Life" movement promoted by Mr. Charles G. Trumbull. Years ago, when I was searching for the truth as to sanctification, I read his tract, "The Life that Wins," in which he goes so far as to say—

"I realized that Jesus Christ was actually and literally within me; and even more than that: that He had constituted Himself my very being. . . . My body was His, my mind His, my spirit His; and not merely His, but literally a part of Him. . . . Jesus Christ had constituted Himself my life—not as a figure of speech, remember, but as a literal, actual fact."

It needs to be said plainly: such talk is *not* Scriptural spiritual-mindedness, but an extrusion beyond the Word. Scripture does *not* teach that Jesus "constitutes Himself my very being", or that my mind becomes "literally a part of Him". Such intense deviation from the sound sense of Scripture may startle us by its seemingly keen spiritual perception, but it betrays the unwary into bogs of make-believe, and leaves faith floundering without any foothold in reality. Apparently, even eradication "of *sin*" is not enough: there is supposedly an *abolition of individuality!*

Similar quotations might be added plentifully, but we forbear. The focal error in this "Higher Life" and "Victorious Life" concept is that it gives Christian holiness a wrongly exaggerated Christocentricity. According to it, the Christian life is not lived by the believer at all, but by Christ Himself in and through the believer. Upon my "letting go and letting God", Christ takes over my life and lives it for me. In reality it is not sanctification, but substitution. We ourselves do not battle against temptation, but (according to Trumbull) "simply let Christ dispose of it, while we stand by like onlookers".

Actually that is no "victorious life" at all. It certainly is not victory for *me*. No, for Christ has supplanted me. *He* is the actor in all my actions. There is absolutely *no* education or development of my own character. Nor is there any victory for Christ Himself, since the temptations aimed at *me*, have no appeal to *Him*, who is already the divine Victor. Nor does Christ have the joy of seeing communicated victory in *me*; for instead of sanctifying me, He is merely superseding me: the human "me" is no longer there to *be* a victor!

One wonders how such strained concepts can secure a hold, but they are like bewitching Delilahs to thousands, at least for a time, until the hard facts of experience hit back in bitter reprisal. Colossians 3: 4 truly enough says that "Christ . . . is our life"; but it does *not* say that "Christ is each of our *selves*". He is our life in the sense that all the sources and resources of our regenerate life are in Him, and in the further sense that He also now indwells us by the Holy Spirit; but community of *life* in Him does not mean personal *identity* with Him. He is He, and you are you, and I am I, as separately conscious individuals, for ever. Destroy that, by supposed fusion into one identity, and at a stroke you have destroyed the very purpose of both our creation and our redemption, i.e. *fellowship*.

Of course, the above-quoted recipe for the "Higher Life" and the "Victorious Life" is inevitably a criss-cross of contradiction. It brings neither a higher life nor a victorious life, for it brings no deliverance from inward sin. Mr. Trumbull's tract, "Victory in Christ," tells us that our sinfulness must unchangeably remain in us: "You must realize that in yourself you are just the same old worthless self—as Billy Sunday has said, so black that you could make a black mark on a piece of anthracite." What a deliverance!—your very self ("yourself") continuously blacker than anthracite. To expect real victory with such an inward corruption is as naïve as expecting an evil tree to bring forth good fruit. The fact is, that despite the ensign, "Victorious Life," the theory offers *no* victory over indwelling *sin*, but only over active *sinning*, and even then the victory is not that of the believer, but of Christ who has taken over the human self.

An Axiomatic Truth

If we are to be truly Scriptural, we simply must believe this, that *THE HOLY SPIRIT DOES A RENEWING WORK WITHIN OUR HUMAN NATURE ITSELF.* This must be axiomatic to all our thinking on this subject of holiness. Take the following texts, which leap readily to mind because they are so well known, each of which denotes a Spirit-wrought effect within our very *nature.*

> "Regeneration and *renewing* of [or by] the Holy Spirit."—Titus 3: 5.
> "Ye are an epistle of Christ, written not with ink but with the Spirit of the living God . . . *in the heart.*"—2 Corinthians 3: 3.
> "We are *transformed* into the same image . . . even as from the Lord the Spirit."—2 Corinthians 3: 18.
> "Be ye transformed by the *renewing* of your mind."—Romans 12: 2.
> "Righteousness and peace and joy in the Holy Spirit."—Romans 14: 17.
> "Strengthened with power through His Spirit in the inward man . . . according to the power that *worketh in us.*"—Ephesians 3: 16, 20.
> "Be *renewed* in the spirit of *your mind.*"—Ephesians 4: 23.
> "The fruit of the Spirit [i.e. produced by the Holy Spirit in and through human character] is love, joy, peace, longsuffering . . ." —Galatians 5: 22, 23.

Mark those verses well, for they represent the teaching of the Epistles in general, that the Holy Spirit not only indwells us or even infills us, but that He effects within us an inwrought renewal, transformation, sanctification. Sad marvel, many Evangelicals seem to begrudge allowing that the Holy Spirit can do any such work in our human nature! They allow that regeneration is indeed a supernatural work, but they minify it into meaning no more than the annexing of a (so-called) "new nature", from which time all the territory formerly existing as "Me" is called the "*old* nature"—an evil "me" which cannot be changed, and with which the (so-called) "new nature" must indecisively wrestle until my last gasp on earth, when, through a mysterious metamorphosis in death, I struggle free, like a butterfly-worm from its pupa-cocoon, and flutter heavenwards on wings of sinless perfection.

It is time we flung that foible to the moles and the bats. It is one of the ragged-urchin errors inflicted on us from the usual misinterpretation of Romans 6: 6 and its fictive by-product of "two natures" (supposedly) in the believer. Are we not going to be sinless in our nature itself amid the heavenly realms? Who will make us so? None other than the Holy Spirit. *Only* He can do it. Then why cannot He change us here and now, at least in degree? Someone may ask: "If the Holy Spirit can effect holiness within us here and now, in degree, why should we not trust Him to do so to the point of sinlessness?" The answer is, that we are not to presume beyond what *Scripture* provides for the present. Nowhere does our New Testament promise or even suggest complete sinlessness either of nature or conduct in this present life yet it *does* teach a true holiness, inwrought by the Holy Spirit. As to the nature and degree and other aspects of this inwrought holiness, we shall say more later. What we are here underlining is, that *the New Testament really does teach an inwrought renovation of our own moral and spiritual nature.*

HOLINESS IS RESTORATION

Finally, if holiness may indeed be thus inwrought by the Holy Spirit, as the New Testament undeniably teaches, then let us gratefully recognise that it is a *restoration*—a restoration of our human nature itself to its truest humanhood. In recognising this, of course, we cut right across the usual holiness teachings, that our natural selves, or what we are in our so-called "old nature", *cannot* be sanctified, but only crucified. As I have said two or three times already, that ghoulish figment of an "old man" supposedly inside our humanhood yet permanently beyond regeneration should be flung away for ever, along with its companion deceit that our human nature is *essentially* and *wholly* evil.

There are those who think that the blacker they make man, the more they glorify God; but they are wrong. To make man more demon than human casts a libel on the God who made him. Although our inherited sin-bent is inborn, it is not a constituent *element* of human nature itself. Let us be as anti-Pelagian as Augustine or Calvin, but let us never allow our doctrine of "original sin" to blur the fact that human nature itself was created entirely *good* (Gen. 1: 31), and that besides transmitted evil, there is transmitted good. We must not make the mistake of saying that the virus and the victim are the same. Because a patient *has* a disease, we must not say that the patient *is* the

disease. However intricately connected the parasite may be
to the living organism *with* and *in* and *on* which it lives, the two
must never be identified as one. We must carefully distinguish
between what our human nature has, and what it *is*. If we say
that our human nature is now fundamentally evil, how explain
all the good in the world—quite apart from those who are
regenerated?

However chronic, adhesive, permeative, sin may be in our
nature, it is not of our human *essence*. The moment we dare to say
that it is, we make our humanhood unredeemable. However
corrupt, vile, wicked, sin may have made us, unless we are to
malign our very Maker we *must* believe that our human nature
itself is not fundamentally rotten, but fundamentally good-ward,
and that this is the "tendency which makes for righteousness"
in our world, despite all its wickedness. Even the modern "lie
detector" tests bear a new scientific witness to the fact that human
nature itself is basically set to the right and true; otherwise a lie
would register no slant of the needle away from the basic moral
nature.

Let no one misunderstand: this is not to say that fallen man
has any goodness or merit which can avail to *save* him, whether
from the guilt or the penalty or the power or the pollution of sin;
for as we have already emphasized, fallen man is spiritually
dead, morally diseased, and physically dying. But we must
believe that human nature itself is still basically good; for it is
that, and only that which makes man redeemable, renewable,
and recoverable.

There are many evidences of this all around us, and pages
might be filled with illustrations; but we mention only two.
First, will anyone deny the basic goodness of self-sacrificing
mother-love? Think carefully: the Bible does not deny it, but
praises it. Second, man cannot regenerate himself, but he can
appreciate and respond to that which *does* regenerate him (indicating a basic moral worth). If we deny this, we make all the
Gospel welcomes and warnings to the unconverted a theatrical
unreality, and charge God with hypocrisy.

These considerations are far more vital to an understanding of
Christian *holiness* than many may realize. It is through dis-
regard of them that holiness teaching has been vitiated by the
morbid misconceit of an incurably vile "old man" or rotten "old

nature" which must co-exist within us, in irreducible filthiness, to the day of our death.

Everything depends on the view which we take of human nature *itself*, basically and essentially. The old saying has it, "We call the chess-board white, we call it black." But what of human nature? What is the foundation colour of the whole? Is our fallen, human nature white spotted on a basic black? or black smeared on a basic white? Is man a child of the devil, whom God is trying to steal? or is he a son of God whom the devil has tricked and fouled?

Some, doubtless, impatiently demur, "What matter, whether it was the bad which intruded on the good, or *vice versa*? Is it not enough to accept and confront the motley and medley just as it now is?" The answer is a capital NO. As has been well said, in this mixed-up world of ours everything depends on whether Peace or War is the intruder; whether Liberty or Slavery has the original right of possession; and in our individual life everything depends on whether it is Falsehood which has invaded the sovereign domain of Truth, or Truth which has intruded into the domain of Falsehood. Unless I strangely misread the New Testament, the vital assumption underlying its whole idea of redemption and salvation is that the realm fundamentally belongs to Truth and Goodness; that the Lie, with all its resultant evil, is everywhere the intruder; that *because* this is so, the invaded territory may be recovered; and that the salvation of our human nature is the restoration of man from his perverted self in sin, to his true self, in Christ.

We need to see it clearly and grasp it firmly: holiness is *RESTORATION*—the restoring of our nature to its true humanhood. It is not a never-ending inward crucifixion of the human self, but a renewing of it. Neither is it a grinding *suppression* of what we naturally *are*, but the purifying and renovating of it into the image of Jesus. Once for all: Christian holiness is not abrogation but *completion*. Sanctification theories have been so occupied with the so-called "old nature" which must supposedly be destroyed, that they have overlooked the native humanity in us which may be restored. How different from them is the New Testament, with its clear ring that Jesus brings to man redemption, restoration, and true fulfilment![1]

[1] See *Excursus* at end of chapter.

But there are those who will still be contradicting me, and bombarding me with the hackneyed old sayings, "God never patches up the *old* nature; He gives us a *new* nature"; and, "What men need is not 'reformation', but *regeneration.*" So stereotyped is their thinking, they cannot even suspect that the rigid "mold" from which it comes may itself be wrong. Let me cordially challenge them. If by the "old nature" they mean a "nature" which is *not* our total human self, but a separable something *within* it, then, as we have shown, they are unscriptural; for neither Romans 6 nor any other passage teaches so. Or, if by the "old nature" they mean all that we are *by nature*, apart from regeneration, then to say that God does not "patch up" *that* is a deceiving slang, for God *does* repair and restore and re-beautify what we are by nature as human beings. He does this by regeneration—which is the infusion of new spiritual life, and through an *inwrought* holiness effected by the Holy Spirit. That old epigram, "What men need is not 'reformation' but regeneration," is a foggy play on words. The real sense of it is that men need more than *self*-reformation. Who would deny that the very purpose of regeneration is our moral and spiritual *re*-formation in Christ?

Regeneration reaches into the *whole* human personality. It diffuses its healthful new life through every part. It is just as coextensive with our whole moral and spiritual being as our hereditary sin-infection is. It does not regenerate merely one part, to the exclusion of an ugly old bag of filth called the "old man", or the "old nature", or the "body of sin", always hanging on me, tied to my mind with strings of hereditary catgut which only death can sever. Regeneration *quickens*, and inwrought holiness *fulfils*, all that is truest and best in what we are by the very essence of our nature as human beings. Christian holiness is the true man; the renewed, restored, completed human character, after the image of the Lord Jesus. In Him, the Son of Man and the Son of God, we are meant to see how *each* son of man is meant to be a son of God.

Here let me register my disapproval of the sharp distinction which is commonly drawn between the so-called "natural virtues" and the "spiritual graces". One gets rather tired of being told that genuine human virtues in the unconverted, such as moral courage, self-denying devotion, patience despite provocation, integrity amid temptation, long-suffering love and loyalty, are "of the flesh", or merely of the "natural man", and that even in the regenerate they must be carefully distinguished from the "fruit of the Spirit" ... To talk of holiness as a separate something not belonging to the intrinsic human virtues, and consisting in a certain special sort of qualities which must be injected from outside, makes holiness a foreign country to me—a foreign country occupied by the Peculiarites, and the Superiorites, the Unnaturalites, the Exclusivites, and the Unattractivites. A sense of strangeness and unreality hangs like an obscuring vapour over the entrance port to it, causing me to wonder whether I as an ordinary human being have any business there.

How wrong we are, to make holiness thus remote by a false distinction! Holiness is *not* a foreign country; it is the prodigal coming home, to live where he really belongs. It is the claiming of our life and nature through and through for God again, by the Holy Spirit, and the flowering into Christ-like sublimation of all our natively human possibilities for good. It is not the abrogation, but the *fulfilment* of our true humanity. The more truly a man is holy, the more truly he is *man*. The sad wonder, yes, the *un*-naturalness, is that any child of God should live outside it, and never become that *true* self.

Let us renounce, then, the artificial distinction between the "natural virtues" and the "spiritual graces". Those nobler human impulses, responses, aspirings, volitions, such as moral bravery, long-forbearing, unselfish giving, sacrificial serving, the returning of good for evil, the magnanimous forgiveness of injuries; *those*, I say, quickened by the new life of regeneration, purified in the Shekinah flame of the indwelling Holy Spirit, and supremely motivated by adoring love of Christ, are the true "graces" of Christian holiness. Or, conversely, the "graces" of the Christian life *are* the "natural virtues", baptized into Christ, liberated, refined, enriched, and lifted up into higher and lovelier expression. When I read in Galatians 5: 22, 23, "The fruit of the Spirit is love, joy, peace, longsuffering ..." *whose* love is it? and whose are the *other* eight qualities mentioned? Is it *His* love and *not* mine? Or is it not rather an outreaching capacity already in my own human nature, which He now kindles to purer flame, and awakes to higher impulses, and interpenetrates by His own sanctifying presence?

Can we not now commit ourselves to the following definition? *HOLINESS IS MORAL LIKENESS TO GOD, AS REQUIRED BY HIS WRITTEN WORD, AS REVEALED IN HIS IN-CARNATE SON, AND AS INWROUGHT BY HIS HOLY SPIRIT.* It is inwrought in suchwise as to penetrate and purify our whole moral and spiritual nature, without excluding any part as being imperviously and irrecoverably corrupt—such as that phantom "old Adam" of the usual holiness theories. This inwrought holiness transforms the whole man. It may operate in differing degree, but its *extent* is always the entire moral being. That is why, as earlier noted, in First Thessalonians 5: 23, the apostle Paul prays for the sanctification of the *whole*, without allowing or even hinting, much less suggesting, *any* excludable or *un*sanctifiable part.

In succeeding chapters we shall consider particular aspects of this inwrought holiness; but even now do we not find ourselves longing and praying in such lines as the following?—

> Break through my nature, holy, heavenly love;
>   Clear every avenue of thought and brain;
> Flood my affections, purify my will,
>   Make all I am Thy sanctified domain.
>
> Thus, wholly mastered and by Thee possessed,
>   Forth from my life, spontaneous and free
> Shall flow a stream of tenderness and grace,
>   Loving because Thy love lives on through me.

EXCURSUS ON HOLINESS AS RESTORATION

Let no one equate this restoration with the dictum of Thomas Aquinas and the Thomists, that grace *perfects* nature ("Grace does not abolish nature, but presupposes it and perfects it"). In rejecting the erroneous we must not let slip that which is truly taught in the New Testament. According to the New Testament, holiness is undoubtedly restoration of our true humanhood. It is not, however, a restoration *backward*, to the level of unfallen Adam, but a *forward*-looking development into the likeness of *JESUS*, who, as the "second Adam" (1 Cor. 15:45, 47) and the "File-leader" (Heb. 12:2) of the new humanity, not only restores but sublimates and finally glorifies our redeemed humanhood. JESUS is the new standard. Christian holiness is neither a fixed ethical level nor, as yet, a restoration completed, but a progressive renewal and approximation into Christlikeness. It has nothing to do with supposedly grace-conveying sacraments or (perish the thought!) supposedly meritorious "works of supererogation." It comes through a moment-by-moment, inwardly realized union with Christ, and by the mind-renewing ministry of the Holy Spirit. It is truly experienced and manifested here on earth, and it will continue progressively in heaven for ever. For even in heaven our holiness cannot be a mechanically fixed state so long as we are free-willed beings; and with Augustine, therefore, we must think even of our heavenly state as *posse non peccare* rather than as *non posse peccare*, i.e. "able not to sin," rather than as "not able to sin." Meanwhile, although inwrought holiness does not reinstate our natural faculties, either mental or moral, into their pristine Edenic perfection, it does bring that deep recovery and blessed transformation indicated in our present chapter. See, also, our supplementary chapter, *Can We Ever Become Dead to Sin?*

I realize, of course, that the foregoing remarks on "able not to sin" versus "not able to sin" in our ultimate heavenly state touches a matter of divided opinion among equally devout and penetrating thinkers. Some reader of these pages may ask: Does not Scripture say that in the consummation we shall be "like Him" (Christ)? Surely *He* is "not able to sin"! How, then, when we are "like Him," shall *we* be "able to sin"? That at once brings up again our Lord's temptations while He was on earth. If there was an absolute impossibility for Him to respond to them, how could they be real?—and how could His not responding be an example to *us*?—and why did those temptations hurt Him even to the point of tears and sweat?

Such reflections touch on the deeply mysterious; and who dare be dogmatic? Our Lord Jesus is absolutely sinless. In the heavenly yet-to-be we shall be "like Him"—yes, *sinless* (glorious wonder!). But does even that give us a built-in, mechanical inability to sin? Lucifer was originally created absolutely sinless. How then could he sin? But he did. So were all the angels created sinless; yet some fell. Does that drive a subtle wedge of uncertainty into the Christian's ultimate heavenly blessedness? No; for God has done a saving and transforming work in us such as no other created beings ever knew; and He has brought us into an indissolubly sacred union with His eternal Son such as no other created beings ever knew; and He has pledged that, having reproduced the very "image" of His Son in us, He will *NEVER* let us go. *That* is our everlasting guarantee.

A CORRECTIVE

It is disconcerting at times, that however clearly one tries to express something, it is somehow taken to mean almost the opposite. One of my most esteemed reviewers of these studies before their American publication writes (appreciatively thinking he correctly represents me): "Dr. Baxter maintains that Scripture holds out to Christians the alluring promise of a deeper work of grace, distinct from and usually subsequent to, conversion; a soul-crisis which results in an *instantaneous* and *permanent* inward sanctification by the Spirit."

Yet any such "instantaneous" or "permanent" holiness (taught by certain widely held theories) is what I argue *against!* As I have said on page 115, the only thing instantaneous is, that in response to a really *full yielding* to Christ there is an immediate full possession by the Holy Spirit—which there cannot be *until* then. And even that does not necessarily include any accompanying, instantaneous, emotional "experience" of it. (See Dr. R. A. Torrey's testimony in our companion volume, *His Deeper Work in Us*, p. 170; also the whole chapter, "Instantaneous Or Gradual?")

As for holiness coming as a "permanent" inward fixture, I thought I had decried that beyond all mistake, as, for instance, on page 115, not to mention other places, especially in my volume, *His Deeper Work in Us*. However gradually or quietly it may be reached, the crisis-point of an utter yielding to Christ is a crisis-*point* (i.e. an instant — instantaneous), but (page 115) "it does *not* effect an all-at-once holiness; it is only the *starting*-point." From then onwards the Holy Spirit has His unhindered opportunity, and there is a really *progressive* holiness. It simply cannot be a permanent fixity. *Any* such "level" or "blessing" or "experience" can be lost again—though it need not be.

HOLINESS: YES, BUT HOW?

NOTE

With this chapter we reach the innermost question of these studies: To what degree may our moral nature be restored in this present life? That very word, "degree", of course, is obnoxious to the ultraistic theories of holiness which dichotomise our inner being into "old man" versus "new man" and then insist that sanctification is the eradication of the old. The early Methodist preachers used to partition believers into (1) justified but not sanctified, (2) justified and also sanctified. That grew out of their eradication theory. There are no degrees in eradication. We have seen, however, that the eradication theory is untenable.

There can be holiness in degree because in our one, indivisible nature there are both the higher reaches and the lower. These coexist inside the one nature, but we must never think of them as two *natures*. In our Lord Jesus there *was* a duality of natures—the divine and the human in one Person. But that must never be thought of as a parallel with the conflicting opposites which coexist in our human nature. Fallen man is indeed internally at odds with himself, but it is not a war of two selves. The big, precious, vital truth which has been too long obscured, but which we must grasp again with a new gratitude to our dear Saviour, is that our nature *itself* may be renewed and refined by the Holy Spirit, so that in greater or lesser degree all that is highest and purest and most God-like may be developed into *radiant ascendancy*.

J.S.B.

HOLINESS: YES, BUT HOW?

WE have made our way, at length, to what may be regarded as the *positive* objective of these studies. It forms itself into two closely related questions:

1. How can we be holy? (i.e. the means).
2. How holy can we be? (i.e. the extent).

Let this be axiomatic to all our thinking about holiness, that *whatever* spiritual change is wrought within us is the work of the Holy Spirit. Many Christians assume, and many preachers have fondly taught, that at death we Christian believers suddenly become sinless at last, on being freed from the mortal body—as though there were some sin-extirpating power in death itself. They are wrong. Whether in this present life or in the Beyond, any such change in our moral nature is exclusively the work of the Holy Spirit. Others, who teach the earnest and attractive "identification" theory tell us, "As you *'reckon'* yourself to be crucified with Christ, and dead in Him to sin, you find that the reckoning makes it real." Let that sincere error also be put away. Neither death nor any suppositionary uni-crucifixion has any power to effect actual change in our moral being. The begetting of holy disposition and experience within us is exclusively the work of the Holy Spirit.

Of course, in the profound mystery of the divine triunity, the Father and the Son and the Holy Spirit are so *one* that the ministry of the Holy Spirit within us may be with truth ascribed both to the Father (as in Phil. 2: 13) and to the Son (as in Col. 1: 21). Indeed, in the climactic last paragraph of Ephesians 3, the Spirit and the Son and the Father are referred to as *together* infilling the sanctified believer (16–19). Nevertheless, as all of us must surely realise, whenever the Father and the Son are spoken of as dwelling or moving within us, we are meant to understand that they do so by the Holy Spirit. Distinctively He is the *Executive* of the God-head in the regeneration and sanctification of the believer.

With that in mind, we may find it helpful at this point to draw certain definite lines of differentiation between the work of Christ and the work of the Holy Spirit in relation to Christian believers. In order to become eternally saved, we sinful human beings needed certain big things done *for* us, and certain vital changes wrought *in* us. By way of general differentiation we may say: it is God the Son who has effected all that needed doing *for* us; it is the Holy Spirit who effects all that needs doing *in* us. Our Lord's work *for* us covers all the *judicial* aspects of our salvation. The Holy Spirit's work *in* us covers all the *experiential* aspects of it. Through the atoning work of the Son we have justification and reconciliation (positional aspects). Through the interior work of the Holy Spirit we have regeneration and sanctification (moral and spiritual aspects). Our Lord's work *for* us especially concerns our Godward *relation*; the Holy Spirit's work *in* us especially concerns our inward *renewal*. Our Lord's work for us has distinctively to do with our standing or *position*; the Holy Spirit's work in us has distinctively to do with our state or *condition*. Through our Lord's Calvary work we have righteousness *imputed* (legal aspect); through the Holy Spirit's regenerative work we have holiness *imparted* (vital aspect). To this it is well to add that our Lord's atoning work *for* us is a finished achievement marked by absolute *finality*, whereas the Holy Spirit's work *in* us is a character-development having *no* limit of finality.

Now the crucial question is: When the Holy Spirit effects experiential sanctification within us, what is it that He does? That is the point at which blurred thinking is easiest, and needs to be clearest. Those who have called this deeper spiritual experience the "second blessing" have always insisted that in it something is done to the very *nature* of the now-consecrated believer. We do well to take careful note of that, for the following reason. Many persons think they can easily dispose of "this second blessing idea" (as they call it) by such remarks as, "Oh, those who talk about the 'second blessing' only mean what we mean by full consecration to Christ." Or perhaps they say, "This so-called 'second blessing' is just a case of *reckoning* yourself to be 'dead indeed unto sin' without actually being so." Those who thus misconstrue it, however, instead of truly explaining it, have not even begun to understand "second blessing" doctrine. They think there is nothing more to it than the merely human side, i.e. "consecrating" or "reckoning" or "claiming", whereas advocates of the "second blessing" have always testified that holiness is a deeper work of the Spirit *Himself* in which He actually *does* something to the believer's *nature*.

Perhaps that needs saying all the more clearly in these days when in much popular evangelism even *conversion* to Christ tends to be represented as merely becoming "committed" or "decided" rather than as a regenerating divine miracle inside the human personality. So, let it be realized once for all: "second blessing" doctrine is, that a sanctifying transformation really happens in the consecrated soul. Surely any teaching of holiness which carefully adheres to the New Testament must teach the same, even if we reject the disliked term, "second blessing."

What, then, *is* this transfused sanctification? Some will at once reply: Imparted holiness consists in being filled with the Holy Spirit. For, inasmuch as He is the *Holy* Spirit, that which He fills becomes holy too. As to that, let me utter my heart with deepest reverence, remembering of whom we speak. On such a sacredly sensitive point the last impression one would wish to give is that of dialectic hair-splitting. But there is a real difference between my being filled with the Holy Spirit, and my having a holiness which is inwrought by Him in my own nature.

The Holy Spirit "came upon" and indeed overpowered the hireling soothsayer, Balaam, causing him to prophesy exaltedly; but that double-minded man was not changed thereby in his moral nature. Similarly, the Holy Spirit came upon the "seventy elders" in the camp of Israel, with supernatural afflatus, but there is not a wisp of suggestion that they were thus renewed in all their propensities. In the Acts of the Apostles it would seem that there were recurrent "fillings" by the Holy Spirit for successive exigencies (4: 8, 4: 31, 13: 9), and it seems inferable that most believers who comprised those churches of the first days had some experience of the Spirit's enveloping them about the time of their conversion (Acts 10: 44, Eph. 1: 13, 14); yet those fillings and tokens are distinguished from the Spirit's deeper work in the sanctifying of character. Believers who had known in vivid experience the "earnest" (Eph. 1: 14) of the Spirit are urged, all

over the Epistles, to seek the Spirit's further and more penetrating ministry of inward renewal and transfiguration.

Blessedly wonderful though it is, that this unworthy heart of
mine may be infilled by the divine Spirit, yet so long as there is
no more than that, the holiness remains His, not mine. The great
truth is, that He comes not only to infill me, but to *change* me
(Rom. 12: 2, 2 Cor. 3: 18, Eph. 4: 23).

To What Degree?

As to how and in what *degree* the Holy Spirit renews our moral
nature into holiness, we are handicapped by the seeming lack of
any illustration which really illustrates it. I remember being
greatly impressed, in my youth, by the illustration of the pebble
and the stream. The pebble lies dirty amid the silt near the
stream. Then it is picked up and held right in the flow of the
water. All the uncleanness is thereby washed away. So long as
the pebble remains in the stream it remains clean. Take it out of
the stream, and it soon becomes soiled again on the bank. The
illustration is good as far as it goes, but it fails in three respects.
The pebble was unclean only on the outside. It was cleansed
only on the outside. The pebble itself remains altogether
unchanged.

There is the apt illustration of the iron and the refining fire.
You have a bar of unrefined gold. There is dirt on the outside
which perhaps you can remove by soap and water. But suppose
there is impurity inside the metal itself: what then? The gold must
go through the fire, and the fire must go through the gold, and
thus the inside as well as the outside is purified. The illustration
is excellent except that it, too, is inadequate; for although the very
condition of the gold is changed by the fire, that bar of metal is
non-sentient; it does not think, desire, choose, will, and keep producing new impurities within itself.

The nearest and truest simile is that of *health* in relation to the
body. Our very word "holy", comes from the old English, *halig*,
which means healthy or whole. Christian holiness is not even
spiritual maturity, as many mistakenly suppose. It is a state of
health, not a stage of growth.

Let me amplify my simile a little. Here is a man with ailing
health and diseased body; anaemic and toxic blood, symptoms of
tuberculosis in the lungs, enfeeblement of limbs, fits of languor

through nervous exhaustion, pallid face and pasty-looking skin. He dwells in a dank, unhealthy slum. His daily diet not only lacks the required freshness, proteins, vitamins, minerals, but consists of debilitating substitutes. He dodders round, an abject specimen of inanition and emaciation. Then, one day, owing to a sudden turn of circumstance, he is transplanted from that malodorous hovel to a lovely villa on a high hilly slope, with glorious mountains stretching away in the rear, and the wide rolling ocean away in front. The purest air in the world begins to fill those shrunken lungs. The best of nourishing food is now supplied to those starved organs; fresh fruits, rich milk, honey, good bread and butter, plenty of vital vegetables, lean meats and well-prepared fish-meals; and all this week after week. Soon, what a change in our man! There is new vigour. He now climbs those hills, and exercises on that beach. As he now breathes deeply, the invigorating air of sea and mountains expands those lungs. The pallor gives place to rosy countenance and ruddy physique. Inertness of limb gives place to normal mobility, then to developing muscle and sinew and exuberant energy. Some time later, a medical examination reports, *"Thoroughly healthy."*

Is it the same body? There are new corpuscles, new membranes, new nerve-cells, new tissues and tendons, new blood, new protoplasm, new lungs, new reflexes, new co-ordination and organic functioning. It is the same body; yet decidedly *not the same*. New life has invaded and permeated that body, through oxygenation, rich nutrition, and regenerative metabolism. The new energy has interpenetrated every part of the organism, transforming disease into fulness of health. Can we say, then, that through this metabasis the body now has *absolute* health? 'No, for there is no such reality as "absolute health" on earth. What we *can* say is, that this body now has *HEALTH ABOUNDING*.

Yes, "health abounding"; and, by parallel, that indeed is what *holiness* is in our *moral* being. *HOLINESS IS MORAL AND SPIRITUAL HEALTH ABOUNDING*. It is not absolute sinlessness or moral perfection, for there is no such reality as "absolute holiness" on earth. Holiness is the life of the Holy Spirit transfused and interpenetrating every part of my moral and spiritual being, transforming diseased impulses and responses, impure desire and inclination, unholy thought, motive, purpose, temper, imagination, into fulness of moral health; so that hatred becomes love; anger becomes kindness; impure desire becomes holy aspiration; selfishness becomes Christlike otherism; jealousy becomes sincere affection; perverted motive and purpose change into earnest ambition to fulfil only the will of God; evil temper and carnal imagination give place to equanimity and spiritual-mindedness; pride becomes humility; egocentricity becomes Christocentricity. The whole inner life becomes pure, gracious, *healthful*.

I emphasize again that this fulness of moral and spiritual health which comes to us via the "second blessing," or (if we still disavow that term) by the infilling of the Holy Spirit, is "health *abounding*." The new Testament says so. It is the "love of God shed in [or *flooding*] our hearts by the Holy Spirit" (Rom. 5:5). It is a being "*immersed* in the Holy Spirit" (Acts 1:5); a being "full" of spiritual "wisdom" (6:3), and spiritual "joy" (13:52). It is the "perfect love" which "casteth out fear" (1 John 4:18); the "peace which passeth all understanding" (Phil. 4:7); the "love which worketh no evil" (Rom. 13:10), which "abounds yet more and more in knowledge and in all discernment" (Phil. 1:9), which "never envies," "never seeks its own," and "never fails" (1 Cor. 13). It is, indeed, the life "*abundant*" (John 10:10). At our conversion, when we became "born from above," there was a transfusion of new spiritual life into our being. That regenerating *transfusion* is meant to become an entire *suffusion* of our moral nature; and it is *that* which works the lovely miracle of inwrought holiness. Oh, that all of us were living in the experience of it!

At this point, though, a further question may arise in some minds. If such a renewal is effectively wrought in our moral nature, what happens if the infilling of the Holy Spirit is for some reason withdrawn? Does the renewing work remain?—or does one's moral condition immediately revert to what it was before? Such a question may well be asked, for there seem to be elusive problems involved (how could it be otherwise with an intangible, complex integer such as the human mind?). I remember how the question was first forced upon my own mind, years ago, when I still believed in the "two natures" theory, and was wrestling with early misgivings about the Wesleyan eradication doctrine. If we are to have a true answer we must stay close to actual human *experience* in the matter, and try to *interpret* that experience as exactly as possible in the light of Scripture.

Take the case of a Christian woman whom we knew years ago. She had formerly been an awful drunkard and a liar, and had been known among the police for her demoniacal temper—on one occasion she broke three fingers of a policeman as she struggled against arrest. After her conversion to Christ, her growth in grace was wonderful to watch. She attended meetings in our town where the deeper truths of Scriptural holiness were jubilantly expounded. She longed for the blessing of complete inward renewal, of entire victory over sin, and of being "filled with the Spirit". She sought and she found. There was no doubt about it. The lovely evidences became visible in her character and conduct. And so it continued month after month, for two or three years, until, through a complexity of circumstances which I need not here detail, she fell away from prayer, began to compromise, lost the blessing, and slid into reverse. The old appetites began to reassert themselves, the tongue began wagging wickedly again, the fierce glint came back into the eyes, and there were suggestions of the old vehemence. I do not mean that she fully backslid. No, she recovered herself from Satan's snare, and re-entered her spiritual Canaan. Her lapse, however, was long enough to show, or certainly *seem* to show, that the harsh old proclivities had not been quite so refined away as had been assumed.

This "reversion to type", as we may call it, is a far bigger problem to the eradicationist. John Wesley found it so in his day. In the question-and-answer catechesis of the 1759 Methodist Conference, one of the questions was: "But if two perfect Christians[1] had children, how could they [their children] be born in sin, since there was none in the parents?" Wesley's reply was: "It is a possible but not a probable case. I doubt whether it ever was or ever will be. But waiving this, I answer: Sin is entailed upon me, not by immediate generation [i.e. not from my own father and mother only] but by my first parent. In Adam all died; by the disobedience of one all men were made sinners. . . . We have a remarkable case of this in gardening. Grafts on a crab stalk bear excellent fruit, but sow the kernels of this fruit, and what will be the event? They produce as mere crabs as ever were eaten." It was an apt illustration, but it certainly was no reply; for if those two "perfect Christians" (hypothetically) are now completely

---

[1] That is, two fully consecrated believers, "entirely sanctified," with the old nature (supposedly) "eradicated", and the heart now filled with "perfect love".

minus the "old nature" and are "dead indeed unto sin", how *can* generic sin find any passage through them to their offspring?

The misguided eradication doctrine simply has no reply to such a conundrum, nor to the reappearance of obvious sins in those who have professedly been ridded of the sin-bent. Is there, then, a satisfactory explanation? Yes, I think there is, provided we keep closely to the truth that holiness is *health*—not sinlessness through surgery, or (supposedly) a sinless *"new* nature" counteracting an unchanged *"old* nature" which can do nothing *but* sin. When once we grasp firmly the positive truth that inwrought holiness is the infilling Spirit of God renewing our whole moral nature to *fulness of health,* then we begin to see that the problem of those sin-traits which reassert themselves even in the sanctified has a coherent solution.

Go back for a moment to our simile of the emaciated slum-dweller whose sickly weakness became transformed to buoyant health through transplantation to that hillside villa with its invigorating sea and mountain air, its plentiful nourishment and its inducements to recreational exercise. Was something really *effected* in the very blood and bone and tissue of that physical organism? Was there an actual *change* wrought in the quality of that responding constitution? The answer is, Yes; and the body gave evidence of its renewal to fulness of health by *functioning* healthily in arteries, blood-vessels, limb and muscle. But now, take our man away from that environment, and confine him again to the squalid slum, with its lice-breeding putridity, its impure air and malnutrition. Does he *immediately* revert back to his former vitiation and consumptiveness? No; for his system certainly did experience a basic transmutation to health. Those physical organs are still different from what they were before, so there is not a sudden relapse. Yet if his imprisonment in that wretched surround *continues,* health then gradually gives way to the former malaise and physical degeneration.

The illustration may not be perfect, but it is a near parable of those lapses which are sometimes observable in Christian believers who have truly known the experience of "entire sanctification". There is no *sudden* or general declension. The believer's inward renewal cannot be all-at-once voided, for the Holy Spirit has indeed effected a deep and blessed change in the believer's moral nature *itself.* Moreover, the godly soul usually recovers the partly forfeited blessing. If, however, there is continued failure, through prayerlessness, compromise, or other such contrary factors, then the moral and spiritual condition gradually deteriorates to what it was before.

If I may be permitted to make passing reference to my own experience in the matter, that is the very process which I have discerned at different times in my own inner life. To the dear Saviour's praise let me say it, I have known something of this blessedly wonderful inwrought renewal. The weary, unequal struggle against hereditary depravity has given place to what has seemed like a cleansing right down at the very springs of sub-conscious impulse, so that thought and desire and motive and response have become spontaneously gracious, and fellowship with God has been an exhilarating wonder. I have known and felt and proved the inwrought renewal. Nor has it been in any way merely transient, for even when, alas, I have lost the fuller experience of it through foolishly busy prayerlessness, the work which the Holy Spirit has effected in my moral and spiritual being has largely *remained*, being evidenced in purified concepts, longings, aims, and choices.

Earnestly, then, do I covet to make this truth perspicuously plain, that inwrought holiness is moral and spiritual *FULNESS OF HEALTH*. As there can be degrees of health in the body, so there can be degrees of holiness in the soul. As there can be *fulness* of health in the body, so there can be *fulness* of holiness in the soul.

Yes, it is verily possible. Inwrought holiness is a reality. In the words of Ephesians 4: 23, we may be "renewed" in the very "spirit" of our "mind". Is not *that* a penetration to the very core of one's moral and spiritual nature, to the inmost spring of one's thought-life? It is, and it means that we may have, as Charles Wesley hymns it,

> A heart *in every thought renewed*,
> And *filled* with love divine.

This entire renewal of mind and spirit, of desires, motives, impulses, soon begins to affect the functioning and condition of the *body*. We can the more readily appreciate this in these days when medical science demonstrates as never before the influence of the mind over the body. A true experience of holiness in younger years can powerfully normalise overstrong animal appetites, and in older years preserve the nervous system from all-too-common later disorders.

Of course, not even "entire sanctification" in the mind can exempt the body from either functional or organic disease if at the same time the system is weakened by improper feeding, unsanitary habits, or lack of exercise and fresh air; but granted that habits are as they should be, there is nothing like holiness of mind for promoting healthiness of body. I have known persons whose whole health has noticeably improved from the time of their experiencing the deeper work of the Holy Spirit.

Albeit, there is another side which we dare not ignore. This penetrating inward renewal does not necessarily mean that all bodily inclinations, cravings, urges and pullings at once subside into docile servants of sanctification. Often the story is far otherwise. Problematical physical peculiarities may persist, like obstinate bad tenants resisting eviction, or like sleek panthers hiddenly watching for the opportune instant to spring into savage action, e.g. the former drunkard's inhering thirst for liquor, or, in others, the overcharged animalistic urge, or in still others a constitutional physical sluggishness which easily hampers watchfulness in prayer or activity in Christian service.

This touches upon the mystery of "psycho-physical-parallelism" —the exquisitely intricate inter-reaction of mind and body. We know well enough that the body itself, being non-sentient matter, can neither know nor feel, can neither think nor act. As soon as it is vacated by the soul it becomes absolutely insensible. Yet, just as truly, different human bodies act in different ways upon the living persons united to them. An athlete is not just athletic in his mind; he has an athletic *body*. Many another who has a strong mental urge to sports never becomes an athlete because of union with a body which does not have the required kind of reflexes. It is all very mysterious, but this big fact stands out: not only does the mind greatly affect the body; *the body powerfully reacts upon the mind*.

Often the wonderful experience of moral *victory* which accompanies inwrought holiness is *despite* some persisting uncooperativeness of the body. It would seem as though in some ways this *has* to be so, for purposes of character-building. Sometimes, in the glad crisis of spiritual infilling, long-pestering bodily appetites are completely expelled or else they immediately seem to wither, while other equally troublesome propensities are allowed to linger on, wringing many a baffled "Why?" from the sanctified soul which now, more than ever, detests every such proneness.

In a slummy part of Glasgow, Scotland, about sixty years ago, much trouble was caused by a gang of young fellows who drank and gambled, fought and thieved, and became so dangerous that even the police had to go round in pairs or trios. Among other things they decided to smash up a revival which had started at a local mission hall superintended by Mr. J. Wakefield MacGill. Contrary to expectations, most of them became truly converted. Thirty years passed. Then, by a sheer coincidence, two of them who had never seen each other during all those years, attended a meeting in Edinburgh and recognised each other. With unrestrainable eagerness they got to each other as soon as the meeting was over. "Charlie!"—"Jim!"—"Fancy seeing you again after all these years!" Then Charlie said, "Yes, praise the Lord, I'm still going on in the Christian life; and from the day of my conversion nearly thirty years ago until this minute I've never once had any further taste for the wretched drink!" Jim's face clouded a bit at this, and a tear glistened in his eyes. "Well, Charlie," he said, "I'm afraid I canna' say that. I only wish I could. There's never been one single day through all these years that I haven't had the thirst for drink." And then he quickly added, "But, thank God, *I've never touched it from that day to this!*" Which of the two had experienced the bigger victory? Which of our Lord's methods with those two men strengthened character the more?

The point is, our Lord Jesus is not only the omnipotent Saviour, He is the omniscient Psychiatrist and the inerrant Pathologist. He who can pluck out the most innate distemper from our constitution, if He so wills, may wisely leave some such provocation more or less undislodged, for the purpose of developing watchfulness and prayerfulness; or as a means of teaching continuous victory through continuous union with Himself; or as a way of developing character-strength out of some constitutional weakness. Was the Apostle Paul filled with the Holy Spirit and entirely sanctified? Yes. Did *he* have some sort of a "thorn in the flesh"? Yes. Did he suffer by it? Yes. Did he plead with Christ to remove it? Yes. Was it removed? No. Did it impair his sanctification, or lessen the filling of his heart with heavenly love and joy? No; he hoists his banner and leaps forward, saying,

"Most gladly therefore will I glory in my weaknesses that the power of Christ may rest upon [lit. *overspread*] me."

This leads to a further observation. No teaching of holiness can be strictly true to the New Testament which excludes *human effort*. Although the most strenuous human effort is utterly powerless to *effect* inward holiness; and although the Holy Spirit alone can renew our moral nature; yet the Holy Spirit never sanctifies the mind and heart in suchwise as to render human cooperation superfluous. Furthermore, although human effort is equally powerless in itself to *maintain* inwrought holiness after the Holy Spirit has wrought the lovely miracle within us, yet human co-operation is all the while necessary in resisting encroachments of evil upon the sanctified territory, in cultivating prayerful responsiveness to the Holy Spirit, and in carefully culturing those *conditions* which are required for a continuing experience of holiness. The Holy Spirit never restores holiness to the human mind in the way that we repair the inner mechanism of a machine. The mind never is (it never can be) made holy in a way which "fixes it" to *remain* so.

One of the subtler blunders in much holiness teaching has been to play off faith and works as mutually antagonistic. Many have preached that sanctification is exclusively "by faith". Others, in dogged disapproval, have insisted that it is "by works". Both are right or wrong according to aspect. In every spiritual transaction there is an interplay of the divine and the human. Inasmuch as, on the divine side, sanctification is a work which God alone can effect, it *must* be appropriated "by faith". On the human side there must be self-separation from all controllable wrong in the life; complete self-yielding to Christ; obedience to the written Word of God; and a prayerful determination to live only to His glory. Sanctification is not real unless it expresses itself in obedience to the divine law—and obedience means "works".

Throughout the sanctified life, faith and works must go hand in hand. It is another case where we must distinguish between sanctification as a work of God in the soul, and as a life of obedience in the believer. The two must ever be distinguished but can never be separated.

Even in the promised land (which was possessed by "faith") Israel found that faith must express itself in works. There were enemies in plenty—though victory was assured to the "obedience of faith". God fought with them—but never *instead* of them. Israel must *do* as well as trust. So, there is a place for "works" on the human side—not to *enter* the goodly land, but to *remain* there; even as we read in Second Corinthians 7: 1, "Having therefore these promises [i.e. to faith] beloved, let us cleanse *ourselves* from all defilement of the flesh and spirit, completing holiness in the fear of God."

But now, after these cautionary observations, a final comment on the main proposition of this chapter, namely, that inwrought holiness is a reality; a proven experience of renewal into moral and spiritual *FULNESS OF HEALTH*. Away for ever with that counteractionist bogey of an "old man" who, in utterly un-changeable filthiness must foul our moral being to the last day we live on earth! Our "whole spirit and soul and body" may be sanctified! Our whole moral being may be "transformed" into clearer, fuller, lovelier likeness to "the image of Christ".

Let us summarize and clinch this. That which *prepares* on the human side is a resolute renunciation of all known wrong in thought and behaviour over which our will has control, and an utterly honest yielding of our whole being to Christ. That which *occurs* from the divine side is the Holy Spirit's infilling of the yielded believer. That which is thereupon *effected* is an inwrought moral and spiritual renewal into holiness, issuing in perceivable transfiguration of character. Of this character-transformation we shall speak in our next chapters.

Meanwhile, may I ask: Dear Christian believer, are you living in this experience? If not, do you ask how it can become real in *you*? Well, have you *really* yielded everything to Christ? Are you sure? Has the Holy Spirit *really* an unobstructed monopoly of all you are and have? Are you sure? Is it *really* holiness you want?— or a gratifying experience of spiritual power or ecstasy? Are you prepared to be thought narrow, peculiar, extreme (not that true holiness ever makes us so)? Do you long for holiness more than for cleverness, position, money, personal advantages, and all mere personal impressiveness? Is your deepest, highest, keenest motive to please and know and reflect and glorify that unspeakably dear Saviour whose outpoured blood on Calvary and outpoured Spirit at Pentecost have made holiness possible?

If so, get alone with Him long enough, and (if He wisely orders it so) *often* enough in lingering prayer, until you know, as only

prayerful consecration can enable you to know, that there is a
thorough understanding between you and Christ: an understanding that you are *utterly His for ever*.

As soon as you really reach that point, you will find (but not
before) that quite suddenly yet quite naturally it becomes easy to
"claim", to appropriate, what may have seemed elusive hitherto.
The promises of the written Word will fairly *offer* themselves to
you for the taking. All are yours when you are all His. You will
"ask and receive, that your joy may be full" (John 16: 24). What
will you ask? Not any more for the (imaginary) crucifixion of
some (suppositionary) "old man" which is not really you at all; nor
for faith to "reckon" an inward death to sin and temptation which
the Word nowhere promises. No; you will ask (1) that your heart
may be truly filled by the Holy Spirit, (2) that the infilling Holy
Spirit will renew your whole moral being from sinward desire and
inclination, (3) that the Holy Spirit will bear unmistakable witness
in your deepest consciousness, to His sanctifying work within you.
Tarry for that witness; for in the words of Habakkuk 2: 3,
"Though it tarry, wait for it, because it will surely come." Let
this be our heartfelt prayer:

> Enduing Spirit from on high,
> My yielded being sanctify;
> From Thine infinitude impart
> Pure life in fulness to my heart.
>
> Now, all I am do Thou possess
> With mind-renewing holiness,
> Till every aim from sin is clear,
> And perfect love expels all fear.
>
> Let innate dross of wrong desire
> Now disappear in Thy pure fire;
> And even through my mortal frame
> May others catch the living flame.
>
> Disperse self-seeking, and instead
> The love of God within me shed;
> Till all my days, on this intent,
> Become one life-long sacrament.

ENTIRE SANCTIFICATION

NOTE

There are those who may consider this treatise at fault because it does not include any stress on the *social* aspects of holiness; the loving of one's neighbour, with reference to the South African and Rhodesian black man, the refugee, the slum victim, etc. A British theologian writes, "In this country holiness teaching is suspect because it does not back the *social* implication of Biblical teaching . . . A nation which tolerates homelessness among its citizens is greatly sinning. Holiness should campaign that no man be homeless or badly housed while the nation has money to remedy the need."

Our answer is clear, without any need to point out that much poverty and slum wretchedness are due to the individual rather than the government. Before all else, holiness is an individually *personal* matter. Beyond all dispute, in both the Old Testament and the New, the *first* emphasis of the Bible is on the human *individual*. Put a man himself right, and *social* obligations will fall into proper place. You do not bring anyone into the experience of inwrought holiness by expatiating on the "social implications" of holiness, or by inciting campaigns to the government for better housing. There simply cannot be *any* "social outreach" of holiness until there is real holiness itself in the individual heart. Such holiness is exclusively the work of the Holy Spirit in the Christian believer; and that is our *sole* concern in this treatise. That is necessarily *prior* to all "social" questions in relation to holiness.

J.S.B.

ENTIRE SANCTIFICATION

No series of studies in this subject of Christian holiness could be complete if it did not include, at some point, a deliberate encounter with the word, "sanctification." There is scarcely a more precious or meaningful word in our Christian terminology. It is definitely Scriptural; for although it is an English word built from Latin forms, it truly translates to us its New Testament Greek original.

The central idea of the word, both in the Greek and in the English, is *set-apartness*. How many Christian believers there are who have longed that their inner life might be like a temple entirely set-apart to the Lord, and continually filled with the purifying Shekinah of His presence! Well, the Scriptures teach us that such an inward condition is possible. But how many believers there are who have been discouraged from seeking and finding the reality of it because of perplexing theories such as those which we have disapproved in our earlier pages! So long as we still cling to that "counteraction" error of a supposed "old nature" in us which can *never* be sanctified, but must live on inside us like a contaminating lodger to our dying day, we shall never know the joy of "entire sanctification"; but that theory cannot bear the true light of Scripture upon it, as we have seen. (For a thorough discussion of this see our companion volume, *His Deeper Work In Us*.)

What we say here will be very simple. It need not be otherwise. We quote just one text, not to expound it, but simply to show that the Scripture does indeed teach *"entire* sanctification", with no place for a supposed "old nature" which cannot be sanctified. The text is 1 Thessalonians 5: 23, 24.

> "And the .very God of peace sanctify you *wholly*; and may your whole spirit and soul and body be preserved blameless unto the coming of our Lord Jesus Christ. Faithful is He that calleth you [to this entire sanctification] who also will do [or effect] it."

If that resplendent text does not teach in plainest wording an *entire* sanctification of the whole threefold territory—"spirit and soul and body", of which our human constitution is comprised, and if it does not teach an *entire* moral blamelessness as the result of a divine work within the believer, then what language could? Let the very forthrightness of the promise capture our grateful hearts!

Let us grasp the fact that this text teaches an *experiential* sanctification. I stress that because in many verses of Scripture where sanctification is spoken of, the reference is to *positional* sanctification. There is indeed a sense in which the Christian believer becomes positionally "sanctified" from the very first moment of union with Christ through conversion and regeneration. Just as truly as the born-again believer has immediate *justification* in the sight of God through the imputed *righteousness* of Christ, so is there an immediate *sanctification* in the sight of God through the representative, all-covering *holiness* of Christ. Here, however, we are concerned, not with this positional sanctification, but with *practical* sanctification in the believer's heart and life.

On the *human* side this entire sanctification is an entire and continuous yieldedness and obedience (set-apartness) to God. From the *divine* side it is an entire possession and use of the yielded vessel; an unobstructed infilling of the believer by the Holy Spirit, a penetrative renewing of the moral nature which decisively breaks the tyranny of inherent depravity, and lifts the mind into an experience of dominant holiness in all its spontaneous impulses, desires, motives, and inclinations.

This is not any so-called "sinless perfection", but it *is* full suffusion by the Holy Spirit, in which the believer's continuous abiding in Christ is answered by the Holy Spirit's continuous renewing of the believer's moral nature—heart, mind, soul, contemplations, reactions, aspirations, aims and urges. It is the fullest present *abiding* in Christ, accompanied by the fullest spiritual *abounding* in Christ, and resulting in truest *character-likeness* to Christ.

The entirely sanctified believer is not yet in heaven. He does not yet have a supernalized resurrection-body which has no response to animal attractions. He still has a body with response to earthly appeals. Not being yet in heaven, he does not yet have a mind utterly permeated and perfected by dwelling in that ineffable divine light in which sin absolutely cannot exist. He can still feel the pull of temptation. He is still sensitively susceptible to allurements of the flesh. In answer to stimulants or aggravations or injections from without, subtle movings within may pressure him sinwards, unless there is uninterrupted renewal of the mind by the Holy Spirit. Yet the power of "the flesh" is really broken. There is true *release* from bondage. There is indeed an inward transformation and refining. All the highest and best is now greatly strengthened; the base, the mean, the sin-tending is greatly weakened. The mind is now more and more habitually set on the holy. The nature which has been chronically sinward becomes fundamentally Godward.

Sin-response is an exquisitely subtle evil in our nature; often it moves through imperceptibly delicate processes of the mind, and only becomes recognizably sin to our mental perception when it has already in part deceived and drawn us. That is still true even in the entirely sanctified. There will always be sin to resist in this present life. Yet this also is true, that where there is entire sanctification the main *bent* of mind and heart is *against* sin, whether it invades from without or is subtly induced from within. Therefore victory now comes through living above it, rather than fighting it down on its own level.

There can, of course, be fluctuations of abiding in Christ, with suspensions of the Holy Spirit's full operation within the believer; yet there is no necessity for such intermissions, nor need we envisage them. The point which we here make is, that when, on the human side, there is this complete set-apartness to God, then those precious results of "entire sanctification" follow which we have eagerly described.

Accompaniments

As with conversion, so with this inward sanctification: the experience of it is not identical in any two persons. Much has to do with the type of personality and disposition; also the Holy Spirit exercises His gracious sovereignty in continually new patterns. Yet there *are* certain accompaniments of the blessing which seem more or less inseparable from it.

There is the *witness of the Spirit*. Verses like the following leap into vivid experience. "The Spirit himself beareth witness with our spirit that we are the children of God" (Rom. 8: 16). "He which hath anointed us is God, who hath also sealed us, and given us the earnest of the Spirit in our hearts" (2 Cor. 1: 22)—such wording evidently signifying a *conscious* inner realization of the Spirit's indwelling. "He that believeth on the Son hath the witness in himself" (1 John 5: 10).

This inward witness by the Holy Spirit, deep down in the human consciousness, is a joy-inspiring and often vivid reality to the entirely sanctified. It is too definite and recognisable to be confused with any kind of dreamy or excited autosuggestion. It is not necessarily a continuous emotional attestation. More often, perhaps, it is the presence of an unmistakably God-given *assurance* which steadies, sustains, uplifts, and gladdens the mind. It confers no infallibility of knowledge. It is no mere visitation of visions and impressions. All such notions are far astray. In times of busy mental activity or other workday absorptions it is often more-or-less subconscious, but it is *there*, giving a soul-deep, unbroken awareness of God and of divine guidance. One cannot read the New Testament references to this witness of the Spirit without seeing that in the first days it was a definite reality to the early Christians, and that it is meant to be known by all the Lord's people. Where there is entire sanctification it is still a wondrous reality.

Then, again, entire sanctification brings the promised *enduement of power*; the "power from on high". Did not our Saviour say, "Behold, I send the promise of my Father upon you; tarry ye . . . until ye be endued with power from on high"? (Luke 24: 49). Did He not also say, "Ye shall receive power after that the Holy Spirit is come upon you; and [in that power] ye shall be witnesses unto Me"? (Acts 1: 8). Entire sanctification brings with it, in one way or another, that "enduement"—and how indispensable it is, if there is to be a prevailing witness for Christ! How unspeakably vital it is to those of us who are in whole-time Christian ministry!

Let me not seem to make a distinction which is not real, but this heavenly enduement is specifically a spiritual equipment for Christian service, for *witness-bearing*, for "holding forth the Word of life" (Phil. 2: 16). This enduement was upon Stephen when his traducers were "not able to withstand the wisdom and the Spirit by which he spoke" (Acts 6: 10). This enduement was upon Paul when in Corinth he preached "in demonstration of the Spirit and of power" (1 Cor. 2: 4); the "power" was in the preacher, the "demonstration" was in the hearer. That is how spiritual work is done with maximum "attraction and repulsion"—attraction of faith and repulsion of fraud. There is an eloquence which is not merely natural, and a persuasiveness which is not merely human, and (in individual soulwinning) an indefinable influence which is more than earthly.

This does not mean that all unconverted hearers become immediately converted, though many of them *do*. The power of Satan is strong and deadly; and many proud men are his gullible satraps. Stephen's slayers were not able to resist his *wisdom*, but they did resist his *witness*. Yet although that malicious group fiercely refused his testimony, think how many others were won and blessed by it (Acts 6: 7, 8). Finney, Moody, Torrey, and others have left honest reports how that enduement swept upon *them*; and they were all men unforgettably magnetic and prevailing in the winning of souls to Christ. Oh, this enduement of "power from on high" is no spent force or otiose thought-form. Nor is it only for conspicuous public spokesmen of Christ like those just mentioned. Let no one suppose that it is now (in fashion-store phrase) a "discontinued line". If it seems little in evidence today, that is because of the far-gone breakdown of true holiness teaching in our evangelical churches, and the now comparatively rare experience of this entire sanctification.

Also accompanying entire sanctification there is always a richer, deeper and more constant *communion with Christ*. In a way never known before, those words of Ephesians 3: 16, 17, break into glad experience: "Strengthened with power through His Spirit in the inward man, that Christ may dwell [*katoikeo*: permanently reside] in your hearts through faith." Instead of being only an intermittent Visitor to our mental apprehension, He now becomes the resident Companion of all our thought-life. Instead of being only occasionally recognizable to our inward perception, He now becomes continually luminous to the mind, so that our song of testimony is,

> Lord, Thou hast made Thyself to me
> A living, bright reality;
> More present to faith's vision keen
> Than any outward object seen;
> More dear, more intimately nigh
> Than e'en the closest earthly tie.

As never before, those precious words now flame with rapturous meaning: "Abide in Me, and I in you" (John 15: 4). Yes, it is truly a two-way *"abiding"*: we in Him, and He in us. In the loveliest sense, there is a heart-to-heart *rapprochement* in which our dear Lord "sees of the travail of His soul, and is satisfied", while the believer's inward experience becomes heaven begun below. In a new way He becomes our constant Companion, Comforter, Counsellor, Confidant; our indwelling Sympathizer, Sustainer, Satisfier; our never-failing Refuge in every crisis or disappointment or loss or trial; our ever-sufficient secret of strength and cheerfulness for day-to-day hum-drum routine and testings. In a vivid way which only those know who experience it He guides us and guards us. He shares our life with us through sunshine and shadow, lining every cloud of sorrow with heavenly gold, and painting a rainbow of reassurance over every stormy sky, and making even permitted sickness a secret stairway into richer communion with Himself. In a way known only to the entirely sanctified He becomes, along the pilgrim way, the "Friend that sticketh closer than a brother", with a glorious love surpassing that of Jonathan for David. And, oh, He becomes so much more than words could ever express. In the words of Paul, "Christ is *ALL*" (Col. 3: 11). We find ourselves singing raptures such as

> How blessed, Lord, at last to find
>   Thy glorious love so real to me,
> Now filling all my heart and mind
>   With joy I never thought could be.
> This, this is heav'n begun below,
> This flood-tide of Thy love to know.
>
> What now are words? Who can express
>   The spacious rapture of the soul,
> The mind-refining blessedness
>   As Thy pure love pervades the whole?
> The heart a very heaven knows,
> The earthen vessel overflows.

Perhaps one of the surest accompaniments of entire sanctification is the long-sought experience of true *heart-rest*. Instead of faith being any longer a mere "clinging"—sometimes, perhaps, a rather desperate clinging amid temptations to doubt, it becomes that settled inward confidence which Scripture calls "the full *assurance* of faith". There then ensues a peace of mind, and a rest of heart, and a poise of life, which completely break the misery of worry and the tiring tyranny of habitual hurry. Just as truly as our Lord hushed the raging elements long ago, He speaks an inward "Peace! be still" to the soul.

> Yes, instead of clinging, "resting",
>   Resting in His changeless love,
> And instead of doubts molesting,
>   Sweet assurance from above:
> Gone the needless care and worry
>   Which have long my heart oppressed;
> Gone the anxious, fruitless hurry,
>   Now, in Him, I truly rest.

These are but a few snapshots of this spiritual Canaan. Oh, that thousands and thousands of us were living in it! Then indeed would Springtime revival and Summer fulness and harvest reapings come in our evangelical churches! Then indeed would our cold Winter lose its long-lasting grip, and the ice melt, and the waters flow, and the sun shine, and the flowers appear, and the birds begin to sing again, and bleakness give place to blessedness!

"Let us go up . . . and possess"

What, then, about taking Caleb's advice:—"Let us go up at once, and possess it"? (Num. 13: 30). How many of us would fain do so, but we are hindered by wrong theories of entering and possessing, as, for instance, some of those which we have earnestly but I hope kindly rebutted in these studies!

Not a few Christians are perplexed by having heard entire sanctification referred to as the *"second blessing"*. That, indeed, used to be a very common name for it. The expression, however, is not literally Scriptural, neither is it necessary even as a convenient way of referring to entire sanctification. Cogent objections have been registered against it. Yet John Wesley who coined it, and the many others who since have used it, were not without understandable purpose in doing so, for the following reason.

Usually (though not of unvarying necessity) entire sanctification is entered upon by a post-conversion *crisis*. It is not something gradually grown into or entered piecemeal. The usual "case history" is, that the Christian believer, although rejoicing in sins forgiven, becomes acutely concerned, even dismayed, by reason of inward defeat, unrest, unholy thoughts, impulses, desires, a superficial spirituality and a feeling of unreality in prayer—all coupled with a deep longing to know a complete victory over sin, a clearer fellowship with Christ, and a true purity of heart. This leads to much inward scrutiny, to an earnest consulting of Scripture teaching about holiness, and often to an enquiry into the experience of those believers who testify to a "more abundant" experience of salvation. Thus a crisis-point is reached by the heart set on sanctification. On the human side it is the crisis of an uttermost yielding of heart, mind, will, life, everything, to Christ (which, although in itself the gateway to the "joy unspeakable", is often a very agony to "the flesh" before the believer actually *gets* there). Then, there is the response from the Divine side; the flooding of the heart with "the love which casts out fear", and the making of inward cleansing an unmistakable reality. Is it any wonder that it became called the "*second* blessing" (conversion being the *first*) in contradistinction to all others?

One very confusing mistake made by users of the term, "second blessing," has been their making a too severe demarcation between *regeneration* (at conversion to Christ) and "entire *sanctification*" (by post-conversion crisis). They have often made it seem as though regeneration and sanctification were different in *nature*. What foggy perplexity might have been avoided if only it had always been made clear that sanctification *is* regeneration in fuller or fullest operation! To every Christian believer who may be seeking the blessing of heart-holiness we say: Be under no mistake; when, through your conversion to Christ, you became "born again", "born from above", the new spiritual life which was then regeneratingly infused into your moral and spiritual being was a holy life from the Holy Spirit Himself. That is always the *beginning* of Christian holiness. But that which was then an *infusion* of new life is now meant to become a *suffusion* of your whole mind and personality. That is what comes through entire sanctification (i.e. through entire set-apart-ness on the *human* side, and the infilling of the Holy Spirit as the response from the *divine* side).

Another point of misunderstanding which perhaps should be mentioned here is, the common failure of holiness teaching to

distinguish between sanctification and *"entire* sanctification". As all of us will agree, once the new life has been received through regeneration, there can be *degrees* of that new life in the believer. There can be degrees of spiritual life and health in the soul just as there are degrees of life and health in the body; and that is only another way of saying that there can be greater or lesser degrees of *sanctification,* corresponding to fuller or lesser degrees of yieldedness to Christ. Regeneration is the *fountain.* Sanctification is the *river* (in deeper or shallower degree). *"Entire* sanctification" is the river in *fullest flow.* Once the crisis-point of entire yieldedness is reached, then, to appropriating faith (it can *only* be then) the Holy Spirit's deeper answer of infilling and renewing the mind becomes a living experience.

The only other point we need mention here is the difficulty which some have had in comprehending that entire sanctification is a *gift* to be received by *faith.* Again and again, in his massive treatise on *Perfectionism,* Dr. B. B. Warfield repels what he calls the "mischief" of the teaching "that justification and sanctification are two separable gifts of grace" which are to be "received by two distinct acts of faith". In my judgment, some of his outflings are almost as unfair as his attitude is adamant. But after all his objections we come back to this: (1) Our justification through Christ is a gracious divine *gift*—necessarily so because it is something we could never have procured for ourselves. (2) Equally so, our regeneration is a gift, because we simply cannot regenerate ourselves. (3) Similarly, inwrought holiness or inward sanctification is necessarily a *gift,* for it is an inward renewal which we ourselves absolutely cannot bring about.

Yes, entire sanctification is a gift; a work of the Holy Spirit; and it is to be appropriated by *faith.* It is so exclusively a gift that it can be received only by faith. For Dr. Warfield to protest that this "suspends human salvation on human volition", and makes God dependent on our faith rather than ourselves on Him, has a ring of needless over-Calvinism in it. The written Word of God calls Christian believers to exercise faith for sanctification just as clearly as it calls to the unconverted to exercise faith on Christ for salvation. The unconverted have utterly no power to regenerate themselves, but they do have the moral capacity to appreciate and *receive* what God graciously *offers.* To say that faith comes only where God gives it, yet all who do not believe are condemned for

ever, turns the Gospel into hypocrisy and the redeeming love of God into a theatrical farce.[1]

Let us thank God that the teaching of the New Testament is so plain: (1) Entire sanctification is a *gift*. (2) It is pledged to the fully *yielded*. (3) It is to be received by *faith*. (4) It may be received *immediately* where there is complete yieldedness to Christ. When the learned Dr. Warfield and others object that it cannot be received "immediately" because it is impossible to receive "all at once" something which is meant to be continually progressive, they are differing merely in word, not in reality. Do we not all believe that *regeneration* comes "immediately" in response to faith on Christ? We do; yet the new life which comes at regeneration is meant to develop progressively. At our conversion to Christ we could not receive the new life of regeneration "all at once" any more than a thousand tomorrows could be crammed into today, but it did *begin* "immediately" at that point. So is it with entire sanctification. There is a crisis-point of utter surrender and appropriating faith at which the Holy Spirit enters in fulness, and then *begins* in a way never known before His wondrous work of inward renewal.

Dear Christian, are *you* living in the experience of "entire sanctification"? Are you convinced, from what we have now said in these studies, that such an experience is promised to us in the Word? Do you not hear that Word calling you to "enter in" and "possess"? It is no mere vapoury mirage. The blessing is really there, waiting to be possessed through consecration and faith.

This inwrought sanctification is the highest Christian way of *victory over sin*. It is victory, not by weary struggle, struggle, struggle, against a nature which is all the time wrenching or dragging you the wrong way, but by an inward renewal of that nature itself, so that with glad spontaneity it loves and keeps the divine law. There will always be temptations either loudly or

---

[1] Any theory of the divine sovereignty which makes *all* human volition *only* that which God predetermines, not only confuses the predestining acts of God with the permissive wisdom of God (both equally operate within the divine sovereignty), it takes away all Godward moral value from any and every act of ours (just as much so after conversion as before it). My hungering and thirsting after God and holiness, my looking up to Christ, and saying, "Lord, Thou knowest all things, Thou knowest that I love Thee," my crying to the Holy Spirit for inward renewal so that I may love God with all my heart, mind, soul, strength, and my neighbour as myself; all this can mean nothing of real value to God, for it is only His own disguised coercion looking back at Him!

subtly invading us from without via the senses of the body and the susceptibilities of the mind; but they are largely beaten foes when that condition within us which formerly betrayed us to them has been renewed into predominating holiness. No longer are we like a crippled dwarf struggling against a giant intruder, but, in the words of Zechariah 12: 8, "He that is feeble shall be as David," and in the words of Joshua 23: 10, "One of you shall chase a thousand."

This inward sanctification is also the way to true repose of heart, tranquillity of mind, serenity of spirit, and equilibrium of disposition. It is the way of spiritual power, and wisdom, and joy, and sacredly familiar fellowship with God. It is the life of overcoming and "always abounding in the work of the Lord". It is the life of maximum effectiveness in witness-bearing for our dear Lord. The very personality becomes His living pulpit, and the whole life becomes an incarnate sermon. There is the invisible fire of Pentecost continually tinging our testimony for Christ— altogether unostentatious but unmistakably there. There is liberty without levity, exuberance without frivolity, eager service without demonstrativeness, and a quality of life which speaks of Christ more eloquently than many a brilliant speech. Have we not all known such Christians? This very minute I am thinking of a dear man—not a minister, but a banker—in whose presence I was somehow always made to think of God. Indeed, it was in him that I first saw and learned the *reality* of transfigured character through inwrought sanctification.

Christian, the Word says to you, "Let us therefore fear lest a promise being left us of entering into His rest, any of you should seem to come short of it" (Heb. 4: 1). It also adds, "Let us therefore give diligence to enter into that rest" (verse 11). Do not let some petty prejudice against the expression, "second blessing," keep you (as some do) from that wonderful reality which it has been meant (well-intendedly) to represent. One thing is very plain: the New Testament sets before us a deeper, richer, higher, fuller experience of salvation than most Christians experience. One of Paul's names for it is "the *fulness* of the blessing" (Rom. 15: 29). Another name for it is "heavenly places in Christ" (Eph. 1: 3). Thousands of Christians are not living in that "fulness" or in those "heavenly places". *How* are they to "enter" and "possess"? Do they not need bringing to a post-conversion crisis? Entire sanctification is not something which they drift into, or culture themselves into bit by bit, or gradually grow into without specifically seeking it. Almost all of us need bringing to a major crisis-point, when once we have grasped that the blessing is truly Scriptural. So were those significant people of Israel brought to a crisis-point at Jordan long ago, in order to possess Canaan.

What, then, of yourself, dear believer? Have *you* entered this spiritual "land of promise"? Are *you* living in the "fulness of the blessing"? Perhaps your heart may find the following verses expressing its deepest feelings and longings:

> O Saviour-King, once crucified,
>   I deeply long to be
> A vessel wholly sanctified,
>   Possessed and used by Thee.
>
> I mourn, I hate these sins of mine
>   Which nailed Thee there forlorn,
> Which speared my holy King divine,
>   And weaved the crown of thorn!
>
> O holy Lord, this very day
>   I wrench myself apart
> From every known unholy way
>   Which hurts Thy patient heart.
>
> Here, too, with weeping gratitude,
>   I hand all else to Thee,
> Break every subtle servitude,
>   And set me wholly free.
>
> Thy liberating love in me
>   Let all my life express,
> And thine infilling Spirit be
>   My true heart-holiness.

TRANSFIGURATION OF CHARACTER

"Nature itself is the work of God; and it is the restoration, not the destruction, of <u>nature</u> which Christ came to accomplish. It is not the works of God, but the works of the devil which He came to destroy."

B. B. Warfield

"You are too much occupied in looking at yourself, and too little in beholding the Lord Jesus Christ. It is by the former that you are to be *humbled*; but it is by the latter that you are to be *changed into the divine image.*"

Charles Simeon

NOTE

In this matter of holiness perhaps the central fact which needs rediscovery today is that true, Christian holiness is supernaturally *inwrought*. In other words, the further, deeper experience which we call "sanctification" is nothing less than a divine work which actually effects a *change* in the deepest being of the born-again Christian. If it were not such, would further discussion of it matter much? But if Scripture does indeed teach such a deep-going inward renovation, nothing can be of more moment than to understand it clearly. Such inward renewal is very different from mere counter-action. I have heard the New Testament teaching supposedly represented in the illustration of the diabetic who, by insulin, can live a more or less normal life, i.e. as a *"controlled* diabetic."￼ He is still desperately ill, but his disease is "controlled" by constant antidotes. So human nature "remains to the bitter end selfish and sinful, but there is that from God which can counter it, if day by day the remedy is continually appropriated." But does the New Testament teach *no more* than that? Does it not teach an inward renewal of our nature itself? I believe that the texts (and others) considered in this chapter *do*.

J.S.B.

TRANSFIGURATION OF CHARACTER

WHATEVER other issues may be involved in this subject of Scriptural holiness, never for one moment must we forget that the supreme purpose of the Holy Spirit's deeper work in the believer is the *transfiguration of character*. However often we may fight it down, there is a reassertive tendency in most of us to think that the infilling of the Holy Spirit is mainly an emotional experience. Perhaps this misunderstanding is the more persistent because of our knowing that sudden envelopments by the Holy Spirit have not infrequently been *accompanied* by an eruption of ecstatic emotion. It is important that we distinguish between the purposive and the merely associative.

The human mind is usually conceived of as having three main areas or centres of activity: (1) intellect, or reason, (2) volition, or free-will, (3) emotion, or feeling. Which is the true order of precedence? The intellect is meant to be king; with the will as prime minister, or executive of the crown; and the emotions as obedient subjects. When that order is violated, and especially when the emotions run amok, we are soon in trouble, either physically or psychopathically, or both. We live in an age of suspense and nervous tension. Emotional behaviour patterns and disturbances are receiving more attention than ever. We dare not understate the importance of the emotions. Yet when we have said the most and the last about them it still remains true that they are comparatively the *least* important. They are the most volatile, the most variable, the most unpredictable, the most *superficial* part of us.

Is it thinkable, then, that the Holy Spirit comes to do His deepest work in the least substantial part of us? No; whatever emotional accidence there may or may not be, that major invasion by the Holy Spirit which has been our subject in these pages designs a renovation in the deepest depths of the human personality. It is meant to effect such a purification and refinement within the moral nature that there shall be a transfiguration of *character*.

I have made a distinction between "nature" and "character". Nature is the raw material, so to speak. Character is what we make out of it. In the final consummation, we shall all be presented "faultless" in our nature; but does that mean we shall all be equal in *character*? No; for as "one star differeth from another star in glory" (1 Cor. 15: 41) so will there be greater and lesser resplendencies of character, developed by our voluntary reactions while living on earth in the mortal body. (Oh, how important is this present span on earth!). In that gracious suffusion by the Holy Spirit which effects inwrought holiness, the divine purpose is not only even the correcting of wrong bias, and the cleansing of impure impulse, and the refining of desire; it is that the *nature*, being thus renewed, may be developed into holy *character*.

In other words, inwrought holiness is not only negative; it is both negative and positive. Wonderful as are the aspects of it which we have already mentioned, those more negative features (i.e. cleansing, correcting, renewing, refining) are the clearing away of obstructions, so that all those traits and qualities which are most natively human, "after the image of God", may be unimpededly developed, even sublimated, in the transfiguration of character. Holiness is not only a reclamation of the garden from weeds, but a filling of it with fragrant flowers. It is not only (negatively) a clearing away of obnoxious undergrowths from the orchard, but (positively) a producing of gracious fruit, even "the fruit of the Spirit . . . love, joy, peace, longsuffering, kindness, goodness, faithfulness, meekness, godly self-control" (Gal. 5: 22, 23), and all manner of "good works which God afore prepared that we should walk in them" (Eph. 2: 10).

The kind of character-beauty which true holiness begets is not that of elegant marble statuary, charming in profile, graceful in silhouette, yet cold and hard to the touch, voiceless, uncommunicative, and locked up in itself. Any kind of holiness which turns the inner life into a mental monastery, and the outer life into a walled-off enclosure, is not holiness according to Christ. One of the loveliest traits of character engendered by true holiness is a self-forgetting otherism. Instead of a continually in-looking self-culture, there is an out-looking diffusion of goodness to others.

Genesis 1: 11 tells how God caused the earth to bring forth herb and fruit tree "whose seed is in itself". The miracle of herb and fruit self-propagation has been going on for all the thousands of years since, and it always happens at the point of full development or ripeness. Similarly, holiness in full development or ripeness expresses itself in an outreaching graciousness of character which propagates goodness and moral beauty everywhere. Except where there is Satanic resistance or Pharisaic hypocrisy, it gently "provokes to love and good works" (Heb. 10: 24) in other hearts and lives. It is never self-advertising, yet neither can it conceal itself. It continually reaches out in soul-winning activity, and atmospheres evangelism in the very love of God. It is full of effort, yet somehow it is effort with ease. Its hands are full of "good works". It produces character which visibly incarnates those words of the Apostolic benediction, "the grace of the Lord Jesus Christ, and the love of God, and the fellowship of the Holy Spirit."

Inward Metamorphosis

Now of course there are many New Testament verses which bear on this matter of Christian character; but I here call special attention to two, because of their using a certain Greek verb, i.e. *metamorphŏō*, which, incidentally, seems to have found new vogue today in our rather modern word, "metamorphosis". Both in the Greek and in the English the meaning is to transform. That Paul should speak about a character-*metamorphosis* through inward renewal is, to say the least, arresting. In Romans 12: 1, 2, he writes,

"I beseech you therefore, brethren, by the mercies of God, to present your bodies a living sacrifice, holy, acceptable to God, which is your reasonable service. And be not fashioned according to this world; but be ye transformed [*metamorphosed*] by the renewing of your mind, that ye may prove what is the good and acceptable and perfect will of God."

It is interesting to see how different translators try to bring out the full force of the meaning in these two verses. From a dozen or so, I pick out the rendering given by Weymouth's *New Testament in Modern Speech*.

"I plead with you therefore, brethren, by the compassion of God, to present all your faculties to Him as a living and holy sacrifice to

Him—a spiritual mode of worship. And do not conform to the present age, but be *TRANSFORMED BY THE ENTIRE RENEWAL OF YOUR MINDS*, so that you may learn by experience what God's will is, namely, all that is good and acceptable to Him, and perfect."

This metamorphosis is here connected with certain factors which immediately catch the eye. (1) *Separation* from the world: "Do not conform to the present age." Our Lord could transfigure a Stephen, but never a Demas who "loved this present age". (2) *Consecration* to God: "Present all your faculties to Him as a living and holy sacrifice". Our Lord may bless others in many ways, but it is only the completely yielded whom He transfigures. (3) *Renovation* inside the human personality: "the entire renewal of your minds". Nothing less than this can really transfigure character. (4) *Realization* of the divine will by new perception and in actual experience: "that you may learn by experience what God's will is. . . ."

All these well merit separate consideration, but the central and vital thing to grasp is that this character-transformation is wrought by *"ENTIRE RENEWAL" OF THE MIND*. If anything could unanswerably show to us how astray both the eradication theory and the conventional counteraction theory are, this second verse in Romans 12 does. If, as eradicationism says, the Second Blessing completely extirpates the so-called *"old* nature", leaving only the *"new* nature", then Paul's exhortation here, in Romans 12: 1, 2, must be to that *"new* nature", which, however, makes the exhortation a useless redundance. For if the so-called "new nature" is (according to theory) sinless, why need Paul exhort *it* to separation from the world, and consecration to God, and inward renewal? On the other hand, if, as says the "counteraction" idea, the "old nature" must persist within us as an inerradicable evil entity to our dying day, how could Paul exhort us to *"ENTIRE RENEWAL OF THE MIND"*?

How long must some of us continue to sponsor such exegetically untenable concepts in the name of Scriptural holiness? How long must unsuspicious audiences be a prey to such misguidance and its hurtful after-effects? How long are we to let well-meant theory, venerated names and tenacious shibboleths blindfold us to the true, precious teaching of our New Testament? With such clear guidance flowing to us through Apostolic pens, why are we so slow to see the real truth about regeneration and sanctification? Regeneration, other than being merely the superinducement of a (suppositionary) "new nature" which is not the human "I" or "me", is the Holy Spirit's transfusing of a new spiritual *life* into our human nature itself. And, through His *further* work in us, this new life may fill, may interpenetrate, may "renew" our whole moral and spiritual nature—not to a static ethical absoluteness but to moral and spiritual *fulness of health* in which inward purity, at last, has the upper hand over all animal appetites, over all temptations injected from without, and over every wrong response from within. *That* is the true New Testament teaching as to regeneration, inward renewal, inwrought holiness, and transfiguration of character.

Yes, that is the central, vital thing: true Christian character-transformation issues from this "entire renewal of the mind". Our Lord said of John the Baptist, "He was a burning and a shining light" (John 5: 35). The burning was inward. The shining was outward. There would have been no outward shining without the inward burning. The inward burning was sanctification through the infilling Holy Spirit (Luke 1: 15). The outward shining was that of transfigured character. It is *still* true that there cannot be a true outward "shining" without the same inward "burning". Many of us are needing to learn that more deeply. So, then, let us briefly analyse this character-transfiguration in its *in*wrought and *out*wrought features.

First there is transformation of the *mind*. The word which Paul uses in Romans 12: 2 (metamorphose) is used of our Lord's mountain-top transfiguration: "He was transfigured before them" (Matt. 17: 2, Mark 9: 2). Luke's verbal variation of it is, "the fashion of His countenance was altered" (Luke 9: 29); it was the same face, yet not the same. Correspondently, there can be such a transfiguration of the mind, by the Holy Spirit, that the very "fashion" of its thinking is changed; so that although it remains the same mind as to personal identity, it is no longer the same in its deepest impulses and responses. It means that all the thoughts, imaginations, emotions, motives, ambitions, yearnings, joys and loves of the heart and mind are made to become radiant with "the joy of the Lord". I myself have known persons who have given every convincing evidence, under widely varied testings, of this fundamental refashioning of the mind.

Resultantly, there is transfiguration of the *personality*. This is the very opposite of self-decoration. It is also quite different from a prepossessing natural charm, which in its own way, of course, can be quite delightful. It is no mere exterior impressiveness of figure or feature, nor is it any kind of personal force which is self-achieved. It is an inner radiance which somehow shines through the personality, not in *any* way because of natural appearance or engaging gifts, but, as often as not, despite the *absence* of them. It is an indefinable but unmistakable glow which tinges and lustres one's way of saying and doing things. It is utterly unconscious of itself, yet it *atmospheres* the whole personality, expressing itself most often through the most ordinary activities of the most ordinary days. It shows itself distinctly to the public through the ministry of public men, but it shows itself most clearly to those who live nearest to it and observe it continually in private life.

I remember reading about a man who once went to breakfast with the saintly John Fletcher (whom John Wesley described as "the holiest man in England"). The breakfast was very plain fare, in itself, but the visitor afterwards described the meal in this way: "Do you know, taking breakfast with John Fletcher was like taking the Sacrament"! This transfiguration of the personality is a lovely fulfilment of that prayer in Psalm 90: 17, "Let the beauty of the Lord our God be upon us".

We may go further and say, with all due cautiousness, that this "entire renewal" of the mind often gradually transfigures *the face*. This may not be one of its most solidly important effects, but it is one of its most appealing adjuncts. It must have been transfixing to the gathered members of the Jewish Sanhedrin when they saw Stephen's face become "as the face of an angel" (Acts 6: 15). Of course, it still remained the same human face, but some unearthly sheen must have shown through it.

I never thought I would ever see anything on earth near enough to that to remind me of it, but I did, a few years ago. My dear wife and I were travelling through what was then the Belgian Congo. On the occasion of which I now speak, I was addressing a crowd of between twelve and fifteen hundred negro men and women of varying ages, from several different tribes, many of whom had come, in larger or smaller contingents, two or even three days' trek through the jungles in order to be present at our Conference. I had asked beforehand for guidance as to my type of message, and had been told, "They will go as deep in the Word as you can take them"—which proved to be true. I believe that many of those beaming-faced African brothers and sisters in the Lord knew more about implicit trust in the Word, and about deeply experienced sanctification, than I did myself. My subject was: "Out of Egypt and into Canaan"—and oh, how they listened, even though it had to be through two interpreters, because of different tribal languages.

Because of needing to preach through *two* interpreters, I practised, as closely as possible, one complete thought to each complete sentence. Next to me, on my left, a lady missionary interpreted, and next further left was a negro interpreter. In that way the main two groups of languages were covered. I could not help noticing how the people looked at that negro interpreter. Maybe *they* could not help noticing how *I* kept looking at him. I became so absorbed in watching his face that sometimes when it was time for me to add my next bit, I had momentarily forgotten the thread of my discourse!

Oh, that face! I have seen many beautiful faces in my time, but never one quite like that. I have seen eyes shine and features beam, but never elsewhere quite like that. Using the word in its finest, uttermost sense, that negro's face was *radiant*. If ever I saw the "spiritual glow", I saw it there. As evidently as anything could be, it was the outshining of an inward purity. In Scriptural phraseology, it was "the *beauty* of holiness". I learned afterward that the beauty of his character matched the radiance of his face.

That was not the only thing which we learned afterward. On our way back from the meeting to the missionary's dwelling, we passed a group of naked natives—six or seven men, squatting at the base of a great tree. Never before in our travels had we seen human beings so facially ugly, or with such prominent suggestion of the ape. I suddenly realized how easy it would be, if we had no authentic guidance from the written Word of God, to believe in human evolution from the anthropoid apes. One of those men was so strange-looking, so gorilla-like, it was disturbing to look at him, yet we could scarce turn away our gaze. As soon as we were past them, our missionary friend said, "I know what you were thinking. We missionaries have thought the same at one time or another. You were shocked at the appearance of that big one, with the coarse hair and ugly gorilla face. Well, he is the brother of the man who interpreted your sermon just now; and your radiant-faced interpreter was even *uglier than that* before his conversion to Christ"! For the moment we were dumb-struck. The contrast between the two was so great that such a transformation seemed incredible; but the missionary assured us that similar transfigurations had occurred in tens of hundreds of lives. When, despite their crudeness, those dark-minded people are brought to the point of simple yet vital faith in the Saviour, and become truly regenerated by the Holy Spirit, there is such a sheer contrast between their new life in Christ and what they were before, in their pre-conversion mental darkness and animalism, that the gracious shock of it causes wonderful *facial* transfigurations.

In a gentler, less vivid, yet equally real way, I have seen transfigured character and transfigured faces in England and America. Pure-hearted Christian saints, I think of them now, and my memory of the gentle light shining through some of those dear faces tempts me to fill pages here, telling about them and the gracious witness for Christ which they diffused. But I must forbear. I would only say that those faces, some masculine, some feminine, some younger though perhaps the more of them rather older, some naturally well-featured, others rather peculiar or else of the plain Jane type, have all had a radiance, a light, an expressive something which transfigured whatever kind of natural cast or feature they had. There was that Shekinah light within which tinges with beauty *whatever* it shines through.

Then again, going with this inward renewal and transfiguration of character, there is always transfiguration of *disposition and. behaviour.* "Entire renewal of the mind" inevitably registers itself in refined and tempered attitudes. Hasty verdicts and drastic reactions drop away. The way of looking at things and dealing with things is modified. There is a new interest in others, a new appreciation of others, a new sympathy with others, a new tolerance of others, a new warmth of kindliness toward others. In matters of faith and conviction there is a new firmness which is the more Christlike because it is firmness without fierceness. The very manner of doing things is changed, even in the commonplace duties, chores, and contacts of everyday living; the way of answering questions, the way of conversing, the exhibiting of charitableness to those who differ—oh, in so many ways, transfigured character communicates itself through transformed disposition and behaviour.

Have we not seen such transformation of character, of personality, of countenance, of disposition and behaviour? It sheds abroad the most winsome of all influence for Christ. It is the most magnetic of all apologetics for the Christian faith. It generally shines out with its most victorious splendour amid life's darkest experiences. With heaven-reflecting eyes it smiles upon us even through sickness, and somehow gives the thin, wan face of the wearied invalid a soft, gentle light and beauty which transfigure even the mystery of permitted pain. It is indeed the transfiguration which comes from the Holy Spirit's deeper work in the entirely sanctified believer. It is the inner glory-light of inwrought holiness, gleaming through the outer windows of the consecrated personality. Or, in those words of Romans 12: 2, it is "entire renewal of the mind" expressing itself through a metamorphosis of character.

Progressive Christlikeness

This brings us to a point where we ought to glance at the other place where Paul uses the verb, "metamorphose" in connection with transfiguration of character. It is Second Corinthians 3: 17, 18,

"But we all, with unveiled face, beholding [or, possibly, 'reflecting'] as in a mirror the glory of the Lord, are transformed [metamorphosed] into the same image, from glory to glory, even as from the Lord, the Spirit."

There is some doubt as to whether Paul here means (1) that *we* are the reflecting mirror, or (2) that our Lord Jesus is the mirror, reflecting "the glory of the LORD" i.e. of Jehovah, or (3) that the Gospel, as the "new covenant" (see verses 6-11) is the mirror, reflecting the glory of Christ. Perhaps number three best fits the context, but, yes or no, the central idea remains the same, namely, that *we*, by beholding with "unveiled face", our glorious Lord, are "transformed into the same image".

It is a striking figure, and flashes with meaning for us. Like Romans 12: 2, it certainly teaches a transfiguration (metamorphosis) of character. The phrase, here, "with unveiled face",

means with unveiled eyes of the *mind*. With our outer, physical
eyes, we cannot see our Lord at all, for the present; but with
unveiled *inward* vision, we may see Him as being luminously ever-
present to the mind. Let us be quick to notice the four aspects of
this character-transfiguration which are here indicated and
blended.

(1) It is transfiguration through *communion*. The participle
clause, "beholding-as-in-a-mirror" is all one word in the Greek
(*katoptrizomenoi*), meaning a beholding or mirroring which is
contemporaneous and *going on*. One of the things which we never
dare forget, especially in teaching inwrought holiness through
consecration and faith, is, that no matter what crisis we may
experience or what spiritual elevation may come to us, *no* blessing
of the Christian life ever continues with us unless there is continuous communion with Christ. Moreover, this "beholding" or
"reflecting" is that kind of communion which we call *adoring
contemplation*—of which, in this age of inane rush, there is so little
that we are spiritually poverty-stricken.

(2) This transfiguration is *progressive*. The verb is in the present
tense: "*being* transfigured". In these chapters we have emphasized
that in no sense is inwrought holiness our reaching a fixed point of
static sanctity. No, this deeper renewal within us marks a crisis-
point of new departure into a *progressive* transfiguration of
character. Heart-holiness is never a reservoir, but, in Frances
Ridley Havergal's words, a "river glorious".

(3) This transfiguration is inwrought *by the Holy Spirit*. It is
"from the Lord the Spirit", that is, it is a result from His activity
in the mind. The noteworthy thing is that He effects His trans-
figuring work through the believer's adoring contemplation of "the
glory of the Lord". In Romans 12: 2, the transfiguration begins
with "entire renewal of the mind". Here, in 2 Corinthians 3: 18,
it is developed through communion; through an adoring contemplation, which absorbs into itself the very impress of that beloved
heavenly Lord.

(4) This transfiguration is an approximating *likeness to Christ*—
"transformed into the same image". Yes, that is the supreme
goal of true, Christian sanctification: to become ever-increasingly
conformed in character to the sublime character of Christ, "the
Altogether Lovely". Let it be reiterated yet again: entire sanctification, or restoration to holiness, is *not*, according to the New

Testament, either a man-achieved or God-inwrought ethical top-level, an accomplished *goal* of moral perfectness; it is restoration from moral and spiritual disease to fulness of health, making possible therefrom an ever-developing likeness to the character and beauty of the Lord Jesus, who is the ineffable moral loveliness of God Himself in visible embodiment.

Inwrought holiness through "entire renewal of the mind" certainly *is* both restoration to moral fulness of health and an elevation to a new high plane impossible of attainment by merely human struggling; but instead of its being a high level from which we look *down*, conscious of an exalted superiority, it humbles us with a prostration deeper than any ever caused by the heart-breaking repentance of a prodigal returning from his wallowing in the mire. Why? Because, on that higher level of holiness through "entire renewal of the mind", we see as never before, "with unveiled face", the "heavenly vision" of the ineffable, all-holiness and all-loveliness of Jesus; the very "glory of God in the face of Jesus Christ" (2 Cor. 4: 6); the one, ultimate attraction of all holy heart-longing; the solitary, absolute all-perfection in the universe; the one-and-only, all-eclipsing, ever-alluring *GOAL* which ever fills the gaze of all the truly sanctified. When once, through inwrought holiness, we have seen *that* exquisite Goal, we never again talk about our own holiness, much less of "perfection"!—for the *nearer* we get to that beatific Goal, so the more do we realize how *far* we are from it. The more truly we may approximate to *that* perfection, the less conscious of it we are, and the more humblingly conscious are we of our own *im*perfection. That which lifts us highest brings us lowest.

Is not that the reason why, in this matter of "Christian perfection", John Wesley is far safer as an example than as teacher? However insistently he may have preached and urged "Christian perfection", he never once claimed it. Nay, he *disclaimed* it. In a letter to Dr. William Dodd, he writes, "I tell you flat, I have not attained the character I draw." As time went on, the Wesley teaching of Christian "perfection" became so pared and trimmed that in reality it was no more than a self-contradictory concept of *im*perfect perfection.

So, then, to summarize. The supreme purpose of the Holy Spirit's deeper work in us is transfiguration of character. That inward transfiguration begins through "entire renewal of the mind", or inwrought holiness, and is revealed outwardly through transfigured personality, facial expression, disposition, attitude, and behaviour. It develops especially through communion with God. It is not the suppositionary ethical immaculateness of the religious perfectionist, but a growing *likeness to Christ*.

Oh, for a deeper knowing of such character-transfiguration through "entire sanctification"! Is not this inwrought holiness the "perfect love" which "casteth out fear"? (1 John 4: 18)—and is not this character-transfiguration that which John means when he says, "*AS HE IS*, even so are we in this world"? (17)—and is not the most thrilling prospect of the coming Rapture just this: "When He shall appear, we shall be *LIKE HIM*"?

> Now, O my King above,
>   Now, even more,
> Thee for Thyself I love,
>   Thee I adore;
> For 'tis the glorious
>   loveliness Thou art
> Which captures and subdues
>   my wondering heart.
>
> Now, all my prayer is this:
>   More, more of Thee.
> Thou art the perfect bliss;
>   Live, live through me.
> Let me Thy life absorb,
>   diffuse, express,
> Till heaven itself unveils
>   Thy loveliness.

SUMMARY AND SUGGESTIONS

"I love Calvin a little, Luther more; the Moravians, Mr. Law and Mr. Whitefield far more than either. . . . But I love truth more than all."

John Wesley

"There are deep, deep reasons why no man can say, with all respect to the saintly Fletcher, 'I am freed from all sin'. It is indeed a thing not to say. It is gravely dangerous to utter such sentiments. If it costs any students of this teaching a pang to part with Wesley at this point, it must console them to remember that, if they have rejected his counsel, they have followed his example."

W. E. Sangster

"PROVE ALL THINGS; HOLD FAST THAT WHICH IS GOOD."

1 *Thessalonians* 5: 21

SUMMARY AND SUGGESTIONS

We have reached our last chapter in this restudy and restatement of Christian holiness. Looking back over the foregoing pages, I recognise only too clearly many imperfections which others also will doubtless see. It is a regret with me that I have to omit some of the most delightful positive aspects of the subject, such as the inward "witness of the Spirit", and the "earnest of the Spirit"; also "anointing" by the Spirit, "enduement" by the Spirit, "walking in the light", and the deeper meanings of "fellowship" with God. But our treatise is already longer than intended. I must not further add to it, except these final paragraphs of summary and suggestion.

In this last chapter, as in the first, I mourn that the New Testament insistence on Christian holiness seems little echoed in our churches today; that there is such a dearth in the teaching and experience of sanctification through inwrought renewal; that the wholesome exultation in it which blessed the churches some decades ago has subsided; that the reviving tide which flowed in so fully has ebbed out so far. I lament that the subject became submerged in the grim struggle of the Evangelical faith against the deadly insurgence of rationalistic higher criticism; that the holiness movement became largely strangled by controversy; that in some forms it became such a rejoicing in precious Christian privilege as to become forgetful of evangelism; that it suffered set-backs through upheavals and vast changes brought upon all of us by two world wars.

But I believe that the time is ripe for a new accent on this deeper, further, sanctifying work of the Holy Spirit in Christian believers. The battle still continues with various relays of Modernism, but the great verities of our Evangelical faith have now withstood the main shock of rationalistic attack, and the negatives of the Modernist forces are in recoil today from the re-established positives of "the faith once-for-all delivered to the saints". What our Evangelical churches are most needing *now* is not a new intellectual apologetic but a new invasion by the Holy Spirit, and a new demonstration of the divine Presence in the great old truths, and a dynamic new testimony to the reality of *inwrought holiness.*

This is the hour, so I believe, to recall our Evangelical pastors and pulpits to a new study and exposition of the subject; to fill our churches again with a true, rich experience of the blessing. I am not thinking in terms of mere excitements, but of behaviour-transformation and Christlikeness of character, and divine enduement for powerful Christian witness-bearing. Recall again Spurgeon's word, "A holy church is an awful weapon in the hand of God." It is time to call our people back, not only to a reassured *faith* in the Bible, but to its teachings about maximum spiritual fulness—the "fulness of the blessing of Christ". We have far more to start with than John Wesley had, or, for that matter, General Booth.

It is time for some of us to jettison our cargo of prejudice. Some time ago I was holding meetings at a church in an area disturbed by erroneous teachings about the Holy Spirit and "speaking in tongues". The well-meaning pastor said to me, "It would be better if we did not mention the Holy Spirit in our meetings." I could only reply, "My dear brother, you are saying, in effect, that the only way to answer error is to muzzle truth!" That must never be our attitude. Because the deeper blessing has for too long been beclouded by well-meant controversy and peculiar deviations we must not allow ourselves to be prejudiced against the truth itself, lest we deeply grieve the Holy Spirit who is the living centre of it. If we dislike the expression, "*second blessing*," let us not be so antipathetic that we thereby miss the "*blessing*"! If we know a better name for it, let us use it; but to preserve and experience the real truth is the vital thing. I myself do *not* like the term, "second blessing."

So, then, *is* a post-conversion crisis-work of the Holy Spirit taught in Scripture as being, at least, a usual procedure in the renewing of Christian believers into inward holiness? In our companion volume, *His Deeper Work in Us*, we have tried to show how such a "second" major experience is at least pointed to, if not actually typified, in Abram who later became Abraham; in Jacob who later became Israel; in the two outstanding experiences of

Moses at age forty and age eighty, respectively; in the two major parts of the one "great salvation" by which the Hebrews were (a) brought out of Egypt, and (b) brought into Canaan; also in Gideon (first converted, then, later, suddenly clothed with the Spirit's power); in the two castings of the mantle on Elisha; in Isaiah's post-conversion sanctification; in our Lord's Jordan baptism; in the representative difference between Calvary and Pentecost; in the distinctively twofold experience of the Apostles; and in the two emphasized main aspects of the Holy Spirit's operation in Christian believers as indicated in various statements of the Epistles.

We will not presume to be dogmatic; but do not all these pointers and patterns blend to give us coherent divine direction? Are they not too recurrent and too pronounced to be accidental? And are there not thousands of upright, credible witnesses to this deeper divine work in the soul—witnesses sufficiently varied in denomination and data and country? Yes, there are.

Is this so-called "fuller blessing" always subsequent to regeneration? Is its beginning always instantaneous? Is there not ample evidence that although it is not *necessarily* later than conversion to Christ, it is *usually* so? It is not always instantaneous in the sense of a sudden *emotional* "experience", but the final step to entire consecration and sanctification necessarily *is* a crisis-point.

Have we not seen that the eradication theory, although a product of devout sincerity, is without valid New Testament warrant, as well as having no authentic endorsement in carefully tested human experience? With warm esteem for all our evangelical brethren we have respectfully indicated (so we think) the self-contradictory fallacies of the conventional "counteraction" doctrine. We have tried to show how misleading and engendering of bondage are the usual explanations of Romans 6: 6, and how unscriptural is the supposition of sanctification by a prolonged inner joint-crucifixion with Christ. In a supplementary chapter, also, we show how unwarranted is the usual interpretation of "cleanseth from *all* sin", in 1 John 1: 7.[1]

What then remains? There remains *the real truth*. What is it? We may put it briefly as follows. Holiness is moral likeness to God. What is God like? We know by looking at One who said,

---

[1]For an examination into the idea of "two natures" in the believer, see our companion volume, *His Deeper Work in Us*.

"He that hath seen Me hath seen the Father." In Him the holiness of God is incarnated. Holiness in us is likeness of heart and life to our Lord Jesus. This, the only true holiness, may become an inwrought reality of experience in Christian believers through a deeper work of the Holy Spirit in us; a deeper work clearly promised in the New Testament, but seemingly realised by comparatively few among the Lord's people today. This deeper work of the Holy Spirit is not to be thought of as intrinsically *different* from regeneration, but as a maximum present development and experience of it, in response to consecration and faith. It is holiness through *complete possession by the Holy Spirit*. As we have noted before, there can be *degrees* of yieldedness to Christ, and therefore degrees of sanctification; but the instant we reach the final point of *utter* yieldedness, there is a correspondingly *instantaneous* full-possession of us by the Spirit (though not always with accompanying emotional raptures); and in that sense "entire sanctification" may be said to *begin* instantaneously.

Christian holiness, however, is not only full-suffusion by the heavenly Spirit, wonderful as that is. The Holy Spirit fills us in order to effect a renewing work within *our human nature itself* (Rom. 12: 2, 2 Cor. 3: 3, Eph. 3: 16, 20, 4: 23, etc.). This may be illustrated in part by the useful old figure of the iron in the fire. Here is a bar of iron—cold and black and hard. Put it into the furnace, and let the fire fill it. Soon, what a change! The coldness and blackness and hardness are gone. There is heat and glow and pliableness. It is still iron; yet how different from what it was! If a bar of gold is put into the fire, the illustration goes much further, for in the fire the gold itself is purified and refined. Even so, and more so, the Holy Spirit not only permeates the consecrated heart, He thereupon begins to cleanse, renew, refine all the thought-springs, desires, intents, inclinations, and reactions until, with gracious spontaneity, the heart *thinks* holiness.

There *cannot* be an absolute inward death to sin (let none presume that there can). There will always be inward susceptibility to its deceitful appeals. There will always be subtle liabilities which can be stirred into response by subtle inducements. There will always be that enigmatical sensitivity within us which can be activated by attractive temptation. Yet none-the-less this deeper work of the Holy Spirit in us inflicts a fundamental reverse on hereditary depravity. The power of sin in our nature is really broken. All the innate capacities for good are greatly strengthened, and the Holy Spirit begins to develop them into increasing beauty of character. In this sense, Christian holiness is *restoration to true humanhood*—in its "image and likeness of God" (Gen. 1: 26).

Although we can no longer believe in the "second blessing" as "eradication" or "counteraction" or "inward crucifixion" or as a static "top-level" permanence, this "entire sanctification" wrought in the believer through a full monopoly by the Holy Spirit was pardonably called the "*second* blessing" because of the epochal crisis-point at which it begins? Are there not trustable present-day pens and voices giving witness to it as such? To that let us hold fast, and let us renew our testimony to it again. Always let us keep sanctification doctrine clear from the merely emotional, from the excitable and the extravagant, remembering that all profession of it is spurious unless it authenticates itself in *transfigured character*.

Not only with a sense of urgent conviction, but with true esteem for all who sincerely preach theories disapproved in this book, I now submit, in closing, that our usual presentation of Christian holiness needs revamping. Unless my main arguments in these chapters can be proved wrong, is it not high time that all holiness schools, groups, and teachers threw off, for ever, the mis-founded eradication ultraism? Is it not overdue that many others of us jettisoned the ambiguous usual form of the "counter-action" idea? Is it not time that the holiness campanile rang out a new kind of peal? Is not the true New Testament emphasis that entire sanctification, or inwrought renewal to holiness, comes through union with our Lord *in His risen life*?—not by a suppositionary joint-crucifixion with Him on long-ago Calvary. The eradicationist and counteractionist misconceptions have for too long chained our thinking to fictitious negatives, while the consistent accent of the New Testament is upon dynamic spiritual positives.

Until the teaching of Christian holiness is rescued from those two beloved blunders, "eradicationism" and the "reckon-yourself-dead" form of "counteractionism", we shall keep bringing believers into the bondage of wrong theory, with the heart-rending dismay of eventual disillusionment. Thousands of intelligent but unsophisticated Christian believers become so perplexed by the intricacies and anomalies of eradicationist and counteractionist and other "explanations" of Christian holiness that they sigh for a dragoman to guide them through the maze. Look again at that holiness standard-bearer text, 1 Thessalonians 5: 23, 24.

"AND THE GOD OF PEACE HIMSELF SANCTIFY YOU WHOLLY; AND MAY YOUR SPIRIT AND SOUL AND BODY BE PRESERVED ENTIRE, WITHOUT BLAME AT THE COMING OF OUR LORD JESUS CHRIST."

How clear it is! How unhesitating!—entire sanctification, without the faintest glimmer of a suggestion that there is one part of us (a so-called "old nature") which *cannot* be sanctified! It is so inclusive and so specific—"spirit and soul and body"—"preserved entire"—"without blame". Yes, indeed, "sanctify you wholly"; or as John Wesley was wont to translate it, *"THE WHOLE OF YOU."*

Could it be that some dear reader who has patiently ploughed through these pages is still *seeking* this "entire sanctification"? Then let me point to the divine guarantee which is subjoined to the promise:—

"FAITHFUL IS HE WHO CALLS YOU [TO THIS ENTIRE SANCTIFICATION], WHO ALSO WILL DO IT."

Yes, "faithful is He who calleth you". Let the closing paragraphs of this book be a warm-hearted challenge and incentive to the individual Christian believer. Could it be that through these pages the truth which sanctifies is knocking at your door again? Already, through your soul-saving conversion and spiritual rebirth you are into "the blessing of Christ", but are you yet into "the *fulness* of the blessing"? Already you are out of Egypt; but are you yet living in Canaan? Are you living in complete and continuous victory over sin and "the flesh"? Are you "filled with the Spirit"? Are you living in the radiant experience of that inward metamorphosis, that "entire renewal of the mind" with all its desires and motives and impulses, which the New Testament opens up to us? Have you the "joy unspeakable", the "peace that passeth all imagination", the enduement of "power from on high"? Have you?

Dear Christian, is it not time for *you* to seek that deeper blessing of which we have spoken?—that further, deeper, fuller, richer work of the divine Spirit within you? Does not your heart "hunger and thirst" after inwrought holiness? Do you not long, more wistfully than for anything else to enjoy unclouded fellowship with the heavenly Father and with our risen Lord Jesus? Do you not long to be "pure in heart", to "walk in the light", to be always "abiding" and "abounding" in Christ? Do you not long, with an almost painful longing at times, to "go up and possess" that sunlit Canaan which beckons you?

You ask: *"How* do I possess?" Well, it is an axiomatic law of the spiritual life that we possess by *being* possessed. When Christ has all of me, then I have all of Him to the limit of my capacity. When the Holy Spirit has the *entire* monopoly of my being, then I know in maximum continuance His infilling and renovating of all my inner life. There is no substitute for this utter yielding to God, to Christ, to the Holy Spirit, for the simple reason that there is no equivalent to it. God must really have *all* of you, if you are to know "the *fulness* of the blessing". You must really *want* to give your all to Him. Then you must really *determine* to give your all to Him. Then you must really *give* your all to Him—not in order to get a blessing, but that the God who made you, and owns you, and died for you, and loves you, may be glorified though you in any way He chooses.

The minute you really get there, you will find that many Scripture promises which somehow you could never get hold of before, now suddenly become easy to appropriate. When you trust God enough to give Him everything, then you suddenly discover that *He* has given *you* everything. So, in the words of an unforgettable little aphorism which I saw on the wall of a Sunday School in Dallas, Texas,

GIVE HIM ALL HE ASKS.
TAKE ALL HE OFFERS.

The two always go together. Without the giving all, there can be no taking all; but when we have done the former, we find the latter becomes wonderfully easy.

Be clear in your mind as to what you are asking God to do

within you. No longer entertain any such idea as an eradication of some supposed "old nature" inside you. No longer plead for enablement to "reckon" yourself "dead indeed" to indwelling sin through a supposed inward co-crucifixion with Christ. Such eradication will never be yours; it is not promised to you. Nor by "reckoning" yourself inwardly dead to sin will you ever become so; for neither is that a Scriptural promise. With deep gratitude realize that in the *judicial* reckoning of God you *have* been once-for-all "crucified with Christ"; that in Him Sin *did* exact its death-penalty on you; that you *did* then and there become legally "dead indeed" to Sin the Exactor, and to the avenging Law; so that being thus forever freed from all guilt and condemnation you should have wide-open access to God, and be able to claim all that has been graciously provided for you in Christ, even fulness of spiritual life and inwrought holiness.

The big, rich, *second* major blessing which you are now seeking is complete infilling or *suffusion* by the Holy Spirit, and the *"entire renewal of your mind"*, by Him. You cannot experience the whole process of that renewal all in one minute, but there is one minute in which that deeper work begins, i.e. when the Holy Spirit infills you, and gives you the inward "earnest" of it.

So, get alone with God; and stay alone with Him, until, as He searches you and draws out your heart toward Himself, you reach the point where with utter relief you yield up your whole being to His possession. Then, with a faith and love to which Heaven never says No, you will find yourself appropriating and experiencing "the promises of God" and the "fulness of the blessing". Yes, the blessing will have become yours, and you will know it. You will have no doubt as to its definiteness, though the inward witness to it may not be after the pattern which you had anticipated. If there seems to be *no* inward witness, beware of thinking that the blessing is *denied* because the attestation of it is *delayed*. So long as your motive is altogether the glory of God, persist in prayer, asking Him to give you the inner pledge: and, in some glad moment, "the Lord whom ye seek shall suddenly come to His temple"!

Yes, *persist* in prayer. If there seems to be delayed answer, do not mistakenly suppose that delay is denial. In any seeming hold-back of response from Heaven there is always a wonderfully educative discipline which prepares us for more properly receiving. Remember again our Lord's words, "Ask, and it shall be given you. Seek, and ye shall find. Knock, and it shall be opened unto you. For every one that asketh receiveth; and he that seeketh findeth; and to him that knocketh it shall be opened" (Matt. 7: 7, 8). In the Greek, the latter part of that utterance is in the present continuous tense: "For everyone that is *asking . . . seeking . . . knocking*." Do not ask just once, and lapse into silence. Do not seek only the once, and then give up. Do not knock only the once, and then desist if the door does not at once fly open. God does not always keep us waiting, but when He does, it always makes the coming blessing immeasurably more meaningful.

Remember that other word of our dear Lord: "If ye, then, being evil, know how to give good gifts unto your children, how much more shall your heavenly Father give the Holy Spirit to them that ask Him?" (Luke 11: 13). If that promise was made with such divine good faith away back yonder on the *earlier* historical side of Calvary, how much more will our heavenly Father make it good to the born-again, consecrated Christian believer on this side of *Pentecost*! Do not only wait *on* God: wait *for* Him. If your heart is truly and fully yielded, He will indeed, without one unnecessary moment of waiting, honour your simple faith and prayerful patience. So again, in the words of Habakkuk 2: 3, "Though it tarry, wait for it; because it will surely come."

Let me close by quoting a little hymn I wrote some time ago, expressing my own heart. Perhaps my prayer may now become yours.

With all my longing heart
   Now may I be
Completely set apart,
   Dear Lord, for Thee.

And may there now begin
   The cure divine;
Work miracles within
   This heart of mine.

Enchained by subtle fear,
   My bondage see;
Break in upon me here,
   And set me free.

All dark allure to sin
   In me replace
By holy light within,
   From Thy dear face.

At last, true holiness
   May I now find
In having Thee possess
   And fill my mind.

Let risk seem what it will,
   My *all* I give;
Lord, all my being fill,
   For Thee to live.

SUPPLEMENTARY

THREE BIG QUESTIONS

1. What does Paul mean by "The Flesh"?
2. What is "Cleansing from *All* Sin"?
3. Can We Ever Become Dead To Sin?

NOTE

Inasmuch as our earlier chapters were considerably occupied with what we consider fallacious theories of holiness, I have thought it preferable, for the sake of new readers in the subject, to postpone until here the three questions raised in this addendum, so as to lessen early appearance of complicatedness. Now that our main aim has been fulfilled, however, it is important (so I think) that these three questions should be dealt with, as a further safeguard against easy and common error. Some of these further pages may need a somewhat concentrated reading; but to exercise the mind keenly on such matters is itself rewarding.

J.S.B.

WHAT DOES PAUL MEAN BY "THE FLESH"?

In these present holiness studies, two factors will have emerged prominently to every reflective reader: first, that Paul's teaching has been considerably misapprehended through inexact translation of his verb-tenses in our revered old "Authorized Version"; second, that it is decisively important to understand correctly such Paulinisms as "the old man", "the new man", "the body of sin", "the inward man", and "the flesh". We have halted at some of these already, but so often do we encounter Paul's phrase, "the flesh", that it calls for separate scrutiny. In itself, it is not peculiar to Paul, but its *usage* often is; and I am convinced that we cannot accurately teach Christian holiness unless we rightly interpret his usage of it. My purpose here is to show that he never uses it (as is generally supposed) to mean an "old nature", or a "sinful nature", or an "Adam nature", or a kind of aggregate "body", or separate subsistence of sin within us.

The Greek word behind this expression, "the flesh", is *sarx*. It occurs 91 times in Paul's epistles (excluding Hebrews, where its 5 occurrences do not affect our conclusion). Here are the component figures: 37 times of the physical or bodily; 25 times of humanity or that which is human; 27 times in a recondite way, i.e. of sin in our human nature; and twice in a borderline way. These are the references:

Used of the physical or bodily	Of humanity or that which is human	Of inherent evil in human nature
Rom. 1: 3	Rom. 3: 20	Rom. 7: 5
2: 28	4: 1	7: 18
6: 19	8: 3 (first)	7: 25
9: 3	8: 3 (second)	8: 5
9: 5	1 Cor. 1: 26	8: 5
9: 8	1: 19	8: 6
11: 14	10: 18	8: 7
1 Cor. 6: 16	2 Cor. 1: 17	8: 8
7: 28	7: 5	8: 9
15: 39 (4)	10: 2	8: 12
15: 50	10: 3	8: 13

2 Cor.	4: 11		10: 3			13: 14
	5: 16 (2)		11: 18	1 Cor.	5: 5
	7: 1	Gal.	1: 16	Gal.	4: 23
	12: 7		2: 16		4: 29
Gal.	2: 20		3: 3		5: 13
	4: 13		6: 12		5: 16
	4: 14		6: 13		5: 17
Eph.	2: 11 (second)	Eph.	2: 11		5: 17
	2: 15		6: 5		5: 19
	5: 29		6: 12		5: 24
	5: 30	Phil.	3: 3		6: 8
	5: 31		3: 4		6: 8
Phil.	1: 22		3: 4	Eph.	2: 3
	1: 24	Col.	2: 23		2: 3
Col.	1: 22			Col.	2: 11
	1: 24				2: 18
	2: 1				
	2: 5				
	2: 13				
	3: 22				
1 Tim.	3: 16				
Philem.	16				

Two seemingly border-line occurrences between the human and inherent evil — Rom. 8: 3 (third) Rom. 8: 4

There are also 8 occurrences of the adjectival form *sarkikos*:
Rom. 7: 14, 15: 27, 1 Cor. 3: 1, 3, 3, 4, 9: 11, 2 Cor. 10: 4.

Anyone can easily verify whether or not we have placed the texts of the first two columns where they rightly belong. It is with those 27 in the third category that we are here concerned. Most of us, probably all, would agree that they refer to *a depravity within each human being*.

Romans 7: 5
"For when we were in the flesh, the motions of sins, which were by the law, did work in our members to bring forth fruit unto death."

Here, "the flesh" cannot mean the body, for the past tense, "when we *were* in the flesh" implies that they were no longer in it, whereas they certainly were still in the body. Note, however, the connection of "the flesh" with the "*members*" of the body.

Romans 7: 18
"For I know that in me, that is, in my flesh, dwelleth no good thing; for to will is present with me, but how to perform that which is good I find not."

Observe here the "I know", and "I find not", with the "in *me*" and "with *me*", indicating the one undivided personality all the way through. Then note that the "flesh" is *within* the "me" as somehow *one* with it and *of* it; not as a separate *entity* in it.

Romans 7: 25
"So then, with the mind I myself serve the law of God; but with the flesh the law of sin."

The "mind" here is the "inward man" (vs. 22, 23). That "inward man" is not a "man" *other* than the real man, nor is the "mind" any other than the one, thinking "I"—which is why Paul now says, "with the mind *I myself* . . ." The "mind" is the man which "serves the law of God", and by exact parallel here the "flesh" is the *same* man (not just a part) who serves "the law of sin".

Romans 8: 5, 6, 7
"For they that are after the flesh do mind the things of the flesh; but they that are after the Spirit the things of the Spirit. For the mind of the flesh is death; but the mind of the Spirit is life and peace; because the mind of the flesh is enmity towards God, for it is not subject to the law of God, neither indeed can be."

What are "the *mind* of the flesh" and "the *mind* of the Spirit"? They cannot be two minds co-existent but not identical in one person, for that would be two *persons*, since the mind is the "I myself." No, they are two *states* of mind. The "mind of the flesh" is the mind set on animal gratification. The "mind of the Spirit" is the mind set on spiritual satisfactions. My mind cannot be predominantly set on the physical and predominantly set on the spiritual both at the same time. It may be either the one or the other at any given time, but it cannot be both simultaneously.

Romans 8: 8, 9
"So then, they that are in the flesh cannot please God. But ye are not in the flesh, but in the Spirit, if so be that the Spirit of God dwell in you."

This cannot mean, "They that are in the *body* cannot please God" nor can it mean, "But ye are not in the *body*"—for that is what they actually *were*. Here, again, "the flesh" must mean something *other* than the body, yet closely *connected* with it.

Romans 8: 12, 13
"Therefore, brethren, we owe nothing to the flesh, to live

It is important to see that here Paul *distinguishes* between the after the flesh; for if ye live after the flesh ye shall die; but if ye through the Spirit put to death the activities of the body, ye shall live."

"flesh" and the "body". He says, "If ye live after the flesh ye shall die", therefore, "Make to die the activities of the *body*". Now it is plain as day that here he *cannot* mean the normal functions of the body, but the *animal appetites*.

Romans 13: 14
"But put ye on the Lord Jesus Christ, and make not provision for the flesh, to fulfil the lusts thereof."

This settles it that by "the flesh" Paul sometimes means an *evil propensity* in our nature. The body itself cannot "lust", but only the human self, *through* the body. As James 2: 26 says, "The body apart from the spirit [i.e. the human spirit] is dead". The body itself does not think or desire. So "the flesh" here must mean *an inward perversity of the mind*.

1 Corinthians 5: 5
"To deliver such an one unto Satan for the destruction of the flesh".

This was an exclusively Apostolic act of authority. Note, however, it is not said to have been for the destruction of the *body*, but "for the destruction of *the flesh*". The precise intent is not easy to determine; but the destruction of the *body* would have dealt only with the organ rather than the origin of the evil.

Galatians 4: 23, 29
"He who was of the bondwoman was born after the flesh . . ." "But as then he that was born after the flesh persecuted him that was born after the Spirit, even so it is now."

The "flesh" here cannot mean merely the body, nor even merely the animal appetites (as we know from the Genesis narrative). It must mean, again, a perversity of *mind*, though with somatic expression.

Galatians 5: 16, 17
"This I say then: Walk in the Spirit and ye shall not fulfil the lust of the flesh. For the flesh lusteth against the Spirit, and the Spirit against the flesh."

Here, most definitely "the flesh" is not the body, though the body is the earthly *organ* of "the flesh", as the context shows (19–21). The flesh is here said to "desire"— which is an attribute of mind; of the human *self*. The desiring is evidently earthy, evil, voluptuary, and opposed to the desire of the Spirit. The "flesh" here is plainly *a self-centred perversity within human nature.*

Galatians 5: 19, 24

"Now the works of the flesh are these [17 such are instanced] . . . And they that are Christ's crucified [aorist] the flesh with the passions and the desires."

Of the seventeen "works" of the flesh here given, about half are *mental*, not physical ("hatred", "envyings", etc.); and those which are physical are varied effects from one cause in the mind. When Paul added "They that are Christ's crucified the flesh", he certainly did not mean that they had crucified their *bodies*. It is no longer open to doubt that by "the flesh" Paul means an active perversion within the human mind; *a perversion which uses the body for self-gratification,* sometimes, though not always, grossly.

Galatians 6: 8

"For he that soweth to *his own* flesh shall of the flesh reap corruption; but he that soweth to the Spirit shall of the Spirit reap life eternal."

The reflexive pronoun, "his own", here emphasizes that "the flesh" is no mere generality, but intensively individual. See again, also, how it is the opposite of the "Spirit".

Ephesians 2: 3

"Among whom also we all had our conduct in times past, in the desires of our flesh, doing the things willed of the flesh and of the thoughts, and were by nature the children of wrath, even as others".

Our translation here is rather stricter than in the A.V. The juxtaposition of terms is significant "desires", "flesh", "willed", "thoughts", "nature". Note: the flesh both "desires" and "wills", so it cannot be the body, even though the very word, "flesh" always indicates close *connection* with the body. But crucially important here is the word, *"nature".* The flesh is shown to be, not a kind of separate "nature" within us (as is usually taught) but an active depravity in the one "nature" which we are. Mark well: both the "flesh" and the "thoughts" are *included* in the resultant words, "and were *by nature* the children of wrath".

Colossians 2: 11, 18

"In the divestment of the body of the flesh . . ." "Vainly puffed up by the mind of the flesh". (E.R.V. & A.S.V.).

There are two arresting phrases here:—(1) "The body of the flesh", (2) "The mind of the flesh". So "the flesh" is not *identical* either with "the body" or "the mind".

There we have the data. May we not deduce as follows?

(1) In these passages "the flesh" denotes figuratively an evil reality in man's *moral* being.

(2) Although non-physical, this evil reality is called "the flesh" because of its strong affinity for, and powerful influence over, our actual flesh.

(3) "The flesh" is neither the body itself nor the mind itself; but it inheres *in* the mind, and behaves *through* the body.

(4) "The flesh" is not a mind within the mind, a self within the self, or a nature within the nature; therefore it cannot be removed either wholly or partly like a parasite or an interloper or a malignant growth.

(5) The "mind" and the "flesh" are in sharp contrast yet both are identified with the "I myself" (Rom. 7: 25); so that whether it be through "the mind" or through "the flesh" it is one undivided human ego which acts.

(6) All this surely leads to the conclusion that "the flesh" must be regarded, not as a *locality* of the mind, but as a *disease*, in greater or lesser degree *throughout* the moral system.

(7) The "mind of the flesh" and the "mind of the Spirit" are not two minds in one person, but two sorts or *states* of mind. The "mind of the flesh" is the mind predominantly set on sensory, earthly gratifications. The "mind of the Spirit" is the mind predominantly set on spiritual satisfactions. Therefore, although a human mind may be either of these at any given time, it cannot be predominantly both simultaneously.

Can we find a common denominator for these varied aspects? I think we can. Is it not the *animal and selfish* in our fallen human nature?—or, perhaps, more exactly, the animal and selfish inclination, predisposition, *propensity* within us? The "flesh" is a self-centred perversity and propensity inhering in and coextensive with our moral nature.

Always in cases of this kind, the decisive test is: Does the suggested "common denominator" truly fit all the data? Does it in *this* instance? Let us quickly run through the twenty-seven texts again, and see whether, in each, we may substitute our suggested equivalent, i.e. "the animal and/or selfish propensities". I know, of course, that a cumbersome paraphrase like "the animal and/or selfish propensities" is bound to read clumsily in place of the one familiar word, "flesh". The test here, however, is not elegance, but correctness.

Romans 7: 5. "For when we were in [i.e. living in and for] our animal and selfish propensities, the motions of sins, which were by the law, did work in our members to bring forth fruit unto death."

Romans 7: 18. "For I know that in me, that is, in my animal and selfish propensities, dwelleth no good thing: for to will is present with me, but how to perform that which is good I find not."

Romans 7: 25. "So then, with the mind I myself serve the law of God; but with the animal and selfish propensities the law of sin."

Romans 8: 5, 6, 7. "For they that are [i.e. who live] according to the 'flesh' mind the things of the animal and selfish propensities, but they that are [i.e. who live] according to the Spirit, mind the things of the Spirit. For the mind [or minding of] the animal and selfish propensities is death; but the mind [or minding] of the Spirit is life and peace: because the mind of [i.e. given to] the animal and selfish is enmity towards God, for it is not subject to the law of God, neither indeed can be."

Romans 8: 8, 9. "So then, they that are in [i.e. living in and for] the animal and selfish propensities cannot please God. But ye are not in [i.e. living in and for] the animal and selfish propensities, but ye are in the Spirit, if so be that the Spirit of God dwelleth in you."

Romans 8: 12, 13. "Therefore, brethren, we owe nothing to the 'flesh', to live after the animal and selfish propensities; for if ye live according to the animal and selfish propensities ye shall die; but if ye through the Spirit put to death [such] activities of the body, ye shall live."

Romans 13: 14. "But put ye on the Lord Jesus Christ, and make not provision for the animal and selfish propensities, to fulfil the lusts thereof."

1 *Corinthians* 5: 5. "To deliver such an one unto Satan for the destruction of the flesh [in this case, the animal and selfish *indulgence* spoken of in the context] that the spirit may be saved in the day of the Lord Jesus." (We mention again, however, that the precise intent of the "flesh" here is not easy to decide finally. There are those who hold that it means the flesh *physically*.)

Galatians 4: 23, 29. "He who was of the bondwoman was born of [i.e. by the activity of] the animal or selfish; but he of the free-woman was by promise." "But as then he that was born of [i.e. by the activity of] the animal or selfish persecuted him that was born of the Spirit, even so is it now."

Galatians 5: 16, 17. "This I say then: Walk in the Spirit and ye shall not fulfil the desires of the animal and selfish. For the animal-and-selfish lusts against the Spirit, and the Spirit against the animal and selfish."

Galatians 5: 19, 24. "Now the works of the animal and selfish propensities are these [seventeen are instanced] . . . And they that are Christ's crucified [aorist] the animal and selfish with the passions and desires."

Galatians 6: 8. "For he that soweth to his animal and selfish propensities shall of the same reap corruption; but he that soweth to the Spirit shall of the Spirit reap life eternal."

Ephesians 2: 3. "Among whom also we all had our conduct once, in our animal and selfish desires, doing the things willed of our animal and selfish (will) and thoughts, and were by nature children of wrath, even as others."

Colossians 2: 11, 18. "In the divestment of the body of animal and selfish propensities . . ." "Vainly puffed up by the mind of (i.e. given to) the animal and selfish propensities."

I agree again that our circumlocutory phrase, "the animal and

His figure of light ousting darkness from a room illustrates this, but only at the cost of fatal contradiction. "The darkness disappears at once," he says. Then where is it? If it has completely gone, is not *that* eradication? No, he says, "the *tendency* to darkness persists". It is only "counteracted" for "just so long" as the introduced light abides. What, then, if the light is withdrawn? Is there a return of the darkness which was there before? No, *that* darkness went for ever. It is a *new* darkness!—which parallels with the strange eradicationist vagary, that even though our "evil old nature" may be completely "destroyed", another one may grow in its place, if we "fall from grace"!

The fault in that attractive illustration is: Neither the darkness nor the light are part of the room *itself*. The teaching of the New Testament is that something happens to the *room*, that is, to the human *self*. We think of Romans 12: 2, "Be ye [i.e. yourselves] transformed by the *renewing* of your mind"—not to mention a score of other such texts; and at once we see the poverty, the mis-focus, of the above teaching. It loses (so I believe) a Scripture truth which shines clear as cloudless morn.

What strange solace to a holiness-hungry heart! I am asked to believe that despite regeneration and sanctification my "sinful nature" remains altogether "incurable". I keep looking at the quoted words, "It is not something that has taken place in you, so that you no longer have the tendency to sin." Putting this and the other comments together, what it really says is, that *no change at all* has taken place in the nature and tendencies.

Now with my New Testament open before me, I deny the Scripturalness of such teaching. According to the Word, regeneration and inward sanctification effect a dynamic and deep-going change in *me*, that is, in my moral nature, my desires, my reactions, my inclinations. I deny that regeneration and sanctification bring no more than merely a superinduced "counteraction" without a fundamental renovation in *myself*. What the New Testament teaches is not just "counteraction", but *transformation* —transformation of heart and character through *renewal* of the mind and will.

I submit just one more illustration. Its author was a master in the art of illustration, and I could well envy his ability at appropriating lucid analogies.

"Suppose that I take a rod and attach to it a piece of lead. I drop it into a tank of water. By the law of sinking bodies, it descends; that illustrates the 'law of sin'. Now I get a piece of cork, and fasten that also to the rod; and placing it in the water I see that by the law of floating bodies, it has a tendency to ascend. But the lifting power of the cork is not strong enough to overcome the downward tendency of the lead, so that it may be kept from sinking. It rises and sinks alternately. There you have the 'up and down' life. 'I myself' by the cork serving the law of floating bodies, and 'I myself' by the lead obeying the law of sinking bodies. 'Up and down'.

"Now turn to Romans 8: 2, and we read, 'For the law of the Spirit of life in Christ Jesus *hath made me free from the law of sin and death'*. What has taken place? Let us suppose that I place my rod with the lead and the cork into a little life-belt, and put them into the tank of water. The rod [i.e. the 'I myself'] now does not sink. Why? Because it is in the life-belt. There is sufficient lifting-power in it [the life-belt] to keep it [the 'I myself'] from sinking; but it is only as it is in the life-belt that it has the benefit of that law. It is the power of a superior law counteracting the other law. The lead is not taken away, but the rod has the benefit of a stronger power so long as it abides in the life-belt."

The speaker is solicitous to demonstrate that even "while we are floating in the life-belt, the lead is there all the same"; but he thereby occasions (we speak respectfully) a wry predicament. His illustration is in two parts, with the first part supposedly picturing what regeneration does, and the second part supposedly picturing a fuller deliverance which comes by the counteracting "superior law" of the "Spirit of life in Christ Jesus". The "rod" dropped into the water, he says, is "I myself". The "piece of lead" is "the law of sin", or the evil nature which pulls me down. The "piece of cork" is regeneration. Alas, the "cork" of regeneration is not as strong as the "lead" of the old nature, so there is an "up and down" life, mainly down, because "the lifting power of the cork is not strong enough"! (Surely a poor idea of regeneration!) And not only is the regeneration "cork" insufficient, but neither the "lead" of the old life nor the "cork" of the new is the *rod* (the "I myself"), but something separate!

Strangest of all, in the *second* part of the illustration, victory over the down-pull comes by placing all three—the "rod" and the "lead" and the "cork", into a "life-belt" which represents our Lord Jesus. So now, all three—the "I myself", and the new nature, and even the *old* nature (the lead) which is "incurably evil", are "abiding" in Christ! Yet how *can* that evil old nature "abide in Christ" if it utterly *cannot* be regenerated?

One wonders that congregations have listened so credulously, and that able men have taught such a mix-up of holiness teaching, for it is not true either to Scripture or to experience. The hereditary evil in my nature is no separable lump of "lead", neither is the new life which regenerated me, in Christ, a cork-like attachment.

Take a last glance back over those two illustrations—the light in the dark room, and the rod in the tank; what do they illustrate? There is the usual confusing of "the flesh" with a so-called "old nature"; and there is the usual miserable outlook: the evil thing is linked to us till our very death, with absolutely no possibility of improvement, *"WE"* are to walk "so as to please Christ". *"WE"* —but which part of us, if the "old nature" (which is the self, the *all* that we were before regeneration) *cannot* "walk so as to please Him"? Is it only the imparted *"new* nature" (so-called) which can do so? Then it is not the real *ourselves* at all who so walk; for it is not the real human self or person which has been regenerated.

One wonders how this teaching of the rod and the lead and the cork—the self and the "old nature" and the "new nature" all "abiding" together in the life-belt, ties in with that other component of the teaching, namely, that the "old nature" is "crucified" and "dead" and "buried"! Why do such contradictions arise? It is because, in the usual holiness message, the notion of "two natures" in the believer is unscriptural; and the supposition of an inward joint-crucifixion with Christ is unscriptural; and the assumption that "the flesh" is the so-called "evil old nature" is unscriptural. Yes, however dear the brethren who have taught so, and however sincere their motive, and however honoured their names, and however much we may have loved them, we say it again with deepest respect: such teaching is *unscriptural*.

A Truer Illustration

A much truer illustration is one used by Dr. R. A. Torrey, which we quote from an address given by him at a well-known conference a few years before his death.

"There is nothing that cleanses like fire. If I have a piece of gold, and there is dirt on the outside, and I want to get the dirt off, I can take soap and water, perhaps, and wash it off. But suppose that the dirt is in the very metal itself, there is only one way to get it out—throw it into the fire! Just so with you and me." "The fire of the Holy Spirit consumes those things within us which are displeasing to God—vanity, pride, temper, personal ambition, uncleanness of all kinds."

I too believe in that refining fire of the Holy Spirit. With every fibre of conviction, I believe that the New Testament opens to us an inward purifying and refining of our whole moral nature. I believe that Charles Wesley's famous stanza not only expresses the deepest longing of all Christian hearts, but exactly echoes the accents of the New Testament itself—

> Refining Fire, go through my heart,
>   Illuminate my soul;
> Scatter Thy life through every part,
>   And sanctify the whole.

That stanza is often sung where the "old nature" doctrine is taught; yet how contradictory if (according to theory) there is a whole area inside us—the "flesh", the "old nature", which the refining Fire *cannot* sanctify? According to some, as we have seen, that "old nature" is the *larger* part of us. Indeed, a common implication is that it is stronger than the (so-called) "new nature" received at regeneration; and it must stay within us "to the very end of our earthly course". Let us be frank: if such teaching is true, then there can be no such present reality as *"entire* sanctification".

I sympathize with the sincere *motive*. Through the years there has been commendable concern not to countenance any teaching which might lessen the believer's utter *dependance* on Christ for holiness. Any view, such as "eradication", which might seem to lessen the need for continuous dependance on Him has been watchfully excluded.

But there can be right motive with wrong method. The "eradication" error has been countered by a teaching which in part is *equally* unscriptural. There seems to have been an over-zealous concern to keep that suppositionary "old nature" alive within us, to the bitter end, so as to make sure that we depend on Christ all the more. If our hearts were set entirely free from inward sin, then (supposedly) that would *lessen* our dependance on Him, impairing our praisefulness for victory, our humility as unworthy sinners, and our adoring wonder at divine grace. What a mistake! Do they need some degree of sin in *heaven* to increase trust or praise or humility or adoration? Is it not the inner working of sin which impedes and impairs our trust and praise and humility and adoration? To say that sin in *any* form or degree is contributory to trust or praise or humility or adoration is the strangest of strange daubs on *holiness* teaching!

As the preceding pages of this treatise will have evinced, I am as certain as anyone that the "eradication" theory is unscriptural; but I am just as convinced that other holiness groups will never utter the true corrective until they break free from this equally unscriptural idea that "the flesh" is an "old nature"—a kind of *lodger* inside the Christian believer, distinguishable from the human ego itself. I maintain again that according to aggregate Pauline usage, "the flesh" means our *animal and selfish propensities*. We must not lump these propensities together (not even as a convenient mode of thinking) into an entity, a core, an old "nature", or "body" of sin, with a kind of mind or will or activity of its own —else we link arms with a subtle Gnosticism, and court error. These animal and selfish propensities within us, as members of Adam's degenerate posterity, are *qualities* which inhere in our nature itself. They cannot be dealt with in bulk; but our nature itself may be refined by the Holy Spirit.

As we remarked in a reference elsewhere, possibly that word, "animal", in our definition, may seem scarcely right to someone. Does not the word, "animal" refer to the *body*? And since the body itself cannot think or desire, how can the word "animal" be used of *mental* qualities? The answer is that the term, "animal", refers just as definitely to the mind as it does to the body. Is that dog of yours a dog just because it has a dog *body*? No; it has a dog *mind*. It thinks and reasons, and desires as a dog. Even so, man is not animal only because he has a body. There is a relatedness of *mind*. Also, there can be animal *mindedness*, the mainspring of which is self-gratification of both body and mind through earthly things. That is precisely what Paul denotes in Ephesians 2: 3,— "The desires of the *flesh* and of the *mind* (or thoughts)". See also Romans 8: 6,—"The *mind* (or disposition) of the flesh".

The animals lower than man are self-centred, naturally so, but not sinfully so, for they do not have moral consciousness. In contradistinction, man is moral and spiritual, as well as animal. Therefore, as originally created, he was not self-centred, but God-centred. It is *since* then, and because "by one man sin entered the world", that human nature has become *self*-centred. This self-centredness inevitably emphasizes itself in the selfish and animal. Paul could scarcely have used a more photographic phrase for our gross selfish and animal propensities than *"the flesh"*.

Once we grasp that in Pauline usage "the flesh" means, not a so-called "old nature", but our inborn *selfish and animal urges* which we have inherited along with all the higher and nobler impulses of our total humanhood—once we grasp that, and then realise that the Holy Spirit can refine our whole moral nature, with *all* its propensities, then, as we said earlier, we have taken the first big step toward a truly New Testament doctrine of holiness.

> Whatever evils in my "self" I find,
>   There is an *inmost* longing for the good;
> Tho' treated badly, rudely pushed behind,
>   It reasserts, however oft withstood:
> No psychiatric skill can diagnose
>   This strange duality alive in me,
> This one deep "I" so subtly self-opposed,
>   This civil war from which I'm never free:
> How high I mount in upward, pure desire,
>   And wish all evil thoughts forever gone!
> How low I sink and wallow in the mire!
>   Am I not two? And yet the two still one?
>
> But if one integrated "self" am I,
>   And if the *good* is basic in my mind,
> May I not be, O "Spirit from on high,"
>   In all my thought and impulses refined?
> May not the very *spring* of wish and will
>   Be cleansed by Thine indwelling purity?
> Blest Sanctifier, come, my mind infill,
>   Transforming strife to holy harmony.
> Possess me, penetrate, restore, endue,
>   No lurking evil can Thy light abide;
> My moral being in its depths renew,
>   Let all I am, in Thee, be sanctified.

WHAT IS "CLEANSING FROM ALL SIN"?

"Antagonisms arise not because one side is entirely right, and the other entirely wrong, but because there is right on both sides for which it is worthwhile to contend, and wrong on both sides by which our vision of the other side is obscured. Our problem is not to destroy antagonisms but to transcend and transform them. It is possible to get below, rise above, or pass through them into a higher, nobler unity."

R. C. Brooks

selfish propensities", sounds strange and reads clumsily in some of these verses. It is not suggested as a translation, but as an *interpretation*. The question is: Does it give the true sense? I believe it does.

Some time ago I read a rather abstruse but learned article on Paul's use of the words, "body" and "flesh". It raised the question as to how far he was influenced by Stoic or Gnostic or contemporary Hellenistic ideas. Exploration, however, reveals little (it said) at which, personally, I am not surprised. There is an independent originality about Paul's specialised use of the word "flesh". Whatever concurrent influences may have affected him, the true way to interpret his recurring use of *any* word or phrase under guidance by the Holy Spirit is to compare carefully all its occurrences and contexts. When we do this with his use of the word "flesh", is not the meaning that which we have here abstracted? May we not repeat, with added conviction, that by the "flesh" he does *not* mean a something which is in us as a local or separable entity?

One point which the aforementioned article makes, and with which I thoroughly agree, is, that in this adapted use of the term, "flesh", Paul refers to "the whole man in his fallenness", or "the total self" in its present spoiled condition; not to a canker located somewhere in the system, but to a toxin chronically permeating the whole. This aspective yet inclusive use of the word has many parallels in common speech. We speak of a certain man as a "male", or as an "athlete", or as a "leper", or as an "alcoholic". We do not mean that the man is only partly male or partly athlete or partly leper or partly alcoholic. In each case the description is only aspective, yet from that one aspect it covers the whole man. Just so, "the flesh" aspectively describes our whole human nature in its present state of perverted animal and selfish propensities.

Whether our suggested "common denominator" may not be elegant or precise enough is of very small consequence just here. The emergent fact is: Paul's use of the word "flesh" gives no support to our usual holiness teaching that the "flesh" is an "old nature" or inner "body of sin" which as a thing in itself may be "crucified with Christ", or separately slain, or eradicated by spiritual surgery. That is the point which comes out clearly again and again.

Invalidity of Usual Teaching

The invalidity of the usual teaching, i.e. that "the flesh" is a sinful "old nature", may be seen in the peculiar contradictions which tangle it. I quote part of an editorial written by one of the ablest exponents of the holiness message. So far as I know, although it was written over fifty years ago, it still remains authentically representative of standard teaching.

"The Word of God does not teach us to expect, in this life, either the *eradication* or *improvement* of the 'flesh'. God's provision in Christ for us, in order that we may walk so as to please Him, supposes the existence, the incurableness, and the continuance of the sinful nature within us up to the very end of our earthly course."

Notice, in that quotation, the synonymizing of the "flesh" with the "sinful nature"; also that this so-called old "nature" cannot be either "eradicated" or even "improved". It is "incurable" and "within us" to our earthly end (which is indeed a gloomy picture). That sinful "nature", however, says the same beloved author, may be *counteracted*. But how? In order to show us the more vividly he uses the following effective illustration.

"When a light is introduced into a dark chamber, the darkness disappears at once. But the tendency to darkness persists; it has not been eradicated; and the room is kept illuminated simply because, and just so long as, the light counteracts the tendency. If it were possible for the room to continue in a state of illumination by passing the candle through it once, the room would not be dependent on the continued presence of the lighted candle for its light. Holiness . . . is a condition of life which must be maintained, moment by moment, through living fellowship with Christ. It is a *maintained condition*, never a *state*."

Now the distinction which the illustration draws between "condition" and "state" is merely verbal, for according to dictionary definition there is no practical difference. What is really meant here (and taught elsewhere) is that holiness is *not inwrought*; it is not something which changes *me*; it is only a "maintained" presence which is *not* the real "me", but which inwardly "*counteracts*" the "me". In saying this we are not in any way misrepresenting the writer, for in another article which we carefully quote he says, "It is *not* something that has taken place in *you*" (italics mine: and see fuller quotation below).

with, and communicated life *from*, Christ Himself. Then, as if to clinch the meaning once for all, our Lord finalized His discourse with these emphatic words:

"It is the spirit that giveth life: *THE FLESH PROFITETH NOTHING*. The words that I speak unto you are spirit and are life."

In that first line, I would fain spell the word, "spirit" with a capital S; but the context does not warrant it, and the second occurrence of "spirit" in the verse forbids it. What our Lord is finally impressing on us is, that it is the *spiritual* eating His flesh and drinking His blood which is vital; the *physical* is merely a useful symbol. I wish those words could burn in letters of flame, over every Roman Catholic altar—

"THE FLESH PROFITETH NOTHING"

With physiological literalism the Roman Catholic Mass supposedly implements our Lord's words about His flesh and blood, especially in the consecration and elevation of Host and Chalice. But the Spirit-illumined eyes of the born-again see through its sacerdotal draperies to the pathetic misconceit which in reality it is. If the bread and wine indeed become transubstantiated into the very flesh and blood of Jesus, and are necessary to salvation, then why is the wine now reserved for the priests, and denied to the laity? Why do the people receive only the bread—nay, the thinnest wafer? A special doctrine has had to be invented for twentieth-century convenience; that the benefits of the wine are now included in the wafer!

If our Lord's phraseology about His flesh and blood is to be taken literally, then why not take literally His words, "The water that I shall give him, shall become within him a fountain of *water*" (John 4: 14)? Or why not take literally our Lord's other metaphors, "I am the *door*", and "I am the *vine*" (10: 9, 15: 1)?

How *can* our Lord's words about His flesh and blood be taken literally, when in fact He now has *neither* flesh nor blood? When He rose from the dead it was not because a new supply of blood was poured through those drained arteries and veins! He now had a supernalized physique, which, although it had real corporality, was a body without blood. It was tangible; yet now, instead of earthiness, there was an ethereality which superseded all cosmic laws of gravitation and solid objects. His body was the same, yet *not* the same as before. Though similar in structure, it was different in *texture*. The Adamic flesh-and-blood body in which He suffered crucifixion was gone. *That* "flesh" was discarded; and the only blood He ever had was now poured out once for all. To think of *that* body and blood as being re-eaten and re-drunk by millions, week after week, from then until now, is the absurdest vulgarity ever conceived. Such transubstantiation would involve the preposterously impossible *re*-creation of that already often consumed body and blood in an endless repetition, also in millionfold size and quantity, so that it simply could not be our Lord's long-ago body and blood at all! Even God cannot do the *absolutely impossible*!

Is final proof required that our Lord's words are *not* to be taken literally? Then surely we have it in what He said about the bread and wine at the Last Supper (Matt. 26: 26–29), and in Paul's later comment (1 Cor. 11: 23–26) "This is My body", "This is My blood". Our Lord Jesus could *not* have meant that the bread and the wine on yonder table became His own flesh and blood; for His flesh was still on His bones, and His blood was still in His veins. Nor could He possibly have eaten His own flesh and drunk His own blood from that loaf and cup. The very fact that He spoke the mystic words *then* and not after His resurrection, confirms the obvious, i.e. that the bread and wine were purely symbols. The accompanying fact, also, of His connecting that Supper with the Passover and the old Covenant, confirms it. And especially so does His explanation: "This is My blood of the New Covenant, which is shed for many, for . . ." Well, for what?— for the liquid imparting of His life to those who drink? No; but "for *THE REMISSION OF SINS*"!

Lastly, see Paul's interpretative verdict, in First Corinthians 11: 26, "As often as ye eat this bread, and drink this cup, ye do . . ." Well, what?—eat His body and drink His blood? No; but, "Ye *PROCLAIM THE LORD'S DEATH TILL HE COME*". That is the last word of Scripture on the matter: a feast of *REMEMBRANCE* (24, 25) and of *ANTICIPATION* (26). The bread is *only* bread. The wine is *only* wine. Both are symbols *only*, though, as such, infinitely meaningful.

Thus, nowhere, either in Gospels or Epistles, is there *any* teaching that the blood of our Lord is communicable. Any such

WHAT IS "CLEANSING FROM ALL SIN"?

One of the best-loved texts in the New Testament is I John I: 7, "But if we walk in the light, as He [God] is in the light, we have fellowship one with another, and the blood of Jesus Christ His Son *cleanseth us from all sin.*"

The unwaning wonder and preciousness of such an assurance can scarcely be exaggerated. It is the kind of text one delights to ponder devotionally but shrinks from handling contentiously. I regret, therefore, that in this present study it must be treated somewhat polemically.

The fact is, that in the competition of holiness theories, I John I: 7 is a major pivot. The three battle-centres have been: (1) What is the meaning of Romans 6: 6? (2) What does Paul mean by "the flesh"? (3) What is the cleansing from "*all* sin" in I John I: 7?

The Usual Teaching

The usual teaching is that the clause, "cleanseth from all sin", means *inward* cleansing. Such is the teaching of *all* eradicationists, and of most counteractionists. The former exult in the "all", claiming that it means utter ablution from inhering pollution. The counteractionists find the "all" awkward—though not confessedly so, and become self-contradictory (as it seems to me) in their circumflexions around it.

Everywhere, we find this idea generally accepted, that I John I: 7 refers to an *inward* cleansing. John Wesley deliberates:

"Now it is evident, the apostle here speaks of a deliverance wrought in this world: for he saith not, The blood of Christ *will* cleanse (at the hour of death, or in the day of judgment) but it '*cleanseth*', at the present time, us living Christians 'from all sin'. And it is equally evident, that if any sin remain we are not cleansed from all sin. If *any* unrighteousness remain in the soul, it is not cleansed from *all* unrighteousness" (*Plain Account*, p. 24).

William Booth, the famous founder-general of the Salvation Army, gloried in being "of the household and lineage" of Wesley as to holiness doctrine. In his clear-cut way he asks, "What is the faith that sanctifies?" and answers: "It is that act of simple trust which, on the authority of Christ's word, says, *"The blood of Jesus Christ does NOW cleanse me from all inward sin, and makes me pure in heart before Him.'"* (*Holy Living*, p. 22.)

We need not multiply quotations. A couple from "Counter-action" voices will suffice to show that even where the cleansing is not taught in the eradicationist sense, it is likewise assumed to be *inward*. I quote from a printed address: "There are regions in our being, far beyond the ken of conscience, which constitute us sinners, still needing the blood which *goes on* cleansing." A dignified further pronouncement occurs in the same volume from a beloved leader who is now no longer with us. He speaks out of an evidently deep and thoughtful conviction.

"This cleansing cannot mean only pardon: it must refer to purity also. . . . A purity of heart beyond what our natural thoughts could conceive is open to those who are willing to claim it, through the blood of Christ alone: and we are here to testify to this most blessed power of that blood."

The Witness of the Hymnbooks

The various hymnbooks, also, plentifully endorse and vivify this prevailing idea, that cleansing by the precious blood of Christ is an *inward* cleansing of the believer. Miss Frances Ridley Havergal's well-known lines come readily to mind

> I am trusting Thee for cleansing
> In the crimson flood;
> Trusting Thee to make me holy
> By Thy blood.

Or, picking almost at random from the Sankey Hymnbook, 1200 edition, we find number 133 saying,

> I know Thy precious blood
> Has power to make me clean.
> Oh, take my sinful heart,
> And wash away its sin.

Going away back to Charles Wesley, we find the same concept again and again:

> I cannot wash my heart
> But by believing Thee,
> And waiting for Thy blood to impart
> The spotless purity.

One verse must suffice to represent the vigorous hymnbook of the Salvation Army. It is number 84 in a fairly recent edition from the International Headquarters, London, England.

> It is the Blood that washes white,
> That makes me pure within;
> That keeps the inward witness right,
> And cleanses from all sin.

A well-known conference hymn book comes to us with Horatio Bonar's earnest lines:

> Purge Thou my sin away,
> Wash Thou my soul this day
> Lord, make me clean.

> Lord, let the cleansing blood,
> Blood of the Lamb of God,
> Pass o'er my soul.

I will not be so unkind as to pass any criticism on the literary quality of the verses which we are here requisitioning. They are quoted for one purpose only, i.e. to represent a common concept. I confess to some inward recoil, however, from such histrionicisms as *"plunging"* in relation to our Saviour's precious blood:

> The cleansing Blood I see, I see!
> I plunge, and oh, it cleanseth me!

Eradication by Ablution

Some of the hymns which sing of this inward cleansing through the Blood unhesitatingly proclaim an *utter expurgation* of sin:

> In new creation now I rise;
> I hear the speaking blood!
> It speaks! polluted nature dies!
> Sinks 'neath the cleansing flood!

It is of peculiar interest to notice how unthinkingly (or with what willing blindness) counteractionists slip into singing outright eradicationist hymns about cleansing of the believer's inmost nature from *all* sin! Demarcations between eradication and non-eradication theory, although strongly marked in platform expositions, somehow become baptismally submerged in the devotional flow of the hymnbook. For instance, how strange to find anti-eradicationists singing,

> Lord Jesus, let nothing unholy remain,
> Apply Thine own blood and *extract ev'ry stain*.
> By faith for my cleansing I see Thy blood flow;
> Now wash me and I shall be *whiter than snow*.

Or what about another number?

> So wash me, Thou, without, within
> Or purge with fire, if that must be;
> No matter how, if only sin
> *Die out* in me; *die out* in me.

There is no getting away from it: such hymns envisage, not only an inward cleansing by the blood of Christ, but an *utter* cleansing.

To my own mind, let me say it frankly but cordially, such teaching is plainly as self-contradictory in its gyrations around 1 John 1: 7 as in its treatment of Romans 6: 6. It says that through co-crucifixion with Christ I become "dead indeed" unto sin, yet I must never delude myself into thinking that in actual experience my (so-called) "old nature" can *ever* be dead! As for 1 John 1: 7, I may be "cleansed from *all* sin", yet I am never *actually* all clean; for though my "new nature" (it is said) *never needs* cleansing, my "old nature" can *never* be cleansed. My own names for these two "explanations" are: (1) the "dead-yet-alive" theory, and (2) the "cleansed-yet-never-clean" theory.

Is it Scriptural?

But is this idea of inward cleansing by the blood of Christ truly Scriptural? I do not think so. Does 1 John 1: 7 really teach that our Saviour's blood cleanses us from sin *inwardly*? My answer is, No. I believe that the cleansing is *judicial*, not internal, and that by "sin" the text means sin as *guilt*, not sin as an innate corruptness. Let me not be misunderstood: I believe in the innate corruptness of our fallen human nature; I believe also that through Christ, by the Holy Spirit, God has provided for our inward cleansing and renewing. What I am here maintaining is that the inward cleansing is not effected either by a literal or a figurative application of our Saviour's blood; and that 1 John 1: 7 does not teach so.

In thus frankly declaring myself on this matter, I do not feel so much of a "lone wolf" as I did in my repudiating the usual teaching on Romans 6. I am in good company, with outstanding Evangelicals like R. A. Torrey and Bishop Handley Moule sharing the same view. The decisive test is, "What saith the Scripture?" That shall be our enquiry just here.

OLD TESTAMENT DATA

So, we turn first to the Old Testament, and our question is: Do we find anywhere in its pages that cleansing is ever effected by blood? The word, "blood", in our Old Testament represents a Hebrew word which occurs 341 times (including adjectival and compound forms). It refers 100 times to Israel's religious sacrifices; 30 times to dietary, hygienic, or social regulations; 23 times to the law of the *goel*, or "avenger of blood"; while the remainder are miscellaneously incidental to historical and prophetical passages. Never once is it used of either outwardly or inwardly *cleansing* a person.

Always, in the actual cleansing of a person or object, the cleansing element is not blood, but *water*; and the cleansing act is not sprinkling, but *bathing*. Blood is not a cleansing liquid for purposes of ablution, nor is mere sprinkling an adequate cleansing measure. I freely grant, of course, that although blood-sprinkling in itself cannot cleanse, it may *represent* cleansing in a judicial sense; yet even then it never represents *internal* cleansing.

Use of the Word, "Cleansed".

What, then, about those passages where the word, "*cleanse*" is used in connection with blood-sprinkling? There are nine such instances: Exodus 29: 36, Leviticus 12: 7 and 14: 7, 14, 25, 52, and 16: 19 (with 30), and Ezekiel 43: 18, 20.

Take Exodus 29: 36. It prescribes the ritual for the consecration of Aaron and his sons. They and their priestly garments, and the altar itself, were to be sprinkled by the sacrificial blood. Yet Aaron and his sons must be already "washed" with *water* (4). So, the blood-sprinkling was not for their *personal* cleansing. It was a symbolic removing of something *between* them and Jehovah, i.e. their *guilt* as sinners. The blood was that of "atonement" (36).

So is it with the five references in Leviticus 12 and 14, to the cleansing rites for childbirth and leprosy. The actual cleansing of the *person* precedes the symbolic cleansing by the blood-sprinkling (see 14: 8). Moreover, eight times that word, "covering" (*kaphar*[1]) occurs; and nine times "trespass", or "guilt" (see E.R.V.), indicating again that the blood-sprinkling symbolized cleansing from *guilt*, not from sin inwardly.

But the most decisive witness is chapter 16, which specifies the rituals for Israel's annual "Day of Atonement". Fifteen times *kaphar* ("covering up")[1] occurs. Here, too, note the plural, "sins" (16, 21, 30, 34). That solemn ceremony had to do with the "covering" of "transgressions". The blood-sprinkling symbolized cleansing from *guilt*, not from an innate sin-condition. Key verses are 21, 30, 34,

"And Aaron shall lay both his hands upon the head of the live goat, and confess over him all the *INIQUITIES* of the children of Israel, and all their *TRANSGRESSIONS*, even all their *SINS*" (21).

"For on this day shall atonement [a covering] be made for you, to *CLEANSE* you from all your *SINS*; and ye shall be clean *BEFORE JEHOVAH*" (30).

So, beyond a fleck of doubt, the blood-sprinkling had to do, not with innate sin, but with "iniquities" and "transgressions". The cleansing, or covering up and putting away, was *judicial*. It "removed"[2] *guilt*—not sin within man, but guilt "*before Jehovah*". So far as personal ablution was concerned, it is noticeable that those who took part in the ritual had to be cleansed *in water* (4, 24, 26, 28).

[1] Translated as "atonement" in our King James Version.
[2] See verses 8, 10, in A.S.V. It almost goes without saying that no mere sprinkling, whether of blood or any other liquid could have cleansed (or have been *meant* to cleanse) either the altar or any other object. It is not sprinkling, but *ablution*, which cleanses anything. The fact that the sprinkling was *seven* times indicates that it was symbolical. The altar itself was neither cleaner nor otherwise after the sprinkling; but it was *symbolically* cleansed from "the uncleannesses of the children of Israel" (19).

Is further proof needed? Here is a remarkable fact: from the inception of the Israel theocracy (Ex. 19) to the end of the Pentateuch, the word "sin" (translating variant forms of the Hebrew *chata*) occurs 63 times, and in every instance it means sin as an *act* or as *acts*; never once as an inward condition. The compound, "sin-offering", occurs 98 times, and without exception it concerns sins *committed*, not inward depravity. Thus, throughout Israel's sacrificial system, "cleansing" by blood-sprinkling is solely judicial; it is the "covering" or "removing" of *guilt*. About 45 times in the Old Testament we read of cleansing by *water*; but never once of washing in blood.

Therefore, if we pay due regard to the evidence supplied by the *Old* Testament in this connection, we surely must come to the *New* Testament predisposed to find similar teaching in relation to the shed blood of our dear Lord.

NEW TESTAMENT DATA

In the New Testament the blood of Christ is mentioned 39 times (omitting Col. 1: 14, as doubtful). Of these, six are simply incidental historical references having no bearing on our present enquiry. The remaining 33 classify as follows. By the blood:

1. "Remission"—Matt. 26: 28, Heb. 10: 19 (with 18).
2. "Propitiation"—Rom. 3: 25.
3. "Redemption"—Eph. 1: 7, Heb. 9: 12, 1 Pet. 1: 19.
4. "Reconciliation"—Eph. 2: 13 (cp. 16), Col. 1: 20.
5. "Justification"—Rom. 5: 9.
6. "Purchase"—Acts 20: 28, Rev. 5: 9.
7. "Sanctification"—Heb. 10: 29, 13: 12.
8. "New covenant"—Mark 14: 24, Luke 22: 20, 1 Cor. 11: 25, 27, Heb. 13: 20.
9. "Sprinkling" seal—Heb. 12: 24, 1 Pet. 1: 2 (cp. Heb. 10: 22).
10. "Witness" to God—1 John 5: 6, 8 (with 11), Rev. 12 : 11.
11. Communion symbol—John 6: 53, 54, 55, 56, 1 Cor. 10: 16.
12. "Cleansing" from sin—Heb. 9: 14, 1 John 1: 7, Rev. 1: 5, 7: 14.

The first 10 classes of these texts ("remission", "propitiation", etc.) all pertain either to the *judicial* or to some other equally *objective* aspect of our Lord's shed blood. That is true even of number 7 ("Sanctification"), for it is not sanctification in the inward sense, but from *guilt*, being linked back to the *covenant* blood and sin-offering of Exodus 24: 8, 29: 12. And so it is with number 9 ("Sprinkling"), for its two texts are allusions to the Mosaic blood-sprinkling as an objective token of *covenant* and removal of *guilt*.[1]

The Blood as a Symbol

Only in groups 11 and 12 do we find texts which might seem to imply an effect of our Lord's blood *within* us. These we must examine carefully. Four of them occur in John 6, in our Lord's great discourse on the Living Bread.

"Verily, verily, I say unto you: Except ye eat the flesh of the Son of Man, and drink His blood, ye have not life in yourselves" (53).
"He that eateth My flesh and drinketh My blood hath eternal life; and I will raise him up at the last day" (54).
"For My flesh is food indeed, and My blood is drink indeed" (55).
"He that eateth My flesh and drinketh My blood abideth in Me, and I in Him" (56).

What did our Lord mean by this drinking of His blood? He could *not* have meant it literally; for if there was one thing more than another gravely and repeatedly forbidden to the Jews, it was to imbibe blood (Lev. 17: 10–16, 3: 17, 7: 26, etc.). Our Lord meant it *spiritually*. The two participle clauses in verse 56 lead to this:

"The one eating My flesh and drinking My blood [is he who] *abideth in Me, and I in Him.*"

That such was His meaning is confirmed by the next verse (57) which is an impletion of it:

"As the living Father sent Me, and I live because of the Father [i.e. His living in Me], so the one eating Me, he also shall live because of Me."

In other words, as our Lord lived by appropriative communion *with*, and communicated life *from*, the indwelling Father, so should the believer live in new spiritual life by appropriative communion

[1] There is indeed, one text which *does* speak of inward "sprinkling". See Hebrews 10: 22. But again it is judicial, i.e. sprinkling "from [condemnation by] an evil *CONSCIENCE*", which at once refers to *guilt*. See wording also, and context.

idea is physiologically unthinkable as well as Scripturally disqualified. John 6: 53–56 is to be interpreted *spiritually*.

"Cleansing" by the Blood

This brings us to those last remaining verses, which speak of *cleansing* through our Saviour's blood. Outside of 1 John 1: 7 there are three: Hebrews 9: 14, Revelation 1: 5 and 7: 14.

Hebrews 9: 14 reads: "How much more shall the blood of Christ . . . cleanse your conscience from dead works?" So this is a judicial cleansing of the *"conscience"* from "dead *works*", not an inward cleansing of the nature. The blood of Christ answers for me, wiping out condemnation, and relieving conscience by making me judicially clean. That the cleansing here meant is indeed *judicial*, not internal, is settled by the verses immediately preceding and following. Verse 13 parallels it with the Old Testament *"sprinkling"* of blood and ashes (Num. 19) which, as we saw, was solely judicial. Verse 15 refers it to "redemption from under *transgressions*"—again the legal aspect.

Turning next to Revelation 1: 5, we find: "Unto Him that loved us, and washed us from our sins in His own blood. . . ." Both E.R.V. and A.S.V. alter "washed" to "loosed", as more truly representing manuscript evidence. But in either case the cleansing or loosing is from *"sins"* (plural); not from sin inwardly.

The only other text is Revelation 7: 14, "These are they that come out of the great tribulation, and they washed their robes, and made them white in the blood of the Lamb." This cannot refer to a present inward cleansing, for the following reasons:

(1) It refers to what happens in heaven, not on earth.

(2) It refers to something yet future, not now occurring.

(3) It is apocalyptic symbol, not definitive statement.

(4) "Robes" symbolize the outward rather than the inward; dignity, priesthood, sonship (see O.T. references to robes of kings and priests: also Luke 15: 22).

(5) In Revelation 6: 11, the "white robes" are *"given"* to the disembodied martyrs in *heaven*.

(6) In chapter 19: 8, the robes of "fine linen, bright and pure" are the "righteous *acts* of the saints."

(7) The verb "washed" is aorist, indicating, *not* a continuous cleansing (as in 1 John 1: 7) but a completed past act.

(8) The washing white of those robes was in "the blood of the *LAMB*", the blood poured out in *propitiation*, not for cleansing of the *heart*, but for cleansing from *guilt*—as was so with *every* sacrificed lamb of Old Testament typology.

What then of 1 John 1: 7?

What, then, of 1 John 1: 7, "the *blood* of Jesus Christ, His Son, *cleanseth us from all sin*"? Have we not shown that neither the Old Testament nor the New gives any warrant for interpreting it as an *inward* cleansing? According to the whole force of Scripture evidence, 1 John 1: 7 means a cleansing from sin in the sense of *guilt* and defilement before *God*. Moreover, if we look at the wording and the context, we find still further confirmation of that.

Take that verb, "cleanseth". It has an augmented preciousness by reason of its being in the present tense, which indicates a *continuous* cleansing. Yet the very provision of continuous cleansing presupposes a continuing *need* of it, that is, of continuing *sin*.

Now we are not just argumentatively hair-splitting, we are carefully distinguishing between things which really differ, when we remark that being *cleansed* is not the same as being *clean*. That which is really clean *cannot* be cleansed, for there is nothing in it to cleanse. Also, conversely, that which needs continuously cleansing cannot in itself be really clean. So, then, if the word, "sin", in 1 John 1: 7 means (as most teach, but which I deny) our *inward condition* of sinfulness as members of Adam's fallen race, then this very text which is supposed to promise purity of heart teaches the opposite; for it teaches our need of continual *cleansing* from continual *sin*.

But then that immediately raises the point: *does* that word, "sin", in 1 John 1: 7, mean an inward condition? I claim that it does *not*. This is one of those instances where, according to strict grammatical interpretation, *either* of two translations may accurately transmit the Greek original. We can read it either as "*all* sin", or as "*every* sin". If we translate it as "*all* sin", then it may well seem to mean an inward *condition* of sin; whereas if we translate it as "*every* sin", it plainly refers only to a *committing* of sin. The big difference is between sin-condition and sin-commission. Practically all the controversy on 1 John 1: 7 has arisen from that translation, "all", which, to my own judgment, is unfortunate and misleading.

Over and over again, in our New Testament, that Greek word (*pas*) rendered as "all", in 1 John 1: 7, is translated as "every". There are some places, also, with exactly the same grammatical construction as in 1 John 1: 7 (preposition *apo* and genitive case), where it *must* be translated as "every". For instance:

Acts 2: 5, "Devout men from *every* nation under heaven"
2 Tim. 4: 18, "The Lord will deliver me from *every* evil work"

Once we change the word, "all", to "every", in 1 John 1: 7, not only is the precious text rescued from mishandling by eradicationist theorizers, but it at once harmonizes with the whole teaching of Scripture concerning the sacrificial blood of our Lord and its varied efficacies on our behalf. But if, contrariwise, we insist on the translation *"all* sin", so as to teach thereby an *inward* ablution from sin *utterly*, we are in head-on collision with the very next verse, which reads, "If we say that we have no sin, we deceive ourselves."

Finally, let me clinch the matter by mentioning the little noticed but powerfully significant circumstance that the words, "cleanseth us from all sin", in 1 John 1: 7, are a practically verbatim quotation from Leviticus 16: 30 as translated from the Hebrew into Greek by the famous Septuagint Version, in the third century B.C. That pre-Christian Greek version of the Old Testament is still used in some of the Eastern churches, and is often of great importance in determining the sense of an old Testament passage. Well, away back there, in that third century B.C., John's very words may be seen in the Septuagint's Greek rendering of Leviticus 16: 30—*"cleanse you from all your sins"*; same word for "cleanse"; same word for "all"; same word for "sins"; and the same grammatical construction. John knew that verse well, and knew he was using its very words. Surely, then, he had that Old Testament "day of Atonement" in mind as he wrote its New Testament counterpart, in 1 John 1: 7. And if so, then he most certainly meant cleansing from sin judicially, not internally. Is it not clear, then, that we ought to substitute the word *"every"*, in place of "all", so as to accord with the plural, "sins", in Leviticus 16: 30?

Conclusions

So, from the gathered data, we draw the following conclusions. First, those precious words, "the blood of Jesus Christ cleanseth", do not mean His blood *literally*—any more than the *wood* is meant literally when we are said to be saved by His "cross", or the *fire* is meant literally when we speak of the Holy Spirit as the "refining fire". The "blood" is to be interpreted metonymically, that is, as representing the whole saving sacrifice by which we are cleansed.

Second: in line with the full, clear witness of Biblical teaching as to "sprinkling" and "cleansing" by sacrificial blood, 1 John 1: 7 simply cannot mean an inward cleansing of our nature; but it *does* mean a complete and continuous cleansing from all the *guilt* of sin; and from all the *stain*, or defilement, caused by our sinning, as seen by the holy eyes of God.

Third: for these reasons the doctrine of an inward cleansing from our hereditary sin-condition cannot be founded on 1 John 1: 7. The Gospel does indeed bring us inward renewal and cleansing, but 1 John 1: 7 is *not* one of those texts which teach it.

Fourth: the eradicationist position, therefore, is unmistakably wrong in making 1 John 1: 7 teach an utter expurgation of sin— with all sinward desires and inclinations thereby deterged from our nature. Equally erring is that suggested alternative which teaches from it this inward cleansing, yet reduces the force of the wording so as to gainsay eradicationism.

The truth is, that both Romans 6: 6 and 1 John 1: 7 need lifting right out of further discussion so far as *experiential* holiness is concerned. In both cases, wording and context alike indicate so, as we have shown. It is the common misinterpretation and misapplication of those two texts which, more than any other factor, has *caused* the long-continuing controversy and division in holiness teaching. That division is the biggest and saddest of all obstacles in the teaching of Christian holiness; and it will never be healed so long as those two texts continue to be misinterpreted in the way which we have discussed in these pages.

From wrong interpretation has come wrong theory; and wrong *holiness* theory has begotten false hope, strange frustration, later disillusionment, and sometimes heart-breaking recoil.

The New Testament, like the Old, teaches that the true agent of cleansing is *water* (John 13: 5, Heb. 10: 22, etc.); and this is beautifully spiritualized in Ephesians 5: 25, "Christ also loved the Church, and gave Himself up for it; that He might sanctify it, having *CLEANSED* it by *THE WASHING OF WATER WITH THE WORD*". Similarly, in Titus 3: 5, 6, we find, "According to His mercy He saved us, through the *WASHING OF REGENER-ATION AND RENEWING OF THE HOLY SPIRIT, WHICH HE POURED OUT UPON US RICHLY THROUGH JESUS CHRIST OUR SAVIOUR.*"

Just as all those Old Testament blood-sprinklings which typified cleansing from *guilt* are fulfilled in the precious blood of Christ, so all those type-anticipations of personal cleansing, such as the cleansing water of the laver (Ex. 30: 18, Heb. 10: 22) are fulfilled by the Holy Spirit and His renewing ministry *within* us by the Word.

THE WORD OF TWO SCHOLARS

"My belief is, that in this case [1 John 1: 7] the true meaning of the verse has been missed by learned and pious expositors." "I hold that the words [of 1 John 1: 7] refer to the cleansing of the guilty, from the point of view of *law*. . . . I hold that the words do *not* refer to subjective results *within* the believer."

Bishop Handley C. G. Moule.
Pamphlet, *The Cleansing Blood*, 1889.

"In Bible usage, cleansing by blood is cleansing from *guilt*. Through the shed blood of Christ, all who walk in the light are cleansed continu-ously—every hour and minute—from all the guilt of sin. There is absolutely no sin *upon them*. There may still be sin *in them*: it is not the blood, but the living Christ and the Holy Spirit who deal with that."

R. A. Torrey.

CAN WE EVER BE DEAD TO SIN?

"If one's view of sin were only shallow enough, sinless perfection would not be an impossible attainment."

Steven Barabas

"I have found a far higher standard maintained by believers who intelligently reject the eradication theory than among those who accept it. Quiet, unassuming Christians, who know their Bibles and their own hearts too well to permit their lips to talk of sinlessness and perfection in the flesh, who nevertheless are characterized by intense devotion to the Lord Jesus Christ, love for the word of God, and holiness of life and walk."

H. A. Ironside

CAN WE EVER BE DEAD TO SIN?

THE usual holiness platforms have taught that through sanctification we may become inwardly dead to sin. Proponents of the eradication theory have insisted that this is effected by a ripping out of inborn sin-fibres from our nature. With politic caution others teach: *You* may be dead to *sin*, but *sin* is never dead to *you*; which, however, is an obscurantism—like saying to a phthisis victim, *"You* are dead to the tuberculosis, but the disease is not dead to *you"*; or saying to a corpse, "You are now dead to the physical world, but it is not dead to *you"*. Tested pragmatically, that yes-but-no expedient is an empty artifice. When you are dead to something, there is such utter absence of response to it that *it*, also, has become dead to *you*.

Both these ideas of death to sin are unsound from a Scriptural viewpoint, as further appeal will confirm. Paul's mighty deliberation on the matter occupies Romans 6 and 7 and 8. In those three chapters there are *three* deaths:

> ch. 6   Death to sin.
>
> ch. 7   Death to the law.
>
> ch. 8   Death to the flesh.

"Dead to Sin"

We have seen how clear is the evidence that our death to sin, by identification with Christ, as taught in Romans 6, is not experiential but *judicial*. Unless what we have said can be refuted, then the idea of an *inward* death to sin, by a simulated crucifixion with Christ, should be discarded, for it certainly is not taught anywhere else in the New Testament.

Also, we must reject, as equally illusory, the fond notion that what happened long ago on Calvary, in the judicial reckoning of God, is now (as the saying goes) to be "made real in you and me"—

so that we are now to "reckon" ourselves inwardly "dead indeed unto sin". As we have shown, the "reckoning" in Romans 6: 11 is *not* that we now *become* dead, but that we *became* dead to sin "once for all" (ἐφάπαξ). Clearly our death with Christ *then* was solely judicial; and by it we are cleared from all condemnation, to live a new life through "the Spirit of life in Christ Jesus".

There is no need to argue further into this again here, though maybe a supplemental reminder will not come amiss that the usual misconstrue of Romans 6 throws a noose of self-contradictions round its own neck. The way in which that theoretic "old nature" may supposedly be alternatingly on and off the Cross, transfixed yet never executed; "dead indeed" yet still "warring in my members"; "buried with Christ" yet daily dodging in and out of the grave; is a jack-in-a-box performance beyond compare.

What scufflings of doughty debaters might have been avoided if only Paul's road-signs to holiness had been more carefully observed just where they are posted! How sure is Dr. Asa Mahan, for instance, that he is on the right road, and that all who differ have forked off into error! (Yet what rich experience of Christ he had!)

"All admit that the terms, 'sin that dwelleth in me', 'the body of sin', the 'old man', the 'law of sin and death', the 'body of this death', and 'lusts which war in the members', mean the same thing, and constitute what is called 'indwelling sin'."

Yet four of those six phrases do *not* refer to "indwelling sin". Paul's road-signs are misread. It is Dr. Mahan himself who slants away on a wrong road, from which he reproaches as "unscriptural" all who do not travel thereon!

"What then do the Scriptures mean by such expressions as these— 'that the body of sin might be destroyed'; 'our old man is crucified with Him'? No dogma can be more *unscriptural* than that of the non-destruction of the body of sin in believers."—*Autobiography*, p. 344.

Yet with all respect to that starchy monopoly of interpretation, have we not shown that neither Romans 6 nor any other New Testament passage teaches sin as a "body" of evil in us, much less that it can be "destroyed" as such?

If in these studies I have harped recurrently on that one string it is only because the garbled treatment of Romans 6 is the mischief-centre. Between eradicationists, counteractionists and

others, that chapter has become an *enfant terrible*, whereas Paul intended it to be our out-and-out "Declaration of Independence" from all *judicial* bondage to sin.

"Dead to the Law"

In just the same judicial way, chapter 7 teaches our death to *the Law*. Verse 4 says, "Wherefore, my brethren, ye also *were made dead* to the Law through the body of Christ." Most expositors seem to see *four* "laws" in the passage:

1.	The law of Moses	Verses 7, 8, 9, 12, 22 and others
2.	The law of sin	"The law of sin which is in my members" (23)
3.	The law of the mind	"Warring against the law of my mind" (23)
4.	The law of the Spirit	"The law of the Spirit of life in Christ Jesus" (8: 2).

My own persuasion is that numbers 2 and 3 are *not* separate "laws", but aspects of the one law given through Moses. I incline to think that an observant halting at the eighteen occurrences of the word, "law", from verse 4 onwards will show that it is the law of Moses each time. What then does Paul mean by the "law of *sin*" (23)? Do not verses 5, 7, 8 and 9 explain? They show us *how* the Law of Moses became a "law of sin and death".

"Sinful passions, which were [provoked] through the Law [of Moses] wrought in our members to bring forth fruit unto death" (5). So the Law of Moses *thus* became a "law of sin and death"!

"I had not known sin, except through the Law: for I had not known coveting except the Law had said, Thou shalt not covet; but sin, finding occasion, wrought in me through the commandment all manner of coveting. . . . And the commandment which was unto life, I found to be unto death" (7–9). So, again, the holy Law of Moses became a "law of sin and death"!

Thus, when Paul adds, in chapter 8: 2, "The law of the Spirit of life in Christ Jesus made me free from the law of sin and death", he does not mean free from some inner principle of sin in our nature, as is generally supposed, but a liberation from the Law of Moses which had *become* a "law of sin and death". If even a fleck of doubt should remain as to that, the very next verse surely removes it: "For what the law [obviously Moses' Law] could not do in that it was weak through the flesh. . . ."

In verse 23, where Paul draws a contrast between "the law of my mind" and "the law of sin which is in my members", he does not mean two different "laws" working within him, but the two *effects* of the one Mosaic Law upon the higher and lower reaches of his nature, respectively. To the mind, the higher and spiritual part of him, it is "the Law of *God*" (22). To the flesh, the animal and selfish propensity within him, it has become "the Law of *sin*" —as he has shown.

I refrain from detailing this any further here, for the very explicating of it on paper gives it a discouraging appearance of complicatedness. The big, central fact in chapter 7 is, that by identification with our vicarious Sinbearer, we are forever *dead* to the Law and all its claims upon us (verse 6).

Death to "the Flesh"

A collating of the twenty-seven verses where Paul uses that expression, "the flesh", of the present sin-bent in human nature shows that he never uses it (as already discussed) to mean an "old nature", or aggregate entrenchment of sin within us. No, he means our inborn animal and selfish urges which we have inherited along with all the higher and nobler impulses of our total humanhood; reactions, responses, propensities of our human nature itself in its present condition. The momentous question is: Can we become dead to *them*? Or can they die so as no longer to exist within us?

Now unless we are irrecoverably hallucinated by holiness errors such as those which these pages have disapproved, the crucial significance of the following fact will not be lost upon us. Unlike Romans 6 and 7, with their once-for-all (ἐφάπαξ) judicial death to sin and to the law through the all-including death of Christ, chapter 8, which now deals with "the flesh", teaches *no* such complete death. Only too eagerly we agree that it *does* teach a putting to death, but it is by a markedly different mode from that in chapters 6 and 7.

Romans 8: 1–13 is Paul's most notable paragraph on "the flesh". The phrase itself occurs in it thirteen times (see E.R.V. or A.S.V.); and the concluding comment is:

"So then, brethren, we are debtors, not to the flesh, to live after the flesh: for if ye live after the flesh, ye must die; but if by the Spirit ye *PUT TO DEATH* the doings of the body, ye shall live."

So there is a "putting to death". But what are those "doings of the body" which are to be "put to death"? Paul cannot mean the involuntary processes and normal functions of the body. *They* are not sinful; neither can they be "put to death" except by putting the body itself to death. Clearly, Paul means those uses of the body which are activated by the animal and selfish propensities within us. It is those animal and selfish activities *through* the body which are to be "put to death"; and Paul simply calls them "the doings of the body" because the body visibly expresses them. Note the following five implications in Paul's words.

1. This death to "the flesh", or inborn animal appetites, is *not* a death which our Lord representatively died *for* us, as He died for us judicially to Sin and the Law. It is a death which we ourselves bring about, for the text says, "If *ye* put to death. . . ."

2. This death is *not* a completed death in the past, as in chapters 6 and 7, but a *continual* putting to death in the present; for the verb is in the present tense.

3. This death is effected, *not* by union with our Lord in *His* death, but by an inward union with Him in His risen *life*; for the text says, "If ye through the *Spirit* put to death. . . ." i.e. through "the Spirit of life in Christ Jesus".

4. This death is *not* either a final or a partial death to some supposed lump-evil in our human being, but a successive putting to death of distributed *activities*, or "doings".

5. This death is *not* an absolute death, such as is our judicial death to sin and the Law, through identification with the death of Christ; it is a death conditional upon our living (as the text says) "*by the Spirit*".

From those five factors we may deduce what this "putting to death" of flesh activities actually is in individual experience. We put them to death when the *will* says an implacable "No" to them even though unsanctified desire still lurks in the heart; and more so when the heart itself turns away unresponsively; and still more so when will and heart and the very "spirit of our mind" (Eph.

4: 23) unite in an *aversion* to them. In that way those "doings" of the "flesh" through the body are "put to death".

Now obviously that "putting to death" is not a death to sin *totally*. It is a recurrent "putting to death" of *"doings"*—and, by involvement, of the *urges* which lead to them. Let me speak from my own experience. There are forms of sin which used to awaken vexatious response within me, but now (so far as I can tell) they have become utterly dead to me. Not only has my will always been resolutely set against them, but whatever desire there used to be toward them has become extinct, and my whole being seems dead to them. But am I therefore now dead to *sin*? No, alas. Why? Because, as I become dead to *some* forms of it, sin seeks to awaken responses within me to other and subtler forms of in-veiglement.

As the years go by, or as our spiritual growth progresses, the enticements and innuendoes of temptation usually follow the order of Lucifer's threefold approach to our Lord Jesus (Matt. 4: 1–11). First there is appeal to the *physical* ("Command that these stones be made bread"). Then there is the appeal to the mental ("Cast Thyself down", i.e. in self-display to win popular following). Then there is direct appeal to the *spiritual* ("All these will I give thee, if thou wilt worship me", i.e. your high goal shall be gained by a quicker, easier way). That, I repeat, is the usual order. As we become dead to *some* forms of temptation we become beset by others. This is simply because the inexhaustible versatility of sin corresponds with the exquisitely complex susceptibilities of our human constitution, and the supersensitive interactions between spirit and mind and body.

So, then, there may be a continual "putting to death" of "the flesh", of sinful urges and tendings. Or, conversely, there may be a progressive inward dying to different forms of temptation and sinning. Such progressive deliverance comes, as the text says, "through the Spirit", i.e. by living responsively to Him, and thus experiencing His liberating ministry within our nature.

When we so truly live "*in* the Spirit" (9) that we "*walk* in the Spirit" (4) and habitually "*mind* the things of the Spirit" (5), then, that in itself continually "puts to death" the "doings" of the "flesh" as they successively occur. That is the way of progressive deliverance and victory through "the law of the Spirit of life in

Christ Jesus". It is a true mortification of the *flesh* by a true sanctification of the *mind*. It is no merely theoretical deliverance through an imagined obliteration of some detachable "body of sin", or by the "counteracting" of a miscreant "old man" within us, who may be doubtfully downed, but never expires, and remains ever unclean, and must live inside us till we pass beyond. It is real victory, not merely by struggling against insinuating seductions down on their own level, but a living *over* them, by inward elevation of mind "in the Spirit".

Yes, it is real victory. It is a real "putting to death" of the "flesh", and a real dying to selfism through *inward renewal*. But, let us mark it well: *there is no promise of an absolute inward death to sin.*

WHAT, THEN, OF DEATH TO SIN?

That brings up the whole question as to the possibility of our ever being inwardly *dead* to sin. Can we ever be so in this present life?—or do we become so in the Beyond?

John Wesley and his eradicationist successors have never hesitated to teach that we may become actually dead to sin in this present life. But is the Wesleyan definition of sin ample? Is it either Biblically or psychologically adequate? My own view is that the beguiling Delilah of the eradication theory would never have been countenanced if there had been a more penetrating doctrine of sin. The eradication theory and the early Wesleyan concept of sin are twins. They were born together; they grew together; and they continue together to the present time, wherever that earlier formula of holiness is preached.

In his *Plain Account*, Wesley defines sin (mark this carefully) as "*a voluntary transgression of a known law*"; and to that he adheres throughout his teaching on "Christian perfection". That which is non-volitional, so he deems, lacks the essential element of sin. "Involuntary transgressions," says he, "you may call sins, if you please: I do not." A corollary of this is, that there cannot be *unconscious* sin, for that which is unconscious ("unknowing" would be a better word) cannot be morally blameable.

The fact is, Wesley's definition does not define sin itself, but only sinning, or *a* sin. It touches sin only at the point of its recognizable commission, not in its interior conception. It identifies the expression but not the compulsion. It puts a label on the symptom but does not diagnose the disease. It overlooks that the problem of the "wretched man" in Romans 7 is not just sin as "a voluntary transgression of a known law", but *"sin that dwelleth in me"*.

The Bible uses that awful word, "sin", not only of something which we *do*, but of a state in which we now *are*. Wesley's definition omits the latter entirely. It is like defining alcoholism as "a voluntary drinking of a known glass of beer", without any reference to the thirst *behind* the drink; or kleptomania as "a voluntary stealing of another's property", without any reference to the neurotic impulse *behind* the theft.

Wesley, we sympathetically agree, could scarcely be expected to anticipate the insights of modern psychology. What disappoints us is that his definition does not cover the *Scripture* data. It is far from sufficient even as a definition of *a* sin. Many a sin is *not* "a voluntary transgression of a known law," yet it is none-the-less a sin. There are sins passive as well as active; sins of omission as well as of commission; sins which are not "transgressions" at all, but fallings short. We may resolve the varied aspects into the following six propositions.

(1) *There can be involuntary sin.* "Involuntary transgressions," says Wesley, "you may call sins, if you please: I do not." Yet his wording is self-contradictory, for "transgressions" (as the very word indicates) are *active* offences, therefore "transgressions" *cannot* be "involuntary". What Wesley means is, that involuntary *sins* are not really sins. Even so, he is wrong. Some of the worst sins are involuntary. In the light of New Testament revelation, the damning sin is not active violation of "a known law", but unbelief, which in many instances is passive torpidity. Since Christ came, the greatest sin of all is *not* "a voluntary transgression of a known law", but non-response to the divine love. There are sins negative as well as sins positive. They are not "transgressions", but *omissions*, yet they are just as truly *sins*. Good which I might have done, but did not; responsibility which I should have shouldered, but did not; such are sins of blameworthy *inactivity*. Some of the darkest sins are not "transgressions," but *neglects*.

Nor can Wesley's denial of involuntary sin weather such passages as Romans 7. Was there not some involuntariness in the behaviour of that "wretched man" who wailed, "The good that I

would I do not; but the evil which I would not, that I do"; and "It is no more I that do it, but *sin which dwelleth in me*"? As certain diseases cause involuntary movement of the body, despite all attempted control by the will, so the sin-disease in man's moral nature strangely galvanizes the mind to actions which override the will. Ask some weakened drunkard, dragged down to the gutter by his wretched slavery, whether his sinning is always a "voluntary transgression". Let Sam Hadley of *Down in Water Street* tell you, with grim poetry, how his first glass of whiskey "let loose a legion of demons" within him which dragged his helpless will through the mire like a chained slave behind a despot's chariot. Yes, there is involuntary sin!

(2) *There can be transgression without sin.* Wesley's definition of sin limits it to "a voluntary transgression of a known law"; but *not* all such transgression is sin. A man sees his neighbour's boy entangled in a barbed-wire fencing, and climbs over to free him, ignoring the sign, "No Trespassing". Transgression? Yes. Sin? No; because there is gracious motive.

(3) *There can be sin without transgression.* Here again Wesley's definition of sin as "a voluntary transgression of a known law", is faulty; for there are many sins which are not transgressions. That is the very point which Paul makes in Romans 5:14, "Nevertheless, death reigned from Adam until Moses, even over them that had not *sinned* after the likeness of Adam's *transgression*." Between Adam and Moses, men did not transgress a specific command, for the Law was not yet given through Moses; yet they were none-the-less *sinning*, because every sin is *intrinsically* immoral, whether it transgresses a known commandment or not. That is why Paul says in verse 13, "For until the Law *sin* was in the world; but sin is not imputed [i.e. is not charged as transgression] where there is no law." So there was sin without transgression. When unconverted Paul blasphemingly persecuted the followers of the hated Nazarene, was he sinning? Yes, grievously. But was he transgressing "a known law"? On the contrary, he thought he was "doing God service".

(4) *Unconscious (i.e. unknowing) transgression is still sin.* Wesley asks, if a transgression is committed unconsciously how can it be called a sin? Yet surely there is unknowing sin just as there is unknowing *crime*. A newcomer infringes the law in a certain community. In court he pleads that he offended in

ignorance. The magistrate replies, "We allow that you broke the law unknowingly, but that does not alter the fact that you *did* break the law; and the law demands reparation." An illegal offence against a human being is a crime, whether committed knowingly or unknowingly, because it breaks a law, and therefore has an *objective* aspect as well as its *subjective* aspect in the offender.

Similarly, as crime wrongs man, so sin wrongs God; and just as every crime has its objective aspect, so has every transgression. Therefore, transgression is still a wrong against God even when the perpetrator is unaware of it. This has clear Scriptural confirmation. In Leviticus 5: 17–19 we find: "And if a soul sin . . . though he *wist it not*, yet he is guilty, and shall bear his iniquity. And he shall bring a ram . . . and the priest shall make an atonement for him concerning his ignorance wherein he erred and *wist it not*." (See also Luke 12: 47, 48.)

(5) *Unconscious sin is still sin.* Wesley says that "unconscious sin" is a contradiction in terms. But is it? See yonder heathen in cringing worship before a hideous idol. Is idolatry sin? Is it wronging God? Yes, it is. Do you object, "Ah, but he does not know that he is wronging the Creator, therefore it cannot be sin"? Wrong! for although he does not know that he is wronging God, it still remains in *fact* that he is doing so; for idolatry itself is a grievous wronging of God. The sin, although "unconscious" is still sin. Of course, that idolater is not committing a "transgression" (a legal term) for he is not violating a "known law"; so there is no *"guilt"* (another legal term) attaching to his idolatry. Remember Romans 5: 13 again: "Sin is not imputed [i.e. as guilt] where there is no law". Nay, in many cases there is pathetically good *motive* in the idolater—a groping after the true God (Acts 17: 23).[1]

When the young priest, Isaiah, was prostrated by his vision of the divine Majesty and the flaming holiness of the heavenly throne, he cried out, "Woe is me! for I am undone!" In one revealing flash he now saw that many things which he had esteemed commendable were inwardly corrupt, including his own heart and actions. But he did not cry out, "Oh, what a relief!—I did those things without any consciousness that they were sinful,

---

[1] As a matter of ultimate indictment, that idolater's sin is not his own, but an extension of Lucifer's, who thus further sins through his blinded victim. That, however, is a mystery which we cannot examine here.

so they were not really sin at all!" No, he recognised them as ugly sin, even though perpetrated without consciousness of their being so. Isaiah also saw the moral corruption in his own nature as never before, and recognised it as *sin* notwithstanding that he had hitherto been *unconscious* of it as such.

In the same way, as already noted, Paul refers to sin which *he* had earlier committed without being aware that it was sin. Recalling his vitriolic fury against the Church, he says, in 1 Timothy 1: 13, "Howbeit, I obtained mercy because I did it ignorantly." Yes, he had done it without the slightest consciousness of its grievous sinfulness, yet none-the-less it *was* sin, and it is with reference to it that he immediately adds, "sinners of whom I am chief". Indeed, the most monstrous sin ever committed was that of which our Lord said, "Father, forgive them; for *they know not what they do*."

Do not all these considerations settle it, that the limited definition of sin as "a voluntary transgression of a known law" is a stilted over-simplification? Do not our own experience and observation likewise disqualify it? I remember a certain man who continually tricked the customs officers at the ports. On the first occasion, although his smart twist was entirely successful, his conscience lashed him: his deceit was a wrong, a crime, a sin. As he kept repeating it, however, not only did conscience subside, but all sense of wrongness evaporated; and by the time he chatted with me on an ocean voyage he had come to regard the port regulations which he kept outwitting as a "cruel injustice" to men like himself who had "worked hard to save a bit". The peculiar shock to me was, that so far as I could penetrate his mind, the wrong had really become right to him. Yet though it had ceased to be sin to *him*, was it not *still* sin? Did it become less and less sin because it became less and less so to *him*? Is sin wholly a matter of a man's conscience about it? Is there not sin (as we have said) in an *objective* as well as in a *subjective* sense? Must we not, after all, endorse W. E. Orchard's asseveration, "Sin without sense of sin is still sin, and, indeed deeper sin just because we are unconscious of it"?

(6) *There is sin chronic as well as active.* Scripture speaks of sin as an inward condition as well as a moral violation. We are reminded again of Paul's words, "sin that dwelleth in me". When we scrutinize that *inner* evil, then we have to leave Wesley's

definition of sin altogether. The human mind, with its laby-
rinthine intricacies and sensitivities of the conscious, the subconscious, and the unconscious, is often a baffling complexity.
There are deep-down quiverings of such superfine subtlety as to
make it practically impossible to distinguish where awareness and
volition begin. This, however, is Scriptural, that even "unconscious" sins, so-called, *are* sinful because they are emanations
of that hereditary uncleanness or sin-disease in our moral nature.
Behind the *outflow* of sinning in thought, word, deed, is a secret
upflow from subtle springs of evil in our deepest being.

I readily acknowledge, of course, that Wesley has much to say—
outside his definition—concerning indwelling sin; but why does he
call it "sin", if sin is solely "a voluntary transgression of a known
law"? To be consistent, should he ever have called that inner
condition anything more than an inward *tendency* to sin? However, he does refer to inward depravity as "sin" over and over
again; but because his definition of sin is inadequate, so is his idea
of "sin that dwelleth in me". We are reminded again of Dr. E.
Sugden's complaint that according to Wesley sin is "a *thing* which
has to be taken out of a man, like a cancer." To Wesley, sin
indwelt as a foreign body, rather than inhered as a toxic infection;
it was a distinguishable malignant growth in the system, rather
than a coextensive permeation. Therefore it could not be refined
away; it must be drastically removed—"eradicated". If Wesley
had seen "inward sin" more penetratively as an evil "leaven"
diffused through the "three measures of meal", instead of leaven
in the "*lump*", his conclusions would have been much modified.
It was the latter view which led to his doctrine of perfection. "A
Christian man may be so far perfect as not to commit sin." With
the "extinction" of inborn sin (so he says) there is a cessation of
all, even inward sins.

"*Christian Perfection*"

Thus to criticize so saintly and mighty a servant of Christ as the
venerable founder of Methodism grates on one's sensibilities. Yet
unless I am obtusely misreading the guideposts of Holy Writ, not
only is he astray in his constricted concept of sin, and its by-
product theory of eradication, but also in his resultant doctrine of
"Christian Perfection", which he has to pare and scissor until it is
not moral perfection at all. In his *Plain Account*, page 223, he says:

[1] *Plain Account*, pp. 197 and 188.

"Not only sin properly so called (that is, a voluntary trangression of a known law) but sin *improperly* so called (that is, an involuntary transgression of a divine law, known or unknown) needs atoning blood. I believe there is no such perfection in this life as excludes these involuntary transgressions. . . . Therefore *sinless perfection* is a phrase I never use, lest I should seem to contradict myself."

Note the three inconsistencies: (1) Involuntary transgressions are not properly sins; yet First John 5: 17, says, "*Every* un-righteousness [even a negative "un" or shortcoming] is sin". (2) If involuntary transgressions are not properly sins, and there-fore not morally blameable, why do they (as Wesley avers) "need *atoning* blood"? (3) If Christian perfection is not absence of such sinning, how can it really *be* "perfection"?

It is strange to see how Wesley clings to that word, "perfection", yet continually edges away from it. He writes his brother Charles not to make perfection *too* perfect: "To set perfection *so* high is effectually to renounce it".[1] Actually, the doctrine becomes one of imperfect perfection. There is a smack of unreality about it; and not without reason is the retort that according to it "one may be a perfect Christian without being a perfect man". As one peers into that bottomless abyss of mysterious surprises, the human heart, and then reflects on Wesley's cramped definition of sin, issuing in eradication-yet-not-sinless, and perfection-yet-not-perfect, the old lines from Hamlet swing solemnly before one's inward eyes again:

> "There are more things in heaven and earth, Horatio,
> Than are dreamed of in your philosophy."

Yet to say that yesterday's Wesley was partly wrong does not mean that today's psychology is wholly right! Modern psychology has given us a much more sophisticated comprehension of "sin" and its interwoven patterns in mental behaviour. It has stratified the mind into the "conscious", the "subconscious", and the "unconscious" (subdivided into "primary" and "secondary"); also, according to some, the "pre-conscious" and "super-conscious". It has analysed, classified, tabulated and labelled our instincts, impulses, motivations and actuations. Yet has it really told us much more about sin than we already knew from the simple,

[1] *Letters* 5: 20.

concentrated words which the Bible uses to define or expose it?

Much that modern psychology set out to clarify and simplify it has tantalizingly complexified into "confusion worse confounded". Are we really wiser in learning that sin is "malfunctioning of instincts", or, "unethical imbalance of motives"? I have heard of a young minister who preached a brilliant sermon on the "total depravity" of man, couching it in highfaluting psychological terminology. Afterwards one of his now-enlightened flock remarked, "My! that's a fine doctrine, if only we could all live up to it"!

Modern psychology can tell us much of value about the operational, but little about the *constitutional*. We know now how the machine works; but who is the "hidden hand" turning the levers? We know now how the piano plays; but who is the mysterious pianist bringing such harsh cacophonies from it? We know now how the stream flows; but what of the hidden source-spring which determines it? The fact is, there is a part of man which is beyond psychology. It is that part which Scripture calls the "spirit". Man is not merely bipartite, but tripartite: body and mind and spirit (*pneuma*). It is the "spirit" which is the *ultimate* mystery in man: therefore psychology can never say the last word about him. It is in the *"spirit"* that human sin (the essence) and sinning (the effluence) originate. And who shall vivisect *that* mystery?

On the whole, therefore, we are wiser not to entangle our concepts of sin too verbally with psychology, for in its deepest meaning sin is essentially *spiritual*. It is not so much a wrong behaviour of parts, as a wrong *direction* of the whole; a rotating of our whole moral nature on a slanting axis. Most of us sensed this and groaned over it before ever we saw our first psychology primer. So did long-ago David (without help from Freud) when he scrutinized his "inward parts", and lamented, "Behold, I was shapen in iniquity". The worst shocks some of us have experienced have been our discoveries that behind and below even the apparently good motives in the upper region of the mind there were ulterior motives skulking in the shadowy recesses of the subconscious. And more; in our moments of most penetrating self-perception are we not helplessly aware of an originating sin-towardness, too tenuous, too elusive for psychological pin-pointing or definition, yet insidiously pre-affecting even the embryonic emergence of awareness and thought and desire and motive. When we beat around for a name by which to call it, somehow psychology has none which quite fits. We must needs go back to the wailing wall of the "wretched man" in Romans 7, *"sin which dwelleth in me"*!

All such considerations should surely caution and steady us in essaying an answer to the question, *"Can we be inwardly dead to sin?"*

CAN WE BE INWARDLY DEAD TO SIN?

Well, *can* we? In the sense of eradication, the answer is a categorical *No*. Let it be said yet again, with final emphasis: sin is not just a bad lodger which can be ejected, or a disease sector which can be excised.

Neither can we ever be dead to sin in the split-ego sense of the "two natures" theory, with one part of us (the so-called "new" nature) dead to sin, and another part (the "old") *never* so.

The precise question is: Can you and I, as spiritually reborn Christian believers, become really dead to sin throughout our now-regenerated moral nature? And the first part of our answer must be, *No*, in the sense that we cannot be dead to the *possibility* of sinning. In the famous Methodist hymnbook of 1780, Charles Wesley asks, in hymn 332, for "a heart that *cannot* faithless prove"; and, in 345, he says,

> "When I feel [Christ] fixt within,
> I shall have *no power* to sin."

But it is wishful poetry rather than conceivable reality. Even in the Beyond, when we are presented in sinless rapture before the heavenly Throne, unless we are demoted into non-volitional beings, there will always be the power of choice which is inherent in free-will; and therefore there must always be at least the *possibility* of sin. There cannot be absolute impossibility of sinning. To deny this is to deny free-will and full humanhood.

Further, we cannot be dead to sin in the sense of absolute *insusceptibility* to it. Even where there is utter absence of bias, inclination, desire, and the soul is perfect in holiness, susceptibility to temptation nevertheless inheres. Were unfallen Adam and Eve sinless? They were, with not a fleck of sin-towardness or wrong desire in their whole being. Yet even they were not *insusceptible* to temptation; for unholy response was begotten within them. Likewise, the fallen angels were all originally sinless. There is neither sex nor procreation among purely spirit-beings, nor, therefore, is there among them any such transmitted evil as an hereditary sin-bias. Each of those fallen intelligences sinned without any such inward bent or pull. Why? Because, even in the sinless, where there is intellect, emotion, and free-will, there cannot be mechanical immunity from wrong response.

Was not our blessed Lord Jesus utterly sinless? Then why did He *"suffer*, being tempted" (Heb. 2: 18)? Why did those Satanic solicitations hurt so, even to tears and sweat of blood? It could only be because, even in that sinless, stainless, guileless, perfect manhood (not in His Godhead) there was an inevitable human susceptibility (despite utter holiness of desire) to temptation.

Some years ago, a rigidly Biblical denomination of believers was almost split in two on the question as to whether our Lord could or could not have yielded to temptation. The one part declared it blasphemous to suppose for a moment that He could possibly have yielded to sin. The other part contended that if it was mechanically impossible for Him to yield, then His temptations were theatrical make-believe; His manhood was merely doketic; and His behaviour was not a valid example we can follow, inasmuch as it was not a genuine human victory. It would have been better if both parties had agreed that they were dealing with an insoluble mystery. Christ, as God, could not be tempted, for "God cannot be tempted" (Jas. 1:13). Similarly, Christ, as God, could not die; yet He *did* die, for He was human. Even so, as His humanhood was susceptible to human pain and death, so was it to temptation. We *must* believe so, or make His incarnation artificial, and discredit the written Word (Hebrews 2: 18, 4: 15, 5: 7, Lk. 22: 43, 44). Yes, even *that* perfect manhood was susceptible to temptation, and could "suffer" in resisting.

But although we cannot be dead to sin in the sense of impossibility or insusceptibility, we *can* be so in the sense of *purity of motive*; also in the sense of *holiness of desire*; also in the sense of *unresponsiveness to the unholy*. That, indeed, will ever be our felicitous state in the Beyond, with our glorified Lord. Every effect of hereditary sin will have been forever expurgated from mind and heart; from thought and inclination. There will be no sin-bent; not a quiver of sin-towardness. The once-aslant axis will have been put perfectly straight. Yea, more; not only will there be absolute absence of sin-propensity, but the whole predisposition will be toward the holy, the heavenly, the exquisitely beautiful, the Divine. There will be no temptation there; but only lovely incentives to highest expressions of holiness. The present flesh-and-blood body will have given place to a physique of supernal texture—a perfect vehicle for the spiritual, with no relation to the animal. We shall continually dwell amid that ineffable glory-light which is pure rapture to the holy, but a "consuming fire" to all else. The eradiating light of His glorious face will shine through and through us, so that never a shadow can even momentarily darken a fitting thought. The Holy Spirit will unobstructedly suffuse our whole being. Not only shall we thus be with Christ: "we shall be *like Him*"! It will indeed be *sinless rapture*.

That, however, is then and there. What of here and now? Even though there cannot be inability to sin, or insusceptibility to temptation, can there be, in the present, death to sin in the sense of utter unresponsiveness to it? What kind or degree of death to sin is possible *now*? We may be helped to a true answer by thinking back over our six propositions, on pages 230 to 234.

From these six premises we may safely draw two conclusions: (a) sin, in the sense of that which is blameable, is always a matter of motive; (b) where the motive is pure there cannot be blame.

It may be asked: Is not an utterly pure motive *sinless*? And if *one* motive may be sinless, why not all? And is not that sinlessness? In reply, we need neither affirm nor deny the possibility of such utter purity throughout one's motives. What we need to realize is, that even sinlessness of motives is not sinlessness of *nature*. Motives are among the subtlest functionings of the nature, but they are not the nature itself. What of that underlying region from which they pre-consciously and incipiently arise in continuous flux and flow?—motives, desires, inclinations, urges, tapering off into minutest reactions of the subconscious.

The New Testament certainly does call us to "*blamelessness*", or entire purity of motive (1 Thess. 5: 23); and to a continuous "*renewing of our mind*" (Rom. 12: 2). Motives, desires, propensities, all may be renewed, refined, sanctified, by the Holy Spirit, as He continuously suffuses the consecrated believer. Yet, nowhere does the New Testament promise a *sinless nature* in this present life.

As we have said, our hereditary sin-proneness lives in the very tissues of our moral nature. In imagination, let us peer into the inner life of the holiest man on earth. Every instant of his wakeful hours, in endless succession, through things seen, read, heard, sensed, there are injected into his mind, from the world around him, thoughts, ideas, suggestions, many of which are more or less evil. They are not emanations from his own mind; they flit in or force entry through the senses of the body or the susceptibilities of the mind; but they all provoke reactions or awaken responses, for he is still human, and still in the flesh; and there is always that within him which will succumb if given opportunity. Yet over against all this, and just as continuously, there is the interpenetrating "Spirit of life in Christ Jesus", renewing his mind, refining his desires, elevating his motives, replenishing his will, so that instead of response to evil there is aversion, and instead of sinning there is holiness.

That kind of continuous dying to sin and living in holiness is truly realizable in the experience of the consecrated, prayerful Christian; and those who have lived in it have testified what a sunlit Canaan of heavenly joy and fellowship with God it is. Does someone ask: If the Holy Spirit can purify and refine our desires, impulses, motives to *that* extent, why not to the point of *absolute sinlessness?* As to the theoretic possibility of that, we are not concerned to answer; but as to its present practicality our reply is unhesitating: it is presumption to go beyond what Scripture promises. We might just as well ask: If the Holy Spirit can heal our bodily sicknesses, as many believers have proved, then why not restoration to utterly diseaseless health, with never a need for even minor medical aid? That the Holy Spirit *could* do this we well know, for in the consummation yet to be He *will* do it (Rom. 8: 11, 23, 1 Cor. 15: 42–45); but we foolishly presume if we try to wrench it into fulfilment *now!*

So, then, can we be inwardly dead to sin, in this present life? *NO*, not in the sense of inability or insusceptibility; nor in the sense of a nature absolutely freed from all hereditary sin-effects, and permanently reconstructed so as to function with moral faultlessness. *YES*, in a dependent, moment-by-moment sense, through the infilling Holy Spirit whose interpenetrating life

BAPTISM AND DEATH TO SIN IN ROMANS 6

As we have said, another factor which indicates that the death to sin which Romans 6 teaches is *not* a present, inward death, but solely a *judicial* death, is its being linked back with the initiatory *baptism* of those Roman believers to whom Paul wrote. It is not a death effected *now*, but a death professed *then*. Observe the verb-tenses again in verses 1 to 4.

"We who *DIED* to sin, how shall we any longer live therein? . . . All we who *WERE BAPTIZED* into Christ . . . *WERE BURIED* therefore with Him through baptism into death."

The verbs in capitals are all aorists, betokening a completed act in the past. Clearly *that* death to sin had been assumed and symbolised as an already finalised act when those long-ago Christians were baptized.

It is generally agreed that the reference in Romans 6: 1–4 is to *water* baptism. As we have said, the reference cannot be to a *spiritual* baptism, for it was an immersion into *death*, whereas spiritual baptism is into new spiritual *life*. That the reference was indeed to water baptism is strikingly confirmed by a most interesting annotation which I here quote, by kind permission, from *The Letter to the Romans*, by Dr. William Barclay, Lecturer in New Testament and Hellenistic Greek at the University of Glasgow.

"But then, having recoiled like that, he [Paul] goes on to something else. 'Have you never thought,' he demands, 'what happened to you when you were baptized?' Now, when we try to understand what Paul is going to go on to say, we must remember baptism in the time of Paul was different from what baptism commonly is today. (a) It was adult baptism. That is not to say that the New Testament is in any sense opposed to infant baptism. . . but infant baptism is the result of the Christian family, and the Christian family could hardly be said to have come into being as early as the time of Paul. A man came to Christ as an individual, often leaving his family behind, in the Early Church. (b) Baptism in the Early Church was intimately connected with confession of faith. A man was baptized when he entered the Church. And he was entering the Church direct from paganism. Baptism marked a dividing line in his life. In baptism a man came to a decision which cut his life in two, a decision which often meant that he had to tear himself up by the roots, a decision which was so definite that for him it often meant nothing less than beginning life all over again.

(c) Commonly, baptism was by total immersion, and that practice lent itself to a symbolism which sprinkling does not so readily lend itself to. When a man descended into the water, and the water closed over his head, it was like being buried in a grave. When he emerged from the water, it was like rising from the grave. Baptism was symbolically like dying and rising again. The man died to one kind of life and rose to another kind of life. He died to the old life of sin and rose to the new life of grace. He went down into the water a man of the world, and rose a man in Christ.

"Now, again, if we are fully to understand this, we must remember that Paul was using language and pictures that almost anyone of his day and generation would understand. It may seem strange to us, but it was not at all strange to Paul's contemporaries. The very language he was using was the very language they used.

"The Jews would understand it. When a man entered the Jewish religion from heathenism it involved three things—sacrifice, circumcision and baptism. The Gentile entered the Jewish faith by baptism. The ritual was as follows. The person to be baptized cut his nails and hair; he undressed completely; the baptismal bath must contain at least forty *seahs*, that is two hogsheads of water. Every part of his body must be touched by the water. As he was in the water he made confession of his faith before three fathers of baptism, and certain exhortations and benedictions were addressed to him. Now the effect of this baptism was held to be complete regeneration; the man was a new man; he was born anew. He was called a little child just born, the child of one day. All his sins were remitted because God cannot punish sins committed before he was born. The completeness of the change is seen in the fact that certain Rabbis held that a man's child born after baptism was his first-born, even if he had had children before baptism. Theoretically it was held—although the belief was never put into practice—that a man was so much a completely new man that he might marry his own sister or his own mother. He was not only a changed man, he was a new man, a different man. Any Jew would fully understand Paul's words about the necessity of a baptized man being a completely new man.

"The Greek would understand. At this time the only real Greek religion was found in the mystery religions. These mystery religions were wonderful things. They offered men release from the cares and sorrows and fears of this earth; and the release was by union with some god. All the mysteries were passion plays. They were based on the story of some god who suffered and died and rose again. The story of the god was played out as a drama. Before a man could see the drama he had to be initiated. He had to undergo a long course of instruction on the inner meaning of the drama. He had to undergo a course of ascetic discipline. He was carefully brought up and prepared. The drama was played out with all the resources of music and lighting, and incense and mystery. As the drama was played out the man felt himself one with the god; he underwent an emotional experience of identification with the god. Before he entered on this he was initiated. Now initiation was always regarded as a death followed by a new birth, by which the man was *renatus in aeternum*, reborn for eternity. One who went through the initiation tells us that he underwent 'a voluntary death'. We know that in one of the mysteries the man to be initiated was called *moriturus*, the one who is to die, and that he was buried up to the head in a trench. When he had been initiated he was addressed as a little child and fed with milk, as one newly born. In another of the mysteries the person to be initiated prayed: 'Enter thou into my spirit, my thought, my whole life; for thou art I and I am thou.' Any Greek who had been through this would have no difficulty in understanding what Paul meant by dying and rising again in baptism, and, in so doing, becoming one with Christ. We are not for one moment saying that Paul borrowed either his ideas or his words from such Jewish or pagan practices; what we do say is that he was using words and pictures that both Jew and Gentile would understand and recognise."

And now, against that background, read again Paul's words at the beginning of Romans 6. "We who *DIED TO SIN*. . . . we who were *BAPTIZED* into Christ were baptized into His *DEATH*. We were *BURIED* therefore with Him through baptism into *DEATH*." Surely it is as plain as can be, that the believer's death which Romans 6 teaches is not a death which has yet to be effected in the believer's inward condition. Much less is it a maintained experience of *dying*. It is a completed death already *past*, which put something away once for all, and is symbolically testified to in the rite of believer's baptism.

ON THE TRUE TRANSLATION OF *ANTHROPOS*

We have shown how the Authorized Version, also the English Revised and the American Standard Versions uniformly translate all 546 occurrences of the Greek word, *anthropos*, in the New Testament as "man" or "men" or "man's". What about more recent versions? Their testimony is just as solid that the true translation of *anthropos* is "man". Not one of them anywhere translates it as "nature", as though it were an "old nature" *inside* man.

We find, however, that some more modern versions have a fondness for breaking away from the phrase, "old man", in Romans 6: 6, as also in Ephesians 4: 22 and Colossians 3: 9. What are we to say about *them*? At the time of my writing these lines I am on far travel, and cannot get to my own bookshelves. The only alternative versions at hand are: the American Revised Standard Version, the Berkeley Version, Weymouth's, Moffatt's, Ferrar Fenton's, the *New Testament in Basic English*, and J. B. Phillips' *Letters to Young Churches*. How, then, do those seven newer versions translate *anthropos* in Romans 6: 6? Not one of them translates it as "nature". Two of them retain "man", four prefer "self", and Phillips, "selves" (a merely arbitrary plural).

Can we let those five get away with the word, "self", in Romans 6: 6? Let the following statistics provide an answer. We have gone through all the 546 texts in the first six of our seven modern versions, and the 154 in Phillips (who covers only the Epistles), a total in all of 3430. Ferrar Fenton and the *New Testament in Basic English* never once in all 546 occurrences of *anthropos* translate it as "self". The R.S.V. and Moffatt give it as "self" only twice out of the 546 (Rom. 6: 6 and 7: 2); the Berkeley Version similarly only twice (Rom. 6: 6 and Eph. 3: 16); Weymouth only four times out of the 546 (Rom. 6: 6, 7: 22, Eph. 4: 24, Col. 3: 9); and Phillips never once outside Romans 6: 6. Could anything more plainly indicate how irregular and suspicious the expression, "our old self" is in Romans 6: 6?

What, now, about "old man" (*anthropos*) in Ephesians 4: 22 and Colossians 3: 9? Two of our seven modern versions retain the word, "man". The R.S.V., Berkeley, Weymouth, Moffatt, have "nature". Phillips has a mere circumlocution in the first text, and returns to "man" in the second. Again we scan the 546 occurrences of *anthropos*, to see if it is translated as "nature" anywhere else. In the A.V., E.R.V., and A.S.V. it is not even once so translated. What of our seven new versions? Three of them never once render it as "nature". As for the

other four, here are the figures: Apart from Ephesians 4: 22–24 and
Colossians 3: 9, the R.S.V. and the Berkeley translate *anthropos* as
"nature" only once (2 Cor. 4: 16); Weymouth only twice (Rom. 6: 6,
1 Pet. 3: 4); Moffatt in one verse only (John 2: 25). Is not this statistical
evidence enough in itself to show that those who turn the "old man"
and the "new man" of Ephesians 4 and Colossians 3 into two "natures"
are importing an altogether alien idea?

Even that is not all. Look at those seven newer versions again. Here
and there, each of them, for the sake of useful variety, uses a variant
from "man" as a translation of *anthropos*. Occasionally in the singular
it is rendered as "person", or "human", or "him", or even as "fellow";
and, in the plural, as "people", or "others", or "everyone", or even in a
uni-plural way as "mankind"; but always, without exception, it means
the total human being; it *never* means a mere *part*, such as might be
called an "old *nature*". Those versions which have substituted the
phrase, "our old self", or "our old nature", in Romans 6: 6, Ephesians
4: 22–24, and Colossians 3: 9, have side-stepped etymological propriety;
for the change which they have thereby effected in our English text
is not merely verbal, but basal. To that degree, at any rate, they have
slipped from strict translation into well-intended but incorrect *interpretation*.

APPENDICES

Excursus: Does Romans 6:6 Have A Counterpart in Our Present Inward Experience?

Soon after the first British edition of this volume and its two companions, a consecrated journalist honoured them by three successive articles in the monthly issues of his magazine. Along with appreciative comments there were some well-expressed animadversions. Admittedly, he had now come to realize the *judicial* nature and bearing of Romans 6, but he was too long wedded to the conventional teachings to give up without a struggle the idea that Romans 6 has *also* a "counterpart" in our subjective individual experience. Let me quote the crucial bits, giving my reply-comments in square brackets.

> "Surely the judicial act of 'crucifying our old man' (verse 6) intended, in the Father's purpose, not only that we should be freed from bondage to sin judicially, but also experientially, and be enabled to 'walk in newness of life' (verse 4) and bring forth 'fruit unto holiness' (verse 22). The purpose of the judicial act of verse 6 was that verse 22 should become our actual experience."
>
> [But where does the chapter itself say so? Nowhere. That is why our well-meaning critic has to begin with the word, "Surely"—indicating merely his own inference. We are just as clear as he, that "the Father's purpose" is our freedom from sin experientially as well as judicially; but the one point here is, that this chapter, Romans 6, *does not teach* any such deliverance through a present, inward, individual co-crucifixion with Christ].

Our journalist friend goes on to express appreciation of my using I Thessalonians 5:23 to teach that in entire sanctification God strikes a "fundamental blow" at sin in the believer's nature. Then, using his inferential "Surely" again, he adds:

> "Surely God's act in striking a 'fundamental blow' at sin in the believer is *based* on His striking a fundamental blow at sin *on the Cross*, which is the basic truth of Romans 6." [We, too, agree that God's dealing with sin in the believer is *"based"* on what He did at Calvary—for, of course, *every* part

of our salvation is "based" on *that*. Our critic's mistake is his wrong inference that because our inward liberation from indwelling sin is "based" on our Lord's crucifixion it is effected directly *by* it, i.e. by a re-inducing of that crucifixion inside the individual Christian as a subjectively realized co-crucifixion. Although he says that this latter is "the basic truth of Romans 6" he has absolutely no warrant for saying so except his own merely inferential "Surely."]

What about the eleventh verse?—"Likewise reckon ye also yourselves to be dead indeed unto sin." Our journalist friend refers to it thus:—

> "We believe that there is something deeper in the 'reckoning' than a mere mental assent to the truth of a *judicial* death to sin. The call in verse 11 to 'Reckon' is a call to believers in Christ to step out in obedience to God, and to believe whole-heartedly that what God did for us at the Cross when 'our old man was crucified with Christ' (verse 6), He can make a blessed reality in our hearts and lives now, and deliver us from all bondage to sin (verse 22).

But *does* God really work in us a death to sin as absolute and final as was our Lord's death in His crucifixion? Yes, or No? See how our critic now backs away from this by alternative wording (and note the word which we italicize):—

> "The injunction to 'reckon' is a call to us to exercise Abraham-ic faith; to trust God to honour our reckoning by doing *something* within our hearts which we could not do for ourselves."

Our journalist friend will nowhere commit himself to saying that God actually *does* effect in us an utter death to sin. He can only say that God "honours" our reckoning by doing "*something*" in us which we could "not do for ourselves."

But most of all he throws his case away in a further comment which admits that this "something" which God does within us is, in reality, the purifying work of the Holy Spirit:

> "Our reckoning is the channel along which flows His mighty power by *the Spirit*, purifying our hearts in the unseen, un-conscious depths, from the pollution of sin; and imparting healing and full health by His *indwelling Spirit*."

So, after all, this inward deliverance is not by an inwrought co-crucifixion with Christ, but *by the Holy Spirit*. Again and again we have noticed that when our co-crucifixion theorists come right down to actual experience, they quietly shift their ground and attribute inward sanctification to the work of the Holy Spirit—and quite rightly so. Of course, some of the dear die-hards would say that it is the Holy Spirit making our Lord's *crucifixion* real in the believer; but that is mere phantasy again, not exegesis, until they show it to us in the written Word.

Perhaps I may usefully add that my journalist reviewer sent me a gracious note along with his three magazine articles. This gave me opportunity, in a cordial reply-note, to ask him "point-blank" about his own experience in the matter. I quote from my letter to him:—

> "You say that in Romans 6:11, the exhortation to us to 'reckon' ourselves 'dead indeed unto sin' is a call to us to trust God to make it a 'reality within our hearts.' Do you, then, seriously teach or believe such a once-for-all and absolute inward death to all sin as the wording inescapably teaches? Do you experience it in yourself? Somehow I cannot think you would resort to the evasion which I have too often heard, i.e. 'Well, *we* are to do the reckoning, and leave God to do the working of it'; for I have not yet met one person anywhere who would *dare* to say that God *had* actually worked such an utter inward death. Besides, the text does not tell us to reckon any such present-tense working, but a completed and once-for-all death. My dear friend, I ask you with utter sincerity: *Do* you, or do you *not*, experience that utter, inward death to sin which you advocate on the basis of Romans 6:6 and 6:11? Or do you even teach it as possible on that basis?"

I thought that by this point-blank question I would sincerely and honourably "hem him in" to an inescapable "Yes" or "No"; but there came back a gracious reply giving an artful new angle! At the same time, however, it was an undisguisable surrender of his earlier position on Romans 6:11. He agreed that the "dead indeed" in verse 11 means an utter, once-for-all death to sin, and rightly linked it with the preceding verse (10), "In that He (Christ) died, He died once for all, but in that He liveth, He liveth unto God." He explained,

> "This death to sin in verse 11 is the same kind of absolute death to sin which our Lord died (verse 10). It is a fixed, final, and indefectible state of sinlessness which is true only of our Lord Jesus Christ in His resurrection glory, because 'death hath no more dominion over Him' (verse 9). Let us term this, '*Resurrection* death to sin.' But death to sin in this absolute sense cannot be true of us Christian believers until we are all in resurrection glory with Christ."

So now, after all, despite Romans 6:11, with its "reckon yourselves to be dead indeed unto sin," there cannot be any such death until our bodily resurrection! Instead of death by *crucifixion* with Christ, it is death by *resurrection* with Christ! That certainly is (to me) a new slant on Romans 6! But he further explains:—

> "Verse 11 cannot possibly mean that we are to 'reckon' ourselves to be in a state of *resurrection* death to sin [of course it cannot: no such thought is anywhere in the chapter]. We must take *the whole context* to find the answer [but are not verses 6 to 11 clear enough in themselves?] The whole chapter is about our *attitude* to Sin, our old taskmaster [Yes, of course it is: our *attitude* to sin because of what God did for us on the Cross; not some crucifixion-death inside us]. We are called to have the mind of Christ toward sin; and in like manner we are to hate and refuse to obey Sin, *thus* reckoning ourselves 'dead indeed' to it [but only in that now very modified way]. We might call the death to sin in verse 11 a *conditional* death to sin, or *Faith's* death to sin, because it is dependent on our continued faith and reckoning."

What a collapse this is, after the earlier enthusiastic insistence that Romans 6:11 warrants us to "reckon" a *real* death to sin within us! It puzzles me that men of such transparent sincerity and logical mind as that gifted writer can take such a view of Romans 6:11 as he earlier contended for, and now backs away from. Think of it: in the end he says that death to sin in the "absolute" sense cannot be true of us until we are all "in the *resurrection* glory." Yet as clearly as words ever stated anything, verse 11 tells us that we are *here and now* to reckon ourselves "dead indeed" unto sin in that absolute sense of verse 10—as the connecting word, "Likewise," settles (and which plainly indicates that the death is solely *judicial*). How strange to read into it, "Likewise, reckon ye also yourselves to be 'dead indeed' unto sin, but only in a modified way, until after the coming resurrection"!

How "off the mark," also, is the idea that the death to sin in verse 11 is (as he suggests) "*conditional*"! Nay, that is exactly what it *cannot* be, for it is *ephapax*, i.e. once-for-all, and "dead *indeed*." Nor can it be (as he suggests) "*dependent*" on our faith or reckoning, for both verse and context teach that it is *aorist* (i.e. past tense), past and over with, and in no sense dependent on *our* continuing to reckon it so.

continuously counteracts the appeal of temptation. *YES*, in the sense that through the indwelling Sanctifier all our conscious desires and motives and inclinations may be so purified and refined as to be continuously unresponsive to sin. *YES*, in the sense that thus, at the very centre of the personality, the upward pull of the desire for holiness may grow stronger and stronger, making the downward pull of sin grow weaker and weaker. *YES*, in the sense that, as we thus live and walk in the light of God, the very springs of our thought and impulse and desire are purified by the Holy Spirit, so that God is the soul's supreme delight, and every thought of sin is *hated*.

This is no *static* level of supposed sinlessness through supposed eradication. Nay, they who walk with God most closely are most keenly aware of inhering liabilities to sin which still linger and would immediately reassert themselves, apart from the continual infilling of the Holy Spirit. Some who read these lines may think we have not gone far enough. Others may think that even what we have said is beyond present experience. There are those, however, not a few, who have left sincere and credible testimony to its reality. Oh, that more of us were living in it, for it is "heaven begun below".

> Not merely pardon, Lord, alone
>   My heart can satisfy,
> But Thou Thyself directly known,
>   A presence always nigh:
> Oh, help me persevere in prayer,
>   Until I always find
> That Thou art luminously there,
>   To my communing mind.
>
> Not merely pardon for my sins,
>   But victory over *sin*,
> The very source where sin begins
>   Renewed and cleansed *within*:
> Not weary strugglings to repress,
>   But all my mind renewed,
> Refined by *inwrought* holiness,
>   By Thine own power endued.

But the strangest thing of all to me is, that such intelligent brethren as my journalist correspondent, even after their fond misconstruings of Romans 6 have been exegetically refuted, can still go on vaguely clinging to the notion that *somehow* God will (as they say) "make it all real in experience." The fact is, of course, that God *never* "makes real in our experience" what He has not promised in His written Word. The crucifixion references in Romans 6, with their past tenses and clear-cut finality, were *never meant* to teach a subsequent *experiential* death to sin inside individual Christian believers by a super-induced co-crucifixion with Christ. God never made any such theatrical mystery the crisis-key to the sanctification of heart and life.

Some dear brethren think, as I myself once did, that to dis-prove this co-crucifixion theory demolishes the whole New Testament doctrine of holiness; but instead, it *liberates* it. Ironically enough, it is their own fond theory which turns plain verities into attractive-looking fetters, and brings believers into puzzling bondage; for the (suppositionary) inward-cruci-fixion-with-Christ theory of death to sin and inwrought holiness never yet worked, and never will.